Three Seconds in Munich

Three Seconds in
Munich

The Controversial 1972 Olympic Basketball Final

DAVID A. F. SWEET

University of Nebraska Press

LINCOLN

Library of Congress Cataloging-in-Publication Data
Names: Sweet, David, 1963– author.
Title: Three seconds in Munich: the controversial 1972 Olympic
basketball final / David A. F. Sweet.
Description: Lincoln: University of Nebraska Press, [2019] |
Includes bibliographical references and index.
Identifiers: LCCN 2019001979
ISBN 9780803299962 (cloth: alk. paper)
ISBN 9781496217363 (epub)
ISBN 9781496217370 (mobi)
ISBN 9781496217387 (pdf)
Subjects: LCSH: Olympic Games (20th: 1972: Munich, Germany)
| Basketball—History—20th century. | Basketball teams—United
States—History. | Basketball teams—Soviet Union—History.
Classification: LCC GV885.49.O43 S84 2019 |
DDC 796.48—dc23 LC record available at
https://lccn.loc.gov/2019001979

Set in Minion Pro by E. Cuddy.

To my Mom and Dad (may they rest in peace)

CONTENTS

ILLUSTRATIONS

ACKNOWLEDGMENTS

NUMEROUS PLAYERS WHO COMPETED in the 1972 Olympic gold medal basketball game generously shared their time and memories with me for this book. Reporters on the scene, broadcast hands, college coaches from the era, and others also tendered their thoughts—including one who watched the game on television as a boy in the Soviet Union and today is an NBA owner, an unimaginable outcome for a Russian youth during the Cold War.

Thank you to Neil Amdur, Charles Bierbauer, Tommy Burleson, Dwight Chapin, Rich Clarkson, Jerry Colangelo, Kenny Davis, Lefty Driesell, Jim Forbes, Tom Henderson, Terry Jastrow, Bobby Jones, Keesha Jones, Kevin Joyce, Marie Lefton, Tom McMillen, Mikhail Prokhorov, Ed Ratleff, and George Raveling for your insights. Quotations attributed to all of them that have no corresponding citation in the endnotes are taken from interviews specifically for this book. Thank you to my longtime friend and former coworker Scott Holleran, who tracked down contact information for a few sources on my behalf and who interviewed one of them. Thank you to Rob Taylor of the University of Nebraska Press who, along with his colleagues, agreed this book should be published.

INTRODUCTION

CERTAINLY IT WAS SPECIAL to be one of the 8,500 or so fans to witness arguably the most famous game of all time.

A team of upstart U.S. collegians knocked off the USSR hockey juggernaut, 4–3, in a jaw-dropping Olympic upset. Before the rest of the country, mired in 1980 tape-delay technology, knew what had happened, Lake Placid partied. Spectators at the game—my father and me included—streamed out of the arena into a celebration of incessant yelling and beer drinking. If memory serves, fireworks exploded in that crisp winter night. Two days later, the United States topped Finland, 4–2, to win the gold medal.

So why write a book about the 1972 USA-USSR gold medal basketball game—which, at age nine, I neither saw in person nor even watched on television?

Some stories are more interesting than others. Indeed, the hockey game offered scintillating drama and triggered streams of tears, but the basketball championship possessed those qualities too—along with time moving backward, as if God had intervened, what appears to be subterfuge to end a thirty-six-year undefeated streak and, finally, an historic refutation by twelve angry men of perhaps the most coveted item in all of sports: an Olympic medal.

There's something about dramatic losses that affix themselves to the soul. The anguish Boston Red Sox fans felt as the ball dribbled through Bill Buckner's legs in 1986, moments after they were one strike away from winning the World Series; Greg Norman's agonizing, historic collapse during the 1996 Masters, blowing a 6-shot lead in the final round, ensuring he would never win the tournament he coveted; and the Atlanta Falcons squandering the biggest lead in Super Bowl history, finally losing to the New England Patriots in overtime. And there are many other similar episodes in the annals of sports.

Thanks in part to my training as a journalist, I approached this story with disinterest, as a judge would. I would be swayed by the facts, not emotions or national pride, while I exhaustively researched the game. While reviewing numerous articles about the gold medal contest and its aftermath, interviewing those who competed, and more, I was initially amazed at how much misinformation about the end of the game is out there. To help compensate, I watched the final seconds of ABC's broadcast (along with the Russian television view) again and again, like a JFK assassination sleuth watching the Zapruder film—trying to gather incontrovertible evidence from a somewhat limited view.

After much research, two conclusions were hard to shake: a purportedly objective, yet powerful, observer who had no authority during the game wedged himself into the outcome by twice demanding time be put back on the clock at the conclusion of the contest, both times with the United States ahead. Also, the decisions of a referee from a Communist country were unnerving. His foul calls near the end of the game were disproportionately against the United States. Then he motioned a U.S. defender away from a Soviet player (who had entered the game illegally under his watch) so the player could clearly inbound a pass down the court in the team's only chance for a victory. To paraphrase a line from an officer in *Hamlet* (a Shakespearean player, but not an Olympic one): Something was rotten in the city of Munich.

Getting players on the U.S. team (eleven out of the twelve are still alive) to return my calls and my emails was not an easy task. A possible reason presented itself when I read Frank Deford's memoir *Over Time*.

Deford related a story of when, well established at *Sports Illustrated*, he had tried to interview Jack Nicklaus about his famous Duel in the Sun against Tom Watson during the British Open at Turnberry in 1977. Deford knew Nicklaus, even writing a Sportsman of the Year piece about him. But Nicklaus didn't want to talk about a torturous defeat by one stroke. As Deford wrote, "Slowly it began to dawn on me that for all his many triumphs, it was still painful for such a champion to talk about a defeat—even one from long ago."[1]

Though heartbreakingly not at the Olympics, all twelve American players ended up, like Nicklaus, champions in their lives—NCAA champions, NBA champions, number-one draft choices, whatever your measure. But most—grandfathers now, young men then—cannot shake the injustice of that late night in Munich nearly fifty years ago.

CAST OF CHARACTERS

1972 U.S. Men's Basketball Olympic Team Roster

PLAYER NAME	POSITION
Mike Bantom	F
Jim Brewer	F/C
Tommy Burleson	C
Doug Collins	G
Kenny Davis	G
Jim Forbes	F
Tom Henderson	G
Bobby Jones	C/F
Dwight Jones	C
Kevin Joyce	G
Tom McMillen	F
Ed Ratleff	F/G

Coaches: Hank Iba (head coach), Johnny Bach (assistant coach), and Don Haskins (assistant coach)

1972 USSR Men's Basketball Olympic Team Roster

PLAYER NAME	POSITION
Alexander Belov	F
Sergei Belov	G
Alexander Boloshev	F
Ivan Dvorny	F
Ivan Edeshko	G
Mishako Korkia	G
Sergei Kovalenko	C
Modestas Paulauskas	F/G
Anatoliy Polyvoda	F
Zurab Sakandelidze	G
Alshan Sharmukhamedov	F
Gennadi Volnov	F

Coaches: Vladimir Kondrashin (head coach), Sergei Bashkin (assistant coach)

Important Principals during and after the Gold Medal Game

R. William Jones, secretary-general, FIBA
Artenik Arabadjian, referee
Renato Righetto, referee
Ferenc Hepp, temporary president, FIBA Jury of Appeal
M. K. "Bill" Summers, U.S. Olympic basketball chair
Herb Mols, U.S. assistant manager
Hans Tenschert, scorekeeper

Three Seconds in Munich

1

THE GUNS OF SEPTEMBER

STROLLING INTO A PACKED McDonald's restaurant in Munich, Tommy Loren Burleson cherished the chance to eat a familiar fast-food meal of burgers and fries far from home. A twenty-year-old North Carolina native abroad for the first time, his gait, along with his occupation, distinguished him from the standard tourist. Not only did he tower over seven feet tall; he and the eleven other young men who accompanied him to Munich were among the best athletes in the world.

Until this day—September 5, 1972—their U.S. Olympic squad had won all of its games, extending its thirty-six-year winning streak in the quadrennial affair to a borderline-ridiculous sixty-two games. In seven contests in West Germany, Burleson had contributed only a handful of points, far short of his performances back home. In his first season playing for the North Carolina State varsity as a sophomore (back then, college freshmen were forced to wait a year before joining the top team, regardless of talent), Burleson averaged more than 20 points and 14 rebounds per game. The big man (the Wolfpack sports information department listed him at seven foot four rather than his actual seven foot two to engender publicity as the tallest player in the land) even nailed a decent percentage of his free throws, making two out of every three over twenty-six games.

Back in that era, even Hall of Fame centers such as Wilt Chamberlain often failed to successfully sink 50 percent of their free throws.

Though unknown among McDonald's customers in Munich, Burleson's fame in the United States reached far: after all, as a teenager, the center had graced the cover of *Sports Illustrated*—an athlete's highest achievement aside from capturing a championship back then—under the billing "Year of the New Giants." The picture featured a serious-looking Burleson, with thick eyebrows and a mop of dark hair, dressed in Wolfpack red while cradling a basketball in his right arm. He gazed straight at the camera through a basketball rim, whose netting had been cut to give a clear view of his face. And in a successful nod to North Carolina State's public relations mavens, he was listed as seven foot four on the cover of the best-selling sports magazine in the nation.

Before that, Burleson had been touted during his high school days as the "Newland Needle," a gangly youngster from that hamlet of five hundred or so best known for being the seat of Avery County, North Carolina. Thanks in part to his prowess inside the paint, Burleson helped the Avery County High School team win more than eighty games while dropping only eight before he graduated.

A work ethic instilled by his father made his size even more imposing. During World War II, William Burleson landed on Utah Beach while serving with the U.S. Army, in a special outfit best known today as the Green Berets. During the next year he battled the Nazi forces all the way to Berlin, where the Germans surrendered in 1945. Only five years later, he served again—this time for the entirety of the Korean War.

"With all that combat time," Burleson said, "he came back here with a lot of discipline."

William instilled that discipline in his son. Often the elder Burleson woke his boy up at 5:30 a.m. so they could head out for a three-mile run. Then, after calisthenics, the younger Burleson and his father milked cows on the family farm. In addition, Tommy's uncle's farm nearby boasted two hundred head of cattle; he worked the fields there starting at age ten.

In addition to his rigorous early-morning schedule, growing up so tall (he wore a size 9 shoe in third grade) in a small town often was painful. In grade school, Burleson was picked on because of his height, teased because he stood a head above some of his classmates.

"Boys would beat me up, and I'd have to go get my head sewn up," Burleson recalled. "My dad would have to come and get me with black eyes and bloody noses. He wanted me to stand up to them.

"My best friend was going to help me stand up to the bullies. One time, we were standing by the agricultural building, all beaten up, and he looked over at me and said, 'It's really hard being your best friend.'"

When Burleson was fourteen and already standing six foot eight, he and his uncle, Ben Ware, visited the open house of the Agriculture and Life Sciences Department at North Carolina State in Raleigh. As an alumnus, Ware knew the campus well. They decided to stop by the basketball office.

"We had heard about him [Burleson] but we didn't know too much about him," said Sam Esposito, an assistant on Coach Norm Sloan's basketball staff. "Burleson walked in and he had to bend down to keep from hitting his head coming in the door. We almost had a heart attack."[1]

Once Burleson's abilities flourished during high school, college recruiters drooled over him; hundreds of letters from interested universities, large and small, jammed the family's mailbox, and legendary basketball coaches such as the University of North Carolina's Dean Smith competed for his services.

But Burleson's lack of self-confidence steered him away from the big-name schools.

"I didn't think I was good enough to play at Carolina. I didn't think I was good enough to play at Duke," Burleson explained about his choice to attend a comparatively unknown basketball school, whose varsity team finished below .500 his freshman year. "I just wanted to be a good ball player."[2]

With the U.S. Olympic basketball trials set to take place in Colorado Springs during the summer of 1972, Burleson seemed to be a realistic candidate to make the team. But he almost blew his chance before the tryouts began. In May, Burleson uncovered a key that could unlock three pinball machines on campus. He and a friend stole more than $100 from them. What happened next was a seminal moment.

Feeling guilty, he entered Sloan's office the next day to confess to his coach, who told Burleson to go turn himself in. To this day, Burleson considers it one of the lowest points of his life, especially after going to court and seeing the two children of the man who owned the machines.

"I realized I was taking food out of their mouths," he said. "I was messing with his livelihood. I've never felt lower in my life."[3]

Forgiven by Sloan after his confession, Burleson arrived in Colorado Springs the next month. Joining him was UCLA center Swen Nater, a six-foot-eleven, 243-pound beast who backed up the best player in college basketball, Bill Walton. Their team had captured six straight National Collegiate Athletic Association (NCAA) titles, a feat that had never before been achieved and is unlikely to be matched. Practically at will Nater scored throughout the scrimmages, meaning Burleson was really contending against Ohio State center Luke Witte for a backup spot during the punishing tryouts, where coaches such as Indiana University's Bob Knight, under head coach Henry Iba's orders, yelled as much as they could at players.

Four months earlier, Witte had been leading the Buckeyes to a crucial Big Ten win in Minneapolis before nearly eighteen thousand fans. After being flagrantly fouled, the Golden Gopher who had knocked Witte to the floor, Corky Taylor, started to help him up—before kneeing the seven-footer. Golden Gopher Ron Behagen leaped off the bench and kicked Witte in the head. Somehow energized by their heroes' ugly display, Minnesota fans stormed the floor with thirty-six seconds left and Ohio State up by 6. Defenseless, despite his sizable height, Witte was further demeaned when, as *Sports Illustrated* reported, "the fans had the audacity to boo Witte as he was helped, bleeding and semiconscious, from the floor."[4]

Recovered from the beating, Witte was forced to fight another tough foe in Colorado Springs. Far from a pushover, Witte's statistics emphasized his proficiency at the center position. During his sophomore year at Ohio State, he had grabbed 331 rebounds, which led the team, and scored nearly 19 points a game. Almost eighteen months older than Burleson, at an age when that represented a huge gap in experience, he seemed to have an advantage.

In their final head-to-head battle in Colorado Springs, with a spot on the twelve-man squad on the line, Burleson excelled. He nailed 18 points to only 3 for Witte and outrebounded him, making the decision easy to put the first Wolfpack player in Olympic history on the team.[5]

Then came training camp at a site of war: Pearl Harbor. Not only were the practices grueling; the accommodations were appalling.

"They put us in a barracks that was partially destroyed during the bombing of Pearl Harbor," Burleson recalled. "We didn't even have mosquito nets and we were getting eaten up. Sailors there who saw us said we had it worse than they did during boot camp."[6]

But Burleson had survived Pearl Harbor and, after a handful of exhibition games on the mainland, flown a Pan Am charter to Munich with his teammates, who (at first at least) basically considered him a hillbilly. Yet here was this country kid in a historic European city, two wins away from a gold medal that would forever mark him as one of the best basketball players of the era.

The night before, Burleson's sleep had been significantly disturbed. Far from worrying about the upcoming semifinal game against Italy, he had been startled awake by a loud sound. When he arose that morning, he learned the truth: an undetermined number of Israeli athletes, coaches, and officials had been taken hostage by Palestinian terrorists. The noise that jolted him from his slumber the previous night was gunfire.

"I had a personal relationship with some of the athletes the terrorists had taken hostage," Burleson said, having met them in the Olympic Village. "One of the Canadian guys asked if I wanted to see the terrorists close up. From his balcony, we could see the terrorists. I realized if they turned and started shooting, that wouldn't be a good place to be."

After he called home following an hour-long wait for a phone to tell his family he was okay, Burleson toured Munich with his fiancée; how often would a farm kid from western North Carolina get a chance to see a spot infamous for its ties to Nazi Germany, after all? Adolf Hitler's beer-hall putsch had shaken Munich in 1923, and the agreement signed fifteen years later by Germany, the United Kingdom, and others led British prime minister Neville Chamberlain to inaccurately declare, "Peace is at hand." (Bolstered by that pact allowing it to annex part of Czechoslovakia, Germany started World War II soon after.) But that age was far removed from Burleson; he had not been alive during those historic events nor had the world-famous restaurant where he was dining even been created.

Soon after enjoying his McDonald's meal with his fiancée (whose presence at the Olympics would curtail one of Burleson's basketball dreams only days later), they visited the Black Forest—where Burleson picked up a Black Forest clock for his mother—and Munich's venerable cathedrals. Daylight began to fade. They took a bus to the apartment where his fiancée was staying, and then he boarded a train heading back to the Olympic Village. He sat in the last car next to two tall Brazilian basketball players. Surprisingly, the train stopped short of its destination.

"We three stood there in the back of the train, with no space between anyone," Burleson said. "Guards were facing forward with their backs to us, and I said to the Brazilians, "There's the parking lot."

Burleson was referring to a shortcut he often took to get back to his apartment. He and his two new friends walked out from the final car, aiming to reach a stairwell that would take them to their rooms.

Soon, a West German soldier encountered the trio in the underground parking garage, saying, "Nein." Burleson said he was simply going to his room, and they all kept walking. Another soldier soon appeared, also speaking German. The young men continued on their path. The soldiers had been instructed to keep everyone away from the parking garage, but the players did not understand.

Then one more soldier approached Burleson—one who spoke English.

"He said, 'Young man, you're in the wrong place at the wrong time. We're bringing the hostages out at this very moment. I want you to face that wall.'"

Burleson complied. He noticed the two Brazilian players were lying on the ground with guns pressed into their backs. Then it was his turn to get a rifle jammed into his back.

Burleson heard some strange language being spoken. He looked over, and he saw the main Palestinian terrorist, Luttif "Issa" Afif. Their eyes met.

"The West German guard saw me looking backward and said, 'I told you to look forward!'" Burleson recalled. "And he stuck the barrel of the gun into my head. I can close my eyes and still see the grooves in that wall."

Burleson began praying. Then, he heard more noise.

"I could hear the Israeli athletes around the corner. I could hear their shoes on the pavement. I could hear the crying and sobbing. I think one of them was hit by a terrorist because I could hear a moan or a cry of pain."

This time, Burleson didn't move. The gun remained shoved against his skull.

Sometimes, recounting a memory freighted with grief is too much to bear. Inconsolable while relating what happened decades ago—before leading North Carolina State to one of college basketball's most epic championships, before becoming a third overall pick in the NBA draft, before returning to the same county where he grew up to live out his days—Burleson summed up what was ahead for those he heard crying.

"They were walking," he said, his large hands pressed to his shuddering face to cover his burst of tears, "to their deaths."[7]

2

A NOBLE HISTORY

NEARLY THREE THOUSAND YEARS ago—well before paved roads, central heating, and yes, even the internet—the Olympics dawned in Greece. The games resembled the twenty-first-century version as much as a weightlifter straining to hoist four hundred pounds resembles a synchronized swimmer.

Recounted David Stuttard, author of *Power Games: Ritual and Rivalry at the Ancient Greek Olympics*, "To compete in this celebration of not just Greek (and later, Greco-Roman) identity but of proud god-fearing masculinity, you had to speak Greek, be free from the pollution of murder—and be male. . . . Until 720 BC, loincloths were de rigueur, but that year [a runner named] Orisippus raced so vigorously that his fell off. When he crossed the line to victory, it was seen as a sign from the gods and henceforth any kind of clothing was banned."[1]

Given the propensity for irrational edicts (such as naked contestants), perhaps it's no surprise that the games petered out in the fourth century AD when a Roman emperor (Greece had been consumed by the Roman Empire by then) shut down pagan festivals. Few ventured to restart the Olympics over the next 1,500 years until, during the 1800s, well-meaning attempts in Greece failed.

Enter Frenchman Pierre de Coubertin, who inspired the resurrection of the Olympics late in the nineteenth century. Born in Paris, on New Year's Day of 1863, Coubertin grew up in a château in Normandy. He was educated in Paris at the Jesuit College of St. Ignatius.

At twenty years old, Coubertin traveled to England, wishing to learn about the British education system. He was struck by the power of sport and its importance in a student's education. "To the merits of this [athletic] education we may ascribe a large share in the prodigious and powerful extension of the British Empire in Queen Victoria's reign," he wrote.[2]

In November 1892, in a hall in the Sorbonne in Paris, a celebration of the fifth anniversary of the Union des sociétés françaises de sports athlétiques took place. Lectures on the history of physical exercise and a talk about antiquity entertained guests. Coubertin was instructed to speak about modern times. In his book *Olympic Memoirs* he recounted,

> Now I had decided to end my talk in sensational fashion with the announcement of the resolution to bring about an early revival of the Olympic Games. The time had come to take the plunge! Naturally, I had foreseen every eventuality, except what actually happened. Opposition? Objections, irony? Or even indifference? Not at all. Everyone applauded, everyone approved, everyone wished me great success but no one had really understood. It was a period of total, absolute lack of comprehension that was about to start. And it was to last a long time.[3]

In fact, about a year after his bold pronouncement, Coubertin barnstormed across America, speaking at universities and clubs to generate enthusiasm for his idea. To his dismay, people yawned. He received the same reaction the following spring in London.

In 1894 he returned to the Sorbonne for the Congress for the Revival of the Olympic Games. The congress approved most of Coubertin's ideas, such as holding the games every four years. He opposed the choice of Athens as the first host, thinking Paris more suitable and financially viable.[4]

Coubertin recalls what lead him to revivify the Olympics:

Their revival is not owing to a spontaneous dream, but it is the logical consequence of the great cosmopolitan tendencies of our times. The XIXth Century has seen the awakening of a taste for athletics everywhere.

At the same time the great inventions of the age, railroads and telegraphs, have brought into communication people of all nationalities. An easier intercourse between men of all languages has naturally opened a wider sphere for common interests. Men have begun to lead less isolated existences, different races have learnt to know, to understand each other better, and by comparing their powers and achievements in the fields of art, industry and science, a noble rivalry has sprung up amongst them, urging them on to greater accomplishments.[5]

The opening ceremonies in 1896 featured choirs singing and cannons booming. About 240 athletes competed in Athens, all of them men. Swimmers thrashed through the frigid Bay of Zea (so cold because the games occurred in April). Track-and-field events were hosted at the Panathenaic Stadium, built three centuries before the birth of Christ, and the route of the first Olympic marathon traced the supposed steps Pheidippides ran from Marathon to Athens to announce a military victory. Boosting the national pride of the Greeks, it was won by a countryman named Spyridon Louis. First-place winners earned silver medals and olive wreaths; gold medals arrived later.

The creator of the Olympic Charter, which championed amateurism, Coubertin served as president of the International Olympic Committee (IOC) from 1896 to 1925. World War I interrupted the quadrennial flow, but the games became increasingly popular, and the choice of host sites provoked little ire—that is, until 1936.

The Summer Olympics were handed to Berlin in 1931, two years before Adolf Hitler's rise to power in Germany. At first, the Führer wanted no part of the extravaganza, believing it might harm his conviction of Aryan supremacy in all aspects of life. But once persuaded that the games could produce a propaganda coup, Hitler backed them strongly.

Though he wanted the world to come see his beloved Deutsch-land in 1936, that didn't stop Hitler from implementing horrific Nazi policies after he was named chancellor in 1933. Jews were excluded from government employment and then stripped of cit-izenship. Homosexuals were arrested. German troops marched into the Rhineland to reoccupy it, violating the Treaty of Versailles. Nations howled at these actions and debated a boycott, question-ing whether their attendance at the games would serve to buoy the Nazi regime. In the end, a record number of athletes traveled to Berlin that August.

Before the games began, Walther Funk, state undersecretary in the Propaganda Ministry in Germany, declared they would bring immense value to the Führer: "There has never before been devel-oped a propaganda campaign equal to that of the Olympic Games ... the foreigner who comes to us shall see the German people united under its leader, Hitler," he said.[6]

During the games, anti-Jewish signs were removed from Ber-lin. People were forced to hoist Nazi or Olympic flags outside their homes. Inside the 105,000-seat main stadium, the first Olympic opening ceremony of the modern games sparkled with pageantry. Hitler walked into the stadium trailed by his entourage and trium-phantly ascended the stands to his viewing spot. The torch relay—a creation of the Nazis—culminated with a runner holding the flame high before lighting the massive bowl at the stadium's crest. On sol-diers' helmets, on bells and elsewhere, the five Olympic rings were clasped within the claws of the German Nazi eagle. Never before had politics been so entwined with world sports.

Because in 1933 the Reich Sports Office adopted an "Aryans Only" policy, no Jews competed for Germany in the 1936 games. Not only that, the Sachsenhausen concentration camp designed for Jews and others Hitler deemed menaces continued to be constructed less than twenty miles from Berlin.

Even without Jewish members, German athletes flourished at the games, earning an Olympic-high eighty-nine medals; the United States finished a distant second with fifty-six. And according to

Minister of Propaganda Joseph Goebbels, the athletes' work carried far greater purpose.

"German sport has only one task," he declared soon after Hitler assumed power. "To strengthen the character of the German people, imbuing it with the fighting spirit and steadfast camaraderie necessary in the struggle for its existence."[7]

Once the games ended, newspapers lauded Germany's capitol and the success of the Nazi-run games. And even though African American Jesse Owens' four gold medals would seem to undermine Hitler's core beliefs, the German leader had captured a far greater prize.

"I'm afraid the Nazis have succeeded with their propaganda," lamented William Shirer, author of *The Rise and Fall of the Third Reich*, in his diary, noting the games had greatly appealed to athletes and visitors alike.[8]

In fact, a two-part documentary created from those games, *Olympia*, is considered a cinematic masterpiece and a powerful piece of propaganda. Directed by Leni Riefenstahl, who had previously put out *Triumph of the Will* about the Nazi Nuremberg rally of 1934, it portrayed a benevolent, beautiful Germany that, as the world would soon see, was a myth. (Amazingly, she served as a photographer for the *London Sunday Times Magazine* during the 1972 games.)

Enraptured by the Olympics, Hitler planned for Germany to host them for all time and approved the idea of a 400,000-seat stadium in Nuremberg. Yet he remained so unimpressed by Jews who had captured Olympic medals on Germany's behalf before 1936 that a number of them perished in concentration camps.

Then came World War II. The German army marched into Poland; its planes bombed London for months. Hitler swallowed swaths of Europe, and his domination of the civilized world seemed possible. But by the end of the war in 1945, he lay dead in a bunker in Berlin, and the city which had hosted the games only nine years earlier had earned the loathing of many countries who had participated—especially the Allied ones.

Because of World War II, the Olympics endured a twelve-year hiatus, the summer version opening again in London in 1948. With memories of the Battle of Britain far too fresh, Germany (now two countries, East and West) was banned from those games, returning in Helsinki four years later.

By the time the Mexico City Olympics began in 1968, Munich had already been chosen as the 1972 host—the first German city since Berlin to invite the world's athletes to compete. Those 1968 games illustrated for the first time that causes promoted around the competitions could beget plenty of worldwide exposure.

Recalled Neil Amdur, a reporter at the time who covered the fortnightly event for the *New York Times*, "You had these student protests in the weeks leading up to the Olympics within blocks of the Olympic Village. You also had the Tommie Smith–John Carlos Black Power expression, which left in the minds of people that politics could garner a lot of attention in the Olympics. It may have given the Palestinians the idea that they could exert a lot more influence taking hostages during the 1972 Olympics."

The idea of displaying a new, tolerant Germany animated the Munich Games. Everything would be 180 degrees from the world's horrific image of goose-stepping, murdering Nazis. Few items would bolster the peaceful image as much as the hosts' decisions about security. With no desire for uniformed police forces to appear anywhere, lest they rekindle memories of Nazism, what security forces ended up wearing seemed almost comical. Hired as the decision-maker on aesthetics was a man named Otl Aicher, whose color and design choices seemed bizarre for a security force:

> Aicher summarily decreed that there must be no red, black, gold or purple at Munich because these were the favored color of dictatorships, old and new, as well as signifiers of German nationalism, past and present . . . the leisure suit–like outfits he came up with for the on-the-ground Olympic security personnel—baby blue polyester pant/jacket ensembles complemented by baseball-style hats and white canvas shoes—definitely ensured that the people wearing this garb would never be confused with the German police forces of old.[9]

Olympic Park—which included the athletes' villages—sat just north of the city center. Though the men's buildings holding three thousand apartments looked bland architecturally, they included a discotheque and massage cabins. Friendliness and goodwill abounded.

"What struck me was how all of these different people from different parts of the world got along, traded pins," said U.S. basketball player Kevin Joyce, a six-foot-three University of South Carolina guard whose sideburns rolled into his dark hair in those days. "I had a little hippie thing in my head—were the governments the problem?"

Bobby Jones, a lanky U.S. forward from the University of North Carolina, wasn't as impressed by tales of goodwill.

"They had food from all over the world, and I loved to eat.

"One day I was eating alone, and I saw another athlete eating alone. I sat beside him. He was wearing a Cuban warm-up jacket. He saw my U.S. jacket, and he left. Where's the harmony?"

Recalled Amdur, "The Germans decided to create an atmosphere in the Olympic Village that this was the new Germany. The music they chose wasn't Wagner; it was light and airy. The decision to downplay security at the village and not have armed guards was so people would not say, 'See that? The Germans are reliving the war.'"

U.S. basketball player Jim Forbes, a six-foot-seven forward from the University of Texas at El Paso who was the last man to join the 1972 team, had already spent six years of his young life around Munich, because his stepfather served in the military. What he remembers about the Olympic Village did not resemble an army base.

"There wasn't an awful lot of security. There wasn't anything confining or suffocating about it," he said. "It was a festive atmosphere in line with the Olympic spirit."

Teammate Ed Ratleff, a six-foot-six forward from Long Beach State, was surprised at the lax arrangements.

"They just about waved you in as long as you had an Olympic logo on," he said.

A chain-link fence—shorter than most basketball players and lacking barbed-wire protection—rimmed the Olympic Village, According to *Sports Illustrated*, a free-for-all ensued that first week:

> With security tossed aside, the Olympics became one big party. Mimes, jugglers, bands and Waldi, the dachshund mascot, gamboled through the Village, while uncredentialed interlopers slipped easily past its gates. After late-night runs to the Hofbrauhaus, why would virile young athletes bother to detour to an official entrance when they could scale a chain-link fence only six and a half feet high? The Olys learned to look the other way. A police inspector supervising security in the Village eventually cut back nighttime patrols because, as he put it, "at night nothing happens." Early in the Games, when several hundred young Maoist demonstrators congregated on a hill in the Olympic Park, guards dispersed them by distributing candy. Indeed, in a storeroom in the Olympic Stadium, police kept bouquets of flowers in case of another such incident.[10]

Negligent security at the Olympic Village—especially in hindsight—is mind-boggling. Not everyone enjoyed the unrestrained atmosphere. Bill Bowerman, the U.S. Olympic track-and-field coach and co-founder of Nike, was appalled by what he saw a few days before the games opened.

"As guards they had boys and girls dressed in pastels, not one with a weapon. The back fence was nothing," he noted. His letter of complaint to United States Olympic Committee chief Clifford Buck went unheeded.[11]

During that first week, of course, plenty was happening away from the Olympic Village. On August 26 the opening ceremony took place during a glorious, warm afternoon. Flags from many nations rippled in the soft wind. Sunlight drenched the long grass oval inside the track. More than seventy-seven thousand fans packed into the stadium, filling its stands that sloped slightly under acrylic glass roofs. They smoked cigarettes and chatted while awaiting the athletes—the most ever to compete in any Olympics.

Within the strictures of the IOC's opening ceremony guidelines,

West Germany's National Organizing Committee tried to ensure the first impression of the games did not hearken in any way to Berlin in 1936. It wanted the ceremony "to appear neither religious, military, nationalistic, nor overly pompous. Instead it was intended to be spontaneous and light and to establish rapport between the performers in the arena and the audience on the tiers," according to its official report.[12]

German folk music played as athletes marched around the stadium, from the youngest, twelve-year-old rower Werner Grieshofer of Austria, to the oldest, seventy-year-old equestrian Hilda Lorn Johnstone of Great Britain. For the first time, artistic programs constituted a big part of the opening ceremonies. Bavarian folk dancers entertained the crowd, and children performed and greeted athletes. American discus thrower Olga Fikotová carried the U.S. flag. Before hoisting the Olympic banner to the top of a flag pole, eight former gold medal winners dressed in white suits walked around the track holding the flag aloft.

As the culmination, Gunther Zahn jogged into the stadium, completing the final stage of the Olympic torch's journey from Olympia to Munich. Far from proceeding in a straight line, the torch had zigged and zagged into the Soviet Union and elsewhere before arriving in Bavaria. Zahn reached the top of the stadium and lit the cauldron.

The Games of Peace and Joy had begun.

In the first nine days, U.S. swimmer Mark Spitz nabbed a record seven gold medals while shattering the same number of world records; effervescent Soviet gymnast Olga Korbut pranced and backflipped into the hearts of millions. More viewers than ever across the world watched the Olympics and couldn't help but be impressed by the athletic excellence amid the splendor of a German city founded in the twelfth century.

After a hectic, glorious start, September 5 was practically designed as a day off. Few competitions were scheduled as the games paused between the end of the swimming and gymnastic events and the beginning of track and field.

Around 2:00 a.m. on that Monday—mere hours before the ter-

rorist attacks began—*Los Angeles Times* sportswriter Dwight Chapin
arrived at the Olympic Village.

"I had a medical problem that required immediate attention, so
I managed to reach the U.S. Olympic team doctors' quarters in the
athletes' village by phone. One agreed to see me," Chapin recalled. "I
walked into the village unchallenged, past what I think was the lone
guard on duty. I flipped up my press badge as I entered the gate, but
there was no way the uninterested guard could have identified me."

Then the commandoes arrived. Formed only one year earlier,
Black September was a militant organization that had broken off
from Fatah, a guerilla group co-founded by Yasser Arafat. Black September hoped to assassinate King Hussein of Jordan; the country
had ousted the Palestine Liberation Organization (PLO) and Fatah
from its borders in 1970. It never accomplished the goal.

The first group approaching the fence at the Olympic Village
around 4:00 a.m. was allegedly helped over by some drunken Americans, while the second group used a stool left by a guard to scram-
ble over. They knew where the Israelis were housed, thanks to some
previous inside work.[13]

Of the country's twenty-eight-member delegation, twenty-one
male Israeli athletes, coaches, and others occupied five apartments in
Connollystrasse 31. Many were about to encounter the same middle-
of-the-night panic in once-safe bedrooms that tormented Jews during
the reign of the Nazis—the difference being this chapter occurred
during a purportedly civilized sports festival.

In apartment one, occupied by seven Israelis, wrestling referee
Yossef Gutfreund heard a key jiggling around the lock a few times.
Then Gutfreund heard voices. He knew it couldn't be Moshe Weinberg, the only Israeli who hadn't returned yet from watching *Fiddler
on the Roof* that night. He placed his 275 pounds against the door
and started yelling. One who heard him from a room in the apartment was Tuvia Sokolovsky, a weightlifting coach:

> When I first heard Gutfreund yell, it was like an electric shock.
> First I went to the door; Yossef had left it open. I took one step into

the hall. I understood the warning; it was terrifyingly obvious. . . . In his underbriefs, Yossef's bull-like mass was holding back the door . . . his knees were bending and then the door swung open, slowly. Gunbarrels and stocks flashed, and that face appeared in the opening, in its black mask. . . . The man aimed a pistol at me, and I was no longer paralyzed. I did what Gutfreund was yelling: I ran into the room, and grabbed a chair. Our French window had been hard to open; the latch stuck. So I smashed the glass with the chair, and out I jumped.[14]

That quick thinking saved Sokolovsky's life; a number of gunshots fired out of the window somehow missed him.

The commandoes were amazingly well-armed, with assault rifles, submachine guns, pistols, and hand grenades. Though their bullets had soared past Sokolovsky, Weinberg wasn't so fortunate. Ambushed outside as he walked back toward the apartment, he was shot in the cheek.

Around 4:30 a.m., a number of hostages from apartment three were brought outside to walk to apartment one, where others were held. One was Gad Tsobari. Given all the commotion, he was stunned more people weren't awake and wondering what was going on: "Picture it: the three Arabs covering us with their submachine guns and rifles, the grenades bulging on them, Moshe Weinberg with his cheek torn away, his blood gushing out . . . and us with our hands on our heads, barefooted, bare-chested, me in pants, the others in their tiny black or white shorts, [David] Berger in his red briefs. I thought if anybody saw this even at a distance, he'd get the idea, wouldn't he?"[15]

Tsobari soon started running. Though a hail of bullets followed him, he climbed a fence and escaped.

Yosseff Romano tried to escape indoors. A weightlifter, he was afflicted with an injured knee, but he, too, was able to avoid gunfire. He headed upstairs, and unfortunately entered a room where five hostages were being held. Somehow, he got hold of a knife and plunged it into the face of one of the terrorists, but they gunned him down. Reporter Serge Groussard entered the same room the following day, where remnants of the horror had begun their disintegration.

"The walls were spattered with matter: some of the spots were sticky, yellow or gray," he noted. "The weightlifter's innards had been splattered on to them under the mad point-blank fire. The ceiling was veined with blood spots, some of them very big."[16]

Moshe Weinberg died soon after, his body riddled with bullets. All of the gunshots at Connollystrasse 31 spurred at least one person into action: an Olympic Village cleaning lady. She alerted the Olympic security office, who sent one person to investigate. He found a masked gunman shortly before 5:00 a.m., contacted headquarters about it, and departed.[17]

Though many were awakened by the gunfire, few American athletes were alarmed—largely because they didn't think it was gunfire. Said Joyce, "I was sick that night. In the early morning I heard the sounds 'kuh kuh kuh.' European cars in the early 1970s would backfire and make sounds like that. I didn't think anything of it."

Recalled Bobby Jones, "The first thing I noticed that night is I thought I heard firecrackers."

Eleven Israelis had been herded into one apartment. Two were already dead. A policeman arrived around 5:25 a.m. He met Afif of Black September at the door (Afif, who spoke German and had lived in West Germany, had been employed inside the Olympic Village before the kidnappings). To underscore the seriousness of the situation, Afif eschewed words; he asked an accomplice to drag Weinberg's dead body for the policeman to view. Paramedics soon arrived to remove the coach's corpse.

The Palestinians shared their ultimatums. They demanded that more than two hundred prisoners held in Israeli jails be released and threatened to execute a hostage an hour if their dictates went unmet.

Amid all of this, the Grand Prix de Dressage kicked off the day's events at 8:00 a.m. as scheduled. That belied the situation at hand. Even though Germany had surrendered twenty-seven years earlier during World War II, the U.S. basketball players woke up to a war zone in Munich.

Doug Collins, a guard on the team fresh from Illinois State, couldn't believe what he was seeing.

"We go to eat and see the terrorists up in the balcony of one of the dorms with hand grenades and machine guns. We see helicopters flying over us, tanks coming in. It's like we're in a movie; it's beyond my comprehension."[18]

While walking to breakfast, team captain Kenny Davis, a guard who had played at Georgetown College in Kentucky, saw a bunch of activity at the Israeli athletes' building, but he had no idea what was going on.

"At the cafeteria, someone told me about it. I immediately lost my appetite," he recalled.

Tom McMillen, a University of Maryland star cut from the final squad before being added at the last minute when UCLA's Swen Nater quit the team, remembers both the horror of the day—and traveling to practice.

"From the Village I watched the tragedy unfold with a front-row view of the terror. . . . I could not shake my mind from the visit by our basketball team to Dachau only a week [before], and I feared the horror of more Jewish sacrifices.

"We talked about it on the bus to practice that day. We didn't know the outcome yet. Some said we should just storm the area where the hostages were."[19]

One of the best-known U.S. Olympians, marathoner Frank Shorter, knew more than most Americans in the chaotic Olympic Village, thanks to a fellow athlete who understood German:

> I heard the early morning gunshots, because I was sleeping on the balcony of our crowded Olympic Village apartment. I didn't know people had just died inside the Olympic Village. Later that morning, we stood in shock as distance runner Steve Prefontaine translated a German telecast. He told of the massacre of Israeli athletes by gunmen who'd surprised them in their apartment, right across the courtyard from us. We all went out to look. How stupid were we?

Over the course of the day, I think we actually saw one of the gunmen in a mask. If he pointed his AK-47 at us, we might have been hit. We climbed over the locked back gate of the village to take our daily training. The guards just shouldered their rifles and smiled as we left and returned. Incredibly, the same way the terrorists had entered.[20]

The warehouse-sized Olympic television complex sat less than one hundred yards from Connollystrasse 31, featuring broadcasters and producers from scores of countries. To interview Israeli weightlifters earlier in the games, ABC reporters had merely walked through an entry gate in the fence to reach them. Terry Jastrow, an ABC producer at the games and all of twenty-three, recalled when he first heard of any trouble.

"I was in our editing compound, putting together three-to-six-minute pieces on the javelin and shot put that Jim McKay would do voiceovers for," he said. "Someone came in and said, 'We need your editing studio! The Israeli athletes are being held hostage.' We moved from being a sports studio to a news studio."

With television cameras set up on rooftops close to the Israeli dormitories, ABC broadcast the crisis live. Chris Schenkel, ABC's genial Olympic host with longtime roots in sports, was soon replaced on air by McKay, who had started his career as a news reporter. The decision by ABC Sports president Roone Arledge upset one well-known TV personality.

"Howard Cosell was furious. He thought he should be the voice of this disaster," Jastrow recalled. "He thought because of the gravity of it, and because of his general-news background in New York, he'd have the mind to give it the proper perspective. But McKay had the heart and soul and spoke with poetry."

In the days before 24/7 cable news and the internet, McKay's calm recitation of what was known served as the world's best source of information. Even when the U.S. players returned from practice, information around the Olympic Village was scant. Television news was broadcast in German, and not everyone possessed a radio to access the Armed Forces Radio Network.

"At times people around the world had a better handle of what was going on [because of TV]," Forbes said. "It was eerie. It was surrealistic."

Joyce's mother, Helen, was staying about an hour away from Munich. She had often visited her son at the Olympic Village, and she appeared again that day.

"My mom sat outside the gate waiting to hear from me," Joyce said. "The house she was at, the people spoke German so they couldn't tell her what was going on."

The morning after his late-night medical treatment, Chapin traveled to downtown Munich to report a story about how the city devastated during World War II had bounced back. He stopped to get lunch, having no idea what had transpired. But a now dying breed—the afternoon paper—filled him in.

"I saw a guy holding a newspaper with the giant headline 'Morte' and what looked like bodies in the village," Chapin remembered. "I ran to get on a rail car, and when I arrived back at the village, it was an armed camp—soldiers, weapons, tanks, barbed-wire closing off everything."

New Yorker writer E. J. Kahn recounted an almost surreal situation at the Olympic Village.

"Seemingly oblivious of what one security man at a locked gate blandly called 'the special situation this morning,' some field-hockey players were whacking away at each other's shins in routine fashion," he wrote. "In the vicinity also were swarms of soldiers and policemen, with armored cars and walkie-talkies and submachine guns, all looking puzzled and helpless. Inside the athletes' compound, not two hundred yards from the hostages, a carefree game of touch football was under way."[21]

In the late morning, the Israeli ambassador to West Germany announced the government's decision not to negotiate with the terrorists nor to release any political prisoners. Despite the terrorists' threats to execute a hostage an hour and another to kill them all at noon, they remained alive as the deadline passed.

Thanks to ABC's cameras, millions saw a terrorist look out of a window, his face covered with a gray ski mask. Aside from the ski mask, the terrorists' outfits were somewhat bizarre and definitely not in line with any stereotypes. A fedora and a cowboy hat sat atop the heads of two of them. One chatted with German authorities outside in a manner so calm that, from afar, it looked as if they were merely discussing the latest discus results.

International Olympic Committee chief Avery Brundage, an octogenarian set to retire after the games, suggested acquiring some sort of gas used by Chicago police in the 1920s to knock out the terrorists. It never happened. As noted in the book *Munich 1972*, "The deployment of gas by German authorities, even in a noble cause, might not have been the keenest idea."[22]

In the early afternoon, Black September released a statement to press agencies and others looking to justify its actions that morning.

"Our revolutionary forces made an entry in strength into the Israeli quarters at the Olympic Village, at Munich, in order to get the Israeli military authorities to adopt a more humane attitude toward the Palestinian people, whether now under Israeli oppression or forced unwillingly into diaspora," it said. "The temporary victory of the Israelis in their conquest of Palestine will never be able to keep the Palestinian people from enjoying their rights in their own country nor give the occupier [Israel] the right to represent Occupied Palestine in a world meet such as the Olympic Games."[23]

Just before 4:00 p.m., the rest of the day's competitions were finally postponed, the first suspension of events in Olympic history. Around the same time, during negotiations with the terrorist Afif, German foreign minister Hans-Dietrich Genscher offered to be taken hostage in return for the Israelis. He was refused.

A rescue attempt named Operation Sunshine was launched by the Germans about thirty minutes later. Unfortunately, it proceeded almost comically, as a handful of policemen dressed in bright track suits and armed with machine guns started crawling up toward the roof of the apartment building, hoping to enter the building through air-conditioning ducts. Their moves were broadcast on live TV—

including in Connollystrasse 31. The Palestinians were furious; the operation was aborted.

A little after 5:00 p.m., Afif agreed to let Genscher up to see the hostages to prove how many existed and that they were alive. What Genscher encountered was an earthly version of hell:

> All the Israelis were tied hand and foot. Each group of three was bound together by a thick rope wound around their arms and attached to the tubular legs of the chairs. . . . Yossef Romano's body lay on the floor in the middle of the room. A soaking bloody towel covered his head. He was horribly wounded, almost cut in two at the waist. . . . Issa warned Genscher to ask only two questions, adding, "If you do not abide by our agreement, we will kill a hostage before your eyes."[24]

Negotiations continued. About an hour later, all parties agreed to fly the terrorists and their hostages to Cairo as soon as a plane could be arranged.

Afif and the other Palestinian leader of the hostage drama, Yusuf "Tony" Nazzal, asked for a bus to the Fürstenfeldbruck military airport. They were told everyone would be transported by helicopter, as the streets were mobbed and it would be dangerous to have them pass through civilian areas.

Negotiators noticed the terrorists were getting increasingly irritable:

> The real reason that made the Fedayeen want to get away from their stronghold at 31 Connollystrasse as soon as possible became apparent when Issa and Tony so quickly agreed to Fürstenfeldbruck. They didn't even look into its ramifications, did not ask for a map of the area, or any details about the air base.
>
> They wanted to get this thing over; they were afraid their nerves were wearing thin. They felt their control of the situation dwindling hour by hour.[25]

The terrorists were right. Authorities tried to stretch out the time, knowing the longer the crisis dragged on, the better the chance the terrorists could slip up somehow as fatigue and strain afflicted them. Around 8:00 p.m., West German chancellor Willy Brandt appeared on two German television stations to give the country an update on the situation.

"These were the Games of Peace and Joy," he said. "Then, this morning, Arab terrorists broke into Olympic Village, and they destroyed the whole thing.

"Our whole country now is in mourning. During all of this day, the directly concerned authorities and I have made every effort to free the hostages, in vain. We offered ransoms, safe-conducts for the attackers out of our territory. Important political leaders offered to become hostages themselves in the place of the Israeli athletes. None of our offers were accepted."[26]

Finally, after 9:00 p.m., the terrorists and hostages walked out of the building. Burleson's memories are bad enough, but a worse scenario was possible. Recalled Bobby Jones, "I remember watching the terrorists parade the hostages past us. I remember thinking, 'What were we doing?' They could have opened up on all of us."

Eventually, the terrorists—with Afif holding a hand grenade—and the captives were ferried to waiting helicopters, walking underground behind the frightened Burleson. Once aboard, they flew to Fürstenfeldbruck in less than ten minutes for the supposed trip to Cairo. A Boeing 727 awaited, but a trap had been set: German policemen were dressed as the flight crew and five sharpshooters crouched in various spots. (Why so few? The Germans were under the impression only five terrorists were involved). By setting up an ambush there, no innocent bystanders would perish.

Yet a lack of proper lighting near the control tower and runways, along with no infrared lighting for the marksmen's weapons, left open the possibility the mission would implode. And an unexpected twist occurred: the members of Black September took the helicopter pilots hostage as they stepped outside. As they wandered near the helicopters for about five minutes, no shots were fired. Then, Afif and a companion walked toward the plane. In retrospect, they made a huge mistake for their own survival: leaving the hostages in the helicopters instead of using them as human shields, the two terrorists were easy targets. Yet despite being shot, they were not instantly killed. Soon, lights across the airport were blown out. Television viewers from Melbourne to Miami could hear repeated gunfire—but see nothing.

Four minutes passed, with the heavily armed Arabs firing wildly. Then, silence.

Unfathomably, for sixteen minutes, quiet descended on the airfield before the terrorists were asked via megaphone to give up. They did not respond, and another thirty-five minutes passed in the dark with little movement.

During this same span of time, the world was being informed, by ABC, Reuters, and by others, that the hostages had escaped, and the terrorists had been captured. Brundage heard as much from Willi Daume, head of the German Organizing Committee.

"I couldn't believe it. I said to myself, 'That's not possible,'" Brundage said. "So I asked Willi to check again and he came back and said, 'Yes, they are safe and the terrorists have all been captured.'"[27]

Rarely in the modern age has more harmful misinformation been transmitted, offering false hope in the extreme. Just past midnight, as reinforcements in armored cars descended upon the airfield, an explosion occurred; a helicopter had been blown up by a hand grenade.

The helicopter had contained five of the nine hostages left; terrorists gunned down the rest in the other helicopter. A total of eleven Israeli athletes, coaches, and referees—all unarmed civilians far from any battlefield—had been murdered. Given the small contingent the country (formed only twenty-four years earlier) had sent to Munich, the fact so many of them had been slaughtered was staggering. Further, some of the terrorists escaped from the airport, though they were later captured.

Incredibly, nearly the exact situation had been considered months earlier. A man named Dr. Georg Sieber had been asked by Olympic organizers to develop worst-case scenarios of ways terrorism could afflict the games. He compiled more than two dozen, and one was chilling in its foresight:

The psychologist had submitted to organizers Situation 21, which comprised the following particulars: At 5:00 one morning, a dozen armed Palestinians would scale the perimeter fence of the Village. They would invade the building that housed the Israeli delegation, kill a hostage or two . . . then demand the release of prisoners held in Israeli jails and a plane to fly to some Arab capital. Even if the Palestinians failed to liberate their comrades, Sieber predicted, they would "turn the Games into a political demonstration and would be prepared to die. . . . On no account can they be expected to surrender."[28]

When McKay took to the airwaves once more, in the middle of the Munich night, he spoke clearly and somberly.

"We've just gotten the final word. When I was a kid, my father used to say our greatest hopes and our worst fears are seldom realized. Our worst fears have been realized tonight.

"They have now said that there were eleven hostages. Two were killed in their rooms. . . . Nine others were killed at the airport tonight.

"They're all gone."[29]

3

"THE GAMES MUST GO ON"

MORE THAN SEVEN THOUSAND athletes from 121 countries gathered at the 1972 Olympics in Munich. Though in theory the games were apolitical, they were a great marketing coup for the host city, offering the chance to express to the world one's best side for two weeks. Thanks to television, Munich held a huge advantage over Berlin, enjoying the ability to beam colorful and happy images around the world.

Terrorism shattered that narrative, usurping those images and replacing them with death and chaos. One day after being the best athlete in the world, in fact, and soon after talking at a press conference about his seven gold medals, Spitz—who is Jewish—found himself hustled out of the Olympic Village amid worries he would be the perfect target for the Palestinians.

The unprecedented calamity numbed the U.S. basketball players. Their apartment building sat near the Israelis'. Just days before, Burleson had eaten in the mess hall with a few of those who now were returning to their homeland in coffins.[1]

"I get sick to my stomach when I think back and remember all the good feelings—that the world was watching, showing love and kindness—and then there's this horrifying attack," he said. "The athletes' families were so excited and proud, and all of a sudden their sons or brothers are coming back in caskets. It's made me very conscious of how fragile life is."

Noted Ratleff, "It was real sad. It's hard to go through that. You feel for them. And you reflect on yourself—it could have been us."

Said Davis, "I grew up quickly. I realized how quickly life can be taken away from you. We were fortunate we weren't targeted—anything could have happened in that Village because it wasn't well protected."

Even though Amdur had been trapped on a hijacked Eastern Airlines plane earlier in 1972 (his account of the ordeal was splashed on the front page of the *New York Times*), during more than four decades covering and editing stories, his memories of Munich stand out for their sheer horror.

"I found the whole episode to be probably the most disturbing series of events in my journalism career," he said. "It's one of those Olympic Games that still lives with me."

Columnist Jim Murray of the *Los Angeles Times*, who would later become one of the rare sportswriters to win the Pulitzer Prize, crafted a memorable opening to his column that ran on September 6:

> I stood on a rooftop balcony on the Connollystrasse in the Olympic village Tuesday and witnessed an Olympic event Baron de Coubertin never dreamed of and the purpose of which is as arcane to me as the discus, the team foil, the hammer, individual epee, or Greco-Roman wrestling.
>
> An Arab rifle team, arriving late, scorned the small bore rifle, three positions, the free pistol (silhouette) and introduced a new event to the Olympic program—murder.[2]

In the other *Times* on the East Coast, fellow Pulitzer winner Red Smith wondered if the Olympics had run their course:

> These global clambakes have come to have an irresistible attraction as forums for ideological, social, or racial expression. For this reason, they may have outgrown their britches. Perhaps in the future it will be advisable to substitute separate world championships in

swimming, track and field, and so on, which could be conducted in a less hysterical climate.

In the past, athletes from totalitarian countries have seized upon the Olympics as an opportunity to defect. During the Pan American Games last summer in Cali, Colombia, a number of Cubans defected and a trainer jumped, fell, or was pushed to his death from the roof of the Cuban team's dormitory.

Never, of course, has there been anything like today's terror. Once those gunmen climbed the wire fence around Olympic Village and shot Moshe Weinberg, the Israeli wrestling coach, all the fun and games lost meaning. Mark Spitz and his seven gold medals seemed curiously unimportant. The fact that the American heavyweight, Duane Bobick, got slugged stupid by Cuba's Teófilo Stevenson mattered to few besides Bobick.[3]

Marie Lefton from Philadelphia served as an usher for horse-riding events during the 1972 games. On the morning of September 6, she put on her Day-Glo orange uniform and left her dormitory with other ushers and headed toward the train station, unsure of what to expect next.

"There's a newsboy there, like something out of the 1930s," she said. "He's holding up the newspaper with the largest headline you've ever seen in German: 16 Tote! [dead]. He was crying and handing them out for free. It was such a profoundly tragic moment."

In the long history of the Olympics, no blueprint existed of how to react to such a tragedy. No longer a handful of athletes running around Greece, competitors from scores of nations traveled tens of thousands of miles to Munich, a city where hundreds of millions of dollars had been spent constructing facilities for the quadrennial event. Canceling the rest of the games would be financially painful for the International Olympic Committee and others and would strip athletes, who had trained for years, of the chance to earn once-in-a-lifetime medals.

Understandably, emotions trumped reason. The U.S. athletes, such as the basketball players, faced a choice. Should they head back to the States, regardless of what Olympic officials decided?

"Our first reaction was just to go home," said Mike Bantom. "It was just scary the way the German police handled everything. It was bad enough that these guys came in and kidnapped these folks and were going to kill them, but then the German solution seemed to be to shoot everybody. It's like, well, this is crazy. We need to get the hell out of here."[4]

Said Bobby Jones, "All I remember thinking in my mind is, 'Surely the Olympics are over.'"

Recalled McMillen, "Originally I felt the Olympics should be canceled. But that would have held the future Olympics hostage."

Beyond that, the world was shocked—if not revolted—by Germany's mismanagement of the entire affair, from the onset of the hostage crisis to the tragic ending at Fürstenfeldbruck. It is hard to point to even one move that made sense or put the hostages closer to freedom. Learning from the Germans' futility, future Olympics organizing committees started to spend hundreds of millions of dollars on security. One of the biggest outlays occurred in Greece in 2004, when about $1.5 billion was earmarked for the efforts, including seventy thousand police and military personnel.[5] In fact, the Athens Games spent more on security than the entire cost of the Munich Olympics. Few cities are even bidding on hosting the games anymore, scared away in part by the expense of security to keep athletes and spectators safe.

Charles Bierbauer, a former senior Washington correspondent for CNN, worked for Westinghouse Radio during the games and was based in Germany. He noticed an immediate impact on security around the country afterward.

"All of a sudden you saw armored cars in embassies around Bonn. At German airports, you'd see police with weapons," he recalled. "I think it was a watershed in terms of political terrorism. It was such a public venue. A handful of terrorists really captured public attention; everyone knew who Black September was.

"That was a demarcation in terms of public officials and the public at large becoming much more vulnerable. Governments started to approach security much differently. Every time in the United

States there's been an attack, the security parameters expand. They never retreat."

For German citizens and their leaders, the whole ordeal was a public relations nightmare, thanks to the hell on earth their fore-fathers had precipitated with the Holocaust. As noted in *Munich 1972*, "The scenario that unfolded on September 5 could not have been worse: Jews, having been invited to the Federal Republic of Germany and placed under the host country's protective care, once again faced political murder on German soil."[6]

Essentially, the final determination of what to do lay in the hands of the person with more Olympic experience than anyone in the world: the IOC's Avery Brundage. Born in the nineteenth century, the American had competed in the Olympics in Stockholm sixty years before, participating in the pentathlon and decathlon (one of the world's greatest athletes ever, Jim Thorpe, won both events). In 1928 he became head of the Amateur Athletic Union, which provided the majority of the U.S. basketball Olympians across the decades. He ran the U.S. Olympic Committee (USOC) for years, championing the controversial decision not to boycott the 1936 games in Berlin in part because during a visit two years before, he was assured there would be no discrimination of Jews. Coubertin wanted Brundage to become part of the IOC; the two men shared great passion for amateur sports and for the Olympic ideal. In 1952 Brundage was elected president of the worldwide organization.

Because of the deaths of the two Israelis in the Olympic Village, already a decision had been made on September 5 to conduct a memorial service in the same spot where the glorious opening ceremony had taken place. No one knew then, of course, that the September 6 memorial would honor an additional nine deceased souls.

Roughly eighty thousand coaches, athletes, citizens, and others trudged into the Olympic Stadium that hot morning, where flags were lowered to half staff. Athletes entered both in civilian clothes and in uniforms.

The Israelis, too, were there. "The stigmata of the ordeal could be seen on the faces of all the survivors," wrote Serge Groussard in his book *The Blood of Israel*: "None had slept for the past twenty-nine hours. . . . They were wearing what was at hand. Those who were housed in Block 31 had not been back there since yesterday's dawn."[7]

The clash of beauty and solemnity struck onlookers. On a gorgeous morning, armed guards monitored the crowd. While tens of thousands united to mourn the dead, no one from the Arab countries participated, nor did any from the Soviet Union. Strains of the second movement of Beethoven's Symphony no. 3, "Eroica," which is designed as a funeral march, began with an oboe solo and mournfully played on.

The Olympic flame still blazed, now surrounded by roses. It was that fire—in Greek mythology, the gift Prometheus had given to human beings, sparking his torture for eternity—that would either be extinguished or keep dancing when the decision on the status of the games was announced that morning.

Ratleff remembered particularly the hush inside the massive venue.

"It was very quiet. The athletes were very respectful. Everybody felt so sorry. You think about what if it was your family or friends."

Speakers strode to the podium. How the chef de mission of Israel, Shmuel Lalkin, could muster any words after the excruciating day and night is known only to him. During a tour before the games, he was surprised and dismayed that the Israeli delegation had been placed on the first floor in the Olympic Village. In Connollystrasse 31 when the terrorists entered, he heard the gunshots. Beset by grief that morning, Lalkin spoke eloquently:

> The Israelis came to Munich for the Games of the XXth Olympiad in the spirit of Olympic brotherhood, friendship, fairness and peace in common with athletes of all the world. Shaken to the core, we mourn the barbaric profanation of the Olympic spirit caused by the malicious raid by terrorists, in which eleven of our athletes were murdered in a criminal fashion. Here are their names:
>
> Berger, David
> Halfin, Elizer
> Friedmann, Zeev

Gotfreund, Josef
Kahat, Schur
Romano, Josef
Shapira, Arnitzur
Slavin, Mark
Spitzer, Andre
Springer, Jacob
Weinberg, Moshe

They were brave and true comrades in sport who died in the prime of their lives. Such a monstrous crime stands without precedent in the history of the Olympic Games and is most forcefully condemned by all civilized men. We deeply mourn our dead and express our deepest sympathy to their families. . . . I can assure you, that despite this base crime the sportsmen of Israel will continue to take part in the Olympic contests in the spirit of brotherhood and fairness. The Israeli delegation leaves this place deeply shocked. We thank all of you for the solidarity you have shown us.[8]

More than an hour into the memorial service, Brundage ascended the podium. Wrote E. J. Kahn of the *New Yorker*, "Some of his remarks were curiously inappropriate. He alluded to his old enemy commercialism, which seemed all the more irrelevant considering that every ticket to these supposedly uncontaminated Games bears on its back advertising for Mercedes-Benz—the make of car, as it happens, that Brundage and his fellow officials ride around in."[9]

Noted Bobby Jones, "As a naïve young man, it was my first understanding that sports was big business."

Brundage—whose words were translated into German and French—also equated the eleven deaths with the fact that Rhodesia had been voted out of the games four days before they began; African nations and others had threatened to boycott if Rhodesia (known later as Zimbabwe) was allowed to compete, alleging racism in the country and other ills.

"Sadly, the greater and more important the Olympic Games become, the more they are open to commercial, political and now criminal pressure," Brundage said. "The games of the 20th Olympiad have been subjected to two savage attacks. We lost the Rhodesian battle against naked political blackmail."[10]

Tom McMillen was stunned.

"Brundage made a callous statement—the equivalence to Rhodesia was so far-fetched it made players question his judgment."

Said Brundage after the games, "I was severely criticized for that . . . but the fact is that I did it on purpose. I had to. There was a principle involved and altho [*sic*] it was a terrible thing that some lives were lost, principles are just as important as human lives."[11]

Whatever the case, the most important words were uttered by Brundage moments later. Said he, in five of the most momentous words ever uttered at the Olympics, "The Games must go on."

Kevin Joyce was relieved.

"The last thing I wanted was for them to cancel the Olympics, to give in," he recalled.

Kenny Davis concurred.

"I think looking back they did the right thing by stopping the Games, paying their respects, and starting them back up," he said. "But at that point, most of us would have said go home. We were tired and homesick."

Soon after, the athletes trudged out and began to prepare for events that would restart that afternoon. Doug Collins was forever thankful for the memorial service.

"We were obviously all devastated," he recalled. "It was hard because there was that part of us that said, you know, we have come this close and we'd love to be able to finish the Games, and then there was that part of us that wanted to show respect for these athletes who had lost their lives. I think the healing process started when we went to the memorial service and got a chance to pay our respects."[12]

Speaking at a Passover seder in Chicago, twelve years after Munich, Willye White—a U.S. track-and-field star who competed in five Olympics—could still not shake what she had seen that morning in Munich.

"It is difficult for me to explain what it feels like to witness and be a part of a memorial service held in the Olympic Stadium watching the Olympic flag of peace flying at half mast," she told friends that night. "You see, in the Olympic Village all the athletes from all nations are family. We are not Americans, not Russians, not Arabs, not Germans, not Israelis. We are one."[13]

Tom McMillen recalled joining a group of Americans who placed a wreath in front of Building 31 before he ventured inside. What he encountered shook him.

"I saw bullet holes in the walls. . . . The stench of fear and death hung like a cloud over the claustrophobic compound."[14]

Marie Lefton—who had spent summers as a child with her grandmother and great-grandmother in the Bavarian Alps—remembers the rules she had been taught then, such as shaking hands before breakfast. One rule was paramount.

"You never, ever, ever mentioned World War II," she said. "Then the massacre brought back to the Germans all of the guilt they had been carrying, the idea that the best of the Jews get murdered."

Terrorism—killing noncombatants in the name of political aims—is practically as old as the human race. But this strain was new in many ways. Before, terrorists had frequently targeted government officials, including the Puerto Rican nationalists who tried to kill President Harry Truman in 1950; never before had they singled out athletes. As well, never before had the goings-on been captured live on global television.

Black September, unfortunately, had created a successful model for evil. Almost thirty years later, an even more hideous terrorist act occurred live on television screens. The parallels between the murders in Munich and the 9/11 slaughter are eerie:

Like the 9/11 attacks, the Munich Olympic Games massacre featured planning, logistics support, and detailed reconnaissance and surveillance conducted within the base area. Preceding both series of attacks, the perpetrators enjoyed a comfort level of living in the base area for an extended time, allowing them to apply that expe-

rience to the operational act. . . . Both the Munich and the 9/11 terrorists were cognizant of the lack of intrusive population controls
and their resultant ability to live and operate in relative obscurity.[15]

When Tommy Burleson was riding in a car on September 11, 2001,
he had a feeling of déjà vu as he listened to the radio.

"I thought to myself, 'I've seen this type of action before,' even
though I couldn't see the devastation," he recalled. "I had to pull
off to the side of the road and just listen. It was just a cold feeling."

Brundage's declaration that the games would continue meant
that, among other events, the basketball tournament, with its four
remaining teams, would run to its conclusion, albeit with the semifinals and gold medal game pushed back one day. The sport had
evolved quite a bit since 1936, where the first Olympics basketball
games were almost comical. Contests were held outdoors, rain or
shine, on revamped tennis courts. And the ball? It was as primitive
as the conditions, lopsided and slippery.

Given that the game was invented by James Naismith in the United
States in 1891 and had not really developed elsewhere (the first European Championships took place in 1935), the United States was
favored in 1936. In the gold medal game against Canada, as rain
drenched the players and the court, the U.S. held its opponent to
single digits in the lowest-scoring final of all time, 19–8. Even some
pro baseball games have featured more scoring.

As World War II intervened, and the Olympics in 1940 and 1944
were canceled, basketball's development outside of the United States
stayed stagnant. In the Soviet Union, the majority initially yawned
at the game. But after the war, citizens of the Soviet Union (which
had not participated in any Olympics at that point) embraced the
sport, as thousands began to attend outdoor games in Kiev and
elsewhere.[16]

By 1951, after capturing the European Championship for the second time, the Soviets' progress in the sport was obvious. To participate in the Olympics, which Russia had not competed in since
the reign of Czar Nicholas II in 1912, became the next logical step.

With no votes against, the IOC approved the new nation in 1951. Emerging from World War II as a great power, the Soviets had also joined the United Nations to become a greater part of the world community, in part to showcase what it believed to be the superiority of its Communist system.

Of course, the IOC possessed valid reasons to reject the Soviets' desires:

The first great obstacle was the notorious amateur rule. The best Soviet athletes were state-supported . . . [and] stellar performances, such as unofficial world records, were richly rewarded with automobiles, apartments and cash bonuses. The second difficulty was that the Olympic Charter called for complete separation between the state and the national Olympic Committee . . . [but] the newly formed National Olympic Committee of the Soviet Union was unquestionably under government control and no one in the IOC was foolish enough to imagine that Stalin was going to grant independence to that or any other organization.[17]

Once the Soviets were approved, they worked hard to get what they wanted. Two Russians, Konstantin Andrianov and Aleksei Romanov, quickly joined the IOC board. The change was extraordinary, as Eastern Europe members voted in lockstep with the duo all the way until the Warsaw Pact fell apart in the late 1980s.[18]

During the 1952 Olympics, the first for the Soviet Union in nearby Helsinki, the men's basketball team grabbed a silver medal after a 36–25 loss to the United States. Though it may be hard to believe, Soviet rulers were satisfied to be runners-up as it could serve as fodder for a bigger propaganda win. Basically neck and neck with the U.S. when the point totals were added up in Helsinki, according to the book *The Big Red Machine*, "*Sovetskii sport* did not hesitate to draw the boldest of conclusions: The victory of Soviet athletes at the Olympic Games is a sharp demonstration of our enormous advances forward; of the development of culture among our people. This kind of growth of talent is inconceivable in any capitalist country."[19]

Basketball quickly became like other Soviet sports, where talented young players were removed from their homes and received training and guidance from the state-sponsored sports complex. At the same time, when Soviet basketball began its ascension after World War II, the nation also embarked on a prolonged struggle—dubbed the Cold War—against the United States. Though they had been allies in their quest to defeat Germany, the political and economic systems of the countries were vastly different, basically incompatible; both emerged from the wreckage of the war as the biggest powers in the world—and also as enemies.

The wariness the nations felt for each other impacted the world. The erstwhile warfront of Europe was divided into free and Communist countries. Berlin became a symbol of the animosity, cleaved into West (free) and East (Communist), as was Germany itself. The Soviets developed an atomic bomb to match the ones the United States dropped on Japan. Given the horror of Armageddon, battling one another in sports was a much safer way to conduct war. As David Foster Wallace wrote, "Men may profess their 'love' of sports, but that love must always be cast and enacted in the symbology of war: elimination vs. advance, hierarchy of rank and standing, obsessive statistics, technical analysis, tribal and/or nationalist fervor, uniforms, mass noise, banners, chest-thumping, face-painting, etc."[20]

The pressure to succeed permeated sports. Soviet failure was unacceptable. As Bela Baram, former columnist for *Sportivna Gazeta*, explained, "The Soviet sports [athletes] had to win in everything because they belonged to the Soviet Union—the strongest, the happiest country. So a Communist cannot lose."[21]

In 1956 a Communist team did lose—in part because of Communism itself. During an uprising in Soviet-controlled Hungary, only weeks before the opening ceremony in Melbourne, the world power dispatched the military. Asked to expel the nation from the games, Brundage refused; a handful of countries boycotted the Olympics because of the Soviets' presence.

The Hungarians faced the Soviets in water polo. The pool turned bloody, as players smacked each other; opponents were kicked and clawed underwater. Even as the contest ended, and Hungary won, the fighting continued:

> The Russian back Valentine Prokopov slammed an elbow into the eye of the Hungarian center Ervin Zador, opening a deep gash. Zador struggled from the water and fell into the arms of a teammate, Hungarian-born spectators rushed toward the pool for revenge, the Russian team formed a protective knot, and police quickly stepped in to enforce peace.
>
> Miklos Martin, youngest of the Hungarian poloists, decided: "They play their sports just as they conduct their lives—with brutality and disregard for fair play."[22]

Despite the war in the pool, the Soviets declared overall victory, claiming the most total points in the Olympics. *Pravda* and others trumpeted this as a win for the Soviet way of life:

> The Soviet press, which snapped critically at Russian athletes (particularly at track and basketball players) during the early days of the Games, suddenly turned benign. *Pravda* jovially noted that the early lead run up by the Americans had finally been "liquidated."
>
> *Pravda*'s use of the familiar Communist term "liquidated" was as revealing as it was doubtless unconscious, since to the rest of the world it carried ironic overtones of slaughter in Budapest. But to the Kremlin brass hats, sport has long been just another form of politics, and the Russians have made it clear that their overriding interest in sports is victory—victory calculated to glorify the Soviet system.[23]

In 1958 the United States and the Soviet Union launched dual track-and-field meets, starting in Moscow. They had taken six years to negotiate the event, exemplifying the level of mistrust between the two nations.

The smallest details were considered. The U.S. officials wondered if the results would be used for Soviet propaganda. After all, in Europe the men's and women's results were combined; in the United States they were not. Officials worried whether the U.S. women could compete with the Soviets. Canceling the event was considered. But finally, according to author David Maraniss, in *Rome 1960*, "U.S. officials concluded that they would look foolish refusing to participate because of the gender issue. Among other things, that would provide the Soviets with more rhetorical ammunition."[24]

Athletes were thrilled to compete. Olympic silver medalist Eddie Southern participated in the first two events in 1958 and 1959, serving as U.S. team captain in the inaugural one. Said he, "[I] would rather die than lose. . . . I wasn't running to get a point or two, I was running to beat the Russians."[25]

The gatherings' popularity was astonishing: By 1962 the dual meets at Stanford University drew more than eighty thousand spectators one day.

The same year that track-and-field meets began, so did a sports exchange in basketball, though it did not get the front-page attention of the former. The Americans won all six games during the first gathering in Moscow. But when the Soviets traveled to the United States in 1960 (having beaten the United States during the 1959 World Championships in Chile), they won four of six games, including one against the AAU champions.

It was a different story in the Rome Olympics later that year. Led by future Hall of Famers Jerry West, Oscar Robertson, and Jerry Lucas, the American team was a juggernaut. Lucas pointed out during the games that there was still a wide gap between the United States and its competitors.

"None are in our class as shooters," Lucas said. "Americans have the feel of a basketball from infancy and develop an instinctive knack of popping the ball into the hoop. With foreigners it's a conscious, studied effort. We're merely doing what comes naturally."[26]

In the last half of the twentieth century, Israeli journalist Noah Klieger covered basketball at nearly every Olympics. The 1960 U.S. squad, he believed, was the best he ever saw.

"I remember when the USA played the Soviet Union, Vladimir Krumminch did not get on the court because he was too slow and too heavy against guys like [Walt] Bellamy and Lucas," he said.

"Both of them could easily outrun the Yugoslav center down the court. Bellamy was outrunning the Yugoslav guards and he was the only player I ever saw who could pick off coins off the top of the backboard.

"In my opinion that American team was the best. Better even than the [1992] Dream Team."[27]

But in the Soviet Union in 1964, the Americans faltered, winning only three basketball games and losing five. Said Harvard University coach Floyd Wilson, "When are we going to realize that we should never send anything less than our best to compete against the Russians? The damage the U.S. image abroad suffers every time one of our teams is defeated by a Soviet team is staggering. . . . Whether we Americans like it or not, the people over there consider any sporting event between the U.S. and Russia to be a struggle between the two nations themselves."[28]

During the 1960s, the Cold War—abetted by television—generated extraordinary interest in athletic events between the United States and the Soviet Union. As ABC's Roone Arledge noted, "It became apparent with the Olympics in those days that if you had an American against a Russian, it didn't matter what they were doing, they could have been kayaking and people would watch it."[29]

On the Olympic stage during that era, the U.S. basketball team continued to rack up golds, gathering its seventh in a row in Mexico City in 1968. Still, its dominance started to falter during other important tournaments.

During a 1967 contest at the World Championships in Uruguay, controversy erupted between the United States and the Soviet Union, foreshadowing Munich in a sense. When American player Jay Miller took a shot with 1:30 remaining, one official said he was fouled; the other claimed the 30-second clock had expired. As a jump ball was called as a compromise, the U.S. team stormed off the court with the game tied at 54. Then Miller was given the free throws, angering the Soviets. With three seconds left, Michael Barret made a layup, giving the United States a 59–58 lead it would hold onto to win, though eventually the Soviets won the gold in the tourney.

At the World University Games in 1970, the country fell to the Soviets for the gold medal in Turin, Italy, its first loss in that event. In a physical battle, the Soviets prevailed, 78–71.

Kenny Davis played on that squad, led by Bob Davis (no relation), his coach at Georgetown College. The United States had not even trailed against any team at halftime until facing the Soviets, and it had averaged more than 90 points a game.

"We played a style where we tried to speed it up," Kenny Davis recalled. "But they were a big, strong team, and they seemed to know what players would do before they did it."

Recalled Bob Davis, "My players went back to the dressing room and cried like crazy after the game . . . we stood there and watched them raise the Communist flag. It was embarrassing. It was heartbreaking."[30]

That same year, Johnny Bach—who served as a U.S. assistant coach during the 1972 Olympics—escorted a group of young U.S. basketball players to Finland, Poland, and Russia to compete. Previously, Bach had traveled to the Soviet Union to teach players the game over there.

"Any city I went to," Bach recalled, "they had only one reel of someone shooting—Jerry West. Who was the best jump shooter of all time? Jerry West. You could see that the Russians were coming."[31]

What Bach observed in 1970 astonished him: "The Soviets' jump shooting, passing, the crispness of what they do is amazing—and alarming . . . their defense is especially admirable, aggressive with great individual responsibility."[32]

Packed with a number of players who would compete in the Munich Games, a Soviet squad traveled to the United States in 1971 to battle American collegiate All-Stars. They won every contest of ten save one, even though they were facing the likes of future Hall of Famers Julius Erving and George McGinnis.

Jerry Colangelo, managing director of the USA Basketball Men's National Team today, remembered when the Soviets appeared in Phoenix in 1971 when he served as general manager of the NBA's Suns.

"It was pretty evident that fundamentally they were sound—they could shoot it, they could set picks and they worked hard," Colangelo said. "It kind of opened my eyes to the players that might be coming out of Eastern Europe." (The Suns eventually drafted six-foot-eight Georgi Glouchkov from Bulgaria in 1985, the first NBA player from Eastern Europe.)

During the 1971 Pan American Games in Colombia, Americans' anxiety about their once unassailable superiority reached new heights. Though the U.S. squad trampled Suriname—a South American country home to fewer people at the time than Toledo, Ohio—by 80 points, it nipped Brazil and fell to Cuba in the opener, snapping a twenty-four-game winning streak at the games.

Then, thanks to the bizarre tiebreaker setup of the Pan American Games, the United States would be eliminated if—and only if—Cuba lost by 5 points or less in its game against Brazil. In that case, Brazil would face Cuba again for the championship. What happened would convince a lay observer that Las Vegas had fixed the outcome:

> With 2:47 left to play, the Brazilians led by 13. But from then until the final buzzer, they took only three shots, coming close on none. And they began to lose the ball on steals. And Cuba started to score. With 10 seconds remaining, Cuba's Alejandro Urgelles Guibot made two foul shots, and Cuba had lost—by five points. The Cuban and Brazilian players embraced and danced around the court. Without a scorecard, you couldn't tell the winners from the losers. When questioned about the strangeness of his team's play in the closing minutes, the Brazilian coach smiled and said, yes, he thought the U.S. team was much stronger than Cuba, and, double yes, he was tickled to death that it was Cuba his team would be facing again in the final round.[33]

Wrote Amdur, "I watched that bizarre late-game point-spread dance between Brazil and Cuba and figured that future United States basketball teams had to realize that politics could trump performance in a close game."[34]

Even before that game, suspicions abounded about anti-American influences. One need look no further than the United States Olympic Committee's recap of what happened in Colombia.

"Questionable 'seeding' of the men's teams by the host Organizing Committee should not be used as an excuse for the elimination of the USA team, but any honest analysis of the tournament must make mention of this seeding in which, for reasons never explained, Argentina was accorded a higher rating than the highly regarded Brazil squad," the USOC wrote. "Thus, Brazil was bracketed with Cuba and the USA in Group B and Argentina assigned to a 'weak' group, including Panama, Canada, the Virgin Islands and the host team, Colombia. There appeared little doubt that the four best teams in the tournament were Brazil, Cuba, Puerto Rico, and the defending champions from the USA."[35]

As the 1972 Olympics rolled around, a thaw in relations, known as détente, was evolving between the Soviet Union and the United States, as both governments realized an unchecked nuclear arms race benefited nobody. Still, players on both teams had spent their entire lives believing the opponents' government would start a war to annihilate them; if not fought on land, the Cold War could be decided, in some ways, on a basketball court.

That suited the Soviet Union, as the popularity of the sport was soaring there. The talent level had jumped tremendously since the 1950s, accompanied by a greater understanding— as Bach observed—of how to successfully play the American-born game. Many top players had been part of the Soviet sports complex for a decade or so, joining it as teenagers, meaning the preferred techniques were ingrained in them by now, and they knew their teammates well. Making the Olympic squad involved fierce competition. Said one of the fortunate ones, Ivan Edeshko, "It was hard to be a Soviet national player . . . it was tough competition to be one of 12. It could end in a fight, but it was a fight for a place in the sun."[36]

Two players stood out on the well-rounded 1972 squad. At age twenty Alexander Belov, a six-foot-eight forward, was one of the team's younger players, but he already possessed vast international experience. He helped the Soviets win the gold twice in the European Championships of 1969 and 1971 (where he averaged 8.5 points per game) while also being a factor in their bronze medal finish at the 1970 World Championships.

Meanwhile, Sergei Belov (no relation), a six-foot-three guard who was twenty-eight when the 1972 games commenced, possessed an even broader background and greater talent. He had competed in the 1968 Olympics, where the Soviets earned a bronze, and had averaged double-digit scoring per game in the same championships Alexander Belov had participated in. Sergei Belov led CSKA Moscow to numerous titles in Russia; his ball-handling abilities, along with his shooting prowess, were already becoming legendary.

"By 1972, we were a very seasoned team," Sergei Belov said. "We understood this was one of the last chances for many of us. Tournaments in 1970 and 1971 let us think we were ready to win."[37]

Guiding the strong squad was head coach Vladimir Kondrashin, who championed a methodical, ball-control offense and a strong defense. Since 1970 he had led the Soviet national team, when he captured a gold medal during the World University Games in Turin. The fact that Kondrashin served as coach, so young at forty-three, was controversial. He had replaced Alexander Gomelsky, who had guided the Soviets to a silver medal in Tokyo in 1964 and to a bronze in Mexico City and who had modeled his charges on the U.S. way of playing, having been awed by the Americans' dedication to ball handling and individual prowess as far back as the friendlies of 1958.[38]

Going into the 1972 Olympics, the combined U.S. basketball teams' fifty-five triumphs in a row—an Olympic record for team sports—could seem almost Globetrotteresque, a superior team manhandling the world's meek in an American-dominated sport. But it's far more admirable than that. The Los Angeles Lakers' thirty-three-game winning streak is a record in the NBA, but that was one team that jelled; the Americans comprised seven different teams, often with different coaches. In 1972, for example, they became a squad a few months before the games during tryouts in Colorado Springs and training camp at Pearl Harbor, played together for about two weeks during the Olympics, then dispersed.

And to not lose a game for thirty-six years? Consider Berlin, site of its first basketball victory. A city at peace in 1936, it became the stronghold of a war-obsessed tyrant, was torn apart by bombs and armies during World War II, and was eventually riven by a wall. The world changed drastically, but the American team's winning streak marched on.

Yet recent Olympics had revealed skepticism that America's dominance could last—even among Americans.

During the 1964 games in Tokyo, Puerto Rican basketball coach Lou Rossini, who had once guided Columbia University to a 21-0 season, favored the Soviet Union in the gold medal game, even though the Americans had just crushed his squad by 20 points in the semifinals.

"The Russians have speed and good size." he said, "and I don't think the U.S. can win if it gets behind."[39]

As *Sports Illustrated* reported, though Russia grabbed an early lead, Rossini's prediction fell short:

> The big difference between the teams is still finesse, and the marvelous mobility good American players develop early. On the other hand, Ivan Krumminch, the 7-foot 2-inch 260-pound Russian veteran of three Olympiads, a massive hulk of a man who might be expected on close inspection to have electrodes at either side of the neck, is still suckered by the most elementary pick. Typical of the entire Russian Olympic contingent, the basketball squad was aging. It averaged 27 years, compared with America's 23, and its old, tired blood was just the kind *Pravda* had spoken of without tenderness when it editorialized, before the end of the Games, on the poor showing the Soviets had made compared with 1960 in Rome, when they had 43 gold medals to 34 for the U.S. A basketball victory would have salvaged much of the lost prestige, but it was not to be.[40]

In 1964 U.S. coach Hank Iba became the first American coach to be picked before the trials, mainly to allow him to get used to international rules. Crucial differences existed between the rules of the International Basketball Federation (known as FIBA, from its French name, Fédération internationale de basket-ball amateur) and those in college basketball. A 30-second shot clock was in play internationally; no shot clock existed at the time in college. FIBA did not implement a bonus free-throw situation, which promoted fouling at will and more bruising play in general.

Iba's methods were a blueprint for the two Olympic teams that followed. Practices—sometimes five hours at a time—were relentless.

"Coach Iba wouldn't let up," said Luke Jackson of the '64 team.[41] Even after demolishing the South Koreans by 66 points, Iba wasn't satisfied. Recalled Jackson, "Iba took us to practice and worked us until our feet fell off. He said that we didn't rebound well. He was just putting it on our mind that every game was important. You have to do things the same way every time. I'm sure we were hot-dogging. And we realized that this guy was serious."[42]

Still, the balanced U.S. team—featuring players such as Princeton University star Bill Bradley—advanced to the gold medal game against the Soviets, who had played well throughout with a fast-paced style. Though the United States trailed early, crisp passing helped it gain a 27–18 lead it never gave up, thanks in part to holding the towering Soviet center Krumminch in check. The United States prevailed, 73–59, for its sixth straight gold medal.

Before the 1968 games, concerns grew. At the U.S. Olympic basketball trials at the University of New Mexico in Albuquerque, only some ninety players showed up from the NCAA, Amateur Athletic Union (AAU), and elsewhere. Apparently, many collegiate players, some of whom had opted to join the National Basketball Association and the recently formed American Basketball Association (which targeted players who hadn't graduated), along with others embracing a potential boycott, seemed to have lost interest in competing in the games. As *Sports Illustrated* reported:

> The U.S. Olympic basketball trials finally reached the showdown stage last week with barely enough candidates for a fast break in a broom closet. . . . The Big E (Elvin Hayes) had taken money (to sign a contract with the San Diego Rockets), Big Lew (Alcindor) had taken a stand (he admits his decision included implicit approval of

the boycott) and many others had just taken a powder of undetermined origin. In addition to Houston's Hayes and UCLA's Alcindor, among the missing were Louisville's Westley Unseld, who said he was tired, Dayton's Don May, who said he was exhausted, and North Carolina's Larry Miller, who said he was injured. Some, by sheer silence coupled with their absence, seemed to be saying best wishes, Olympics, but drop dead.[43]

At six foot eight, center Spencer Haywood shined at the trials, where big men were few, and made the team as a teenager. Flashy players oozing with talent, such as Pete Maravich, did not. The twelve picked traveled to Alamosa, Colorado, for training in air that would resemble the altitude of Mexico City, about 7,300 feet above sea level.

The Soviets believed they had improved since Tokyo. Two players, Vladimir Andreyev and Sergei Kovalenko, towered over seven feet. Said Gomelsky, "The Americans will have at least one equal opponent at Mexico City—our team. . . . I do not contend that we will win for sure, but I do believe that we have equal chance with the Olympic champions."[44]

The Soviets never got the chance to prove it. In the semifinals against Yugoslavia, they lost in a stunning upset 63–62. Though Puerto Rico played them closely, the Americans raced to the gold medal game undefeated.

In front of twenty-five thousand fans during the first half of the championship battle against Yugoslavia, it looked as if the streak, then standing at fifty-four games, might be snapped. The Americans led only 32–29 at halftime. But scoring 17 straight points in the second half guaranteed the country would earn its seventh straight gold medal. Like so many opponents before, Yugoslavia lost by double digits, 65–50. Haywood led all U.S. scorers at the games, averaging more than 16 points a contest and making more than 70 percent of his shots, which exemplified his dominance inside.

The Soviets were devastated. Another four years had passed and, if anything, they seemed to be going backward, earning only a bronze. According to *American Hoops*, "The versatility, and especially the speed and athleticism, demonstrated by the U.S. squad counted as the key difference between it and other top contenders. As a result, the Soviets redoubled their efforts to develop versatile, agile, big men and quick, deft guards who could shoot."[45]

Despite the Americans' success, after the gold medal game top officials, such as Olympic Basketball Committee chair Bill Summers, expressed surprise that the United States prevailed again, given the poor exhibition games it had played in Yugoslavia and Moscow before the Olympics. And the unorthodox way the United States chose its quadrennial basketball team—bringing together scores of NCAA, AAU, military, and other players only a few months before they needed to face the best in international competition, while other countries (such as the Soviets) played together for years—disturbed U.S. coaches. For the first time, in 1970, they created an Olympic basketball development camp to get an early look at potential players for the 1972 games. Opined *Sports Illustrated*, "The reason for all this effort is that the U.S. can no longer dominate international basketball simply by showing up with five gunners from the corner playground. Fielding such teams, we have not won a World Games championship the last six times the tournament was played. . . . We have never lost at the Olympics, but the competition gets tougher each time, and another form of competition—among the professional teams to sign good talent as it becomes available—is a disturbing factor not met in most other countries."[46]

Despite the new development camp, only three players on the U.S. squad from the 1971 Pan American Games—Dwight Jones, from the University of Houston; Jim Forbes; and Kenny Davis—ended up playing in Munich. In fact, by 1971, warning signs of the end of American domination were blinking rapidly. During a cross-country tour, the Soviet basketball team finished 8-1, mainly against top-notch American collegians such as Jacksonville University center Artis Gilmore. Scarily, the Soviets didn't even seem to be playing their best. A number of them had competed in the 1968 Olympics, so their deep experience playing together overwhelmed a slew of different American teams, depending on the locale. The group even traveled to little Paintsville, Kentucky, where the game was close until the Soviets scored 22 of the game's last 34 points. Said ex–University of Kentucky player Phil Argento, who had also competed against the Soviets during their 1969 tour, "They're a lot more poised and polished than before."[47]

Over the years, the United States had generously taught its rival how best to play the game. U.S. coaches would visit the Soviet Union, and their Soviet counterparts would travel to the United States to learn the sport. Recalled Sergei Bashkin, a Soviet assistant coach during the 1972 Olympics, "We'd go to America. They would hold training clinics. We collected basketball books to study. Two big boxes with books, one meter by one meter, we brought home."[48]

The following June of 1972, nearly sixty potential Olympians (out of sixty-six invited) from across the country gathered in Colorado Springs at the U.S. Air Force Academy. What the basketball hopefuls encountered was as militaristic as the academy itself. In the cadet quarters they endured an early wakeup, a complete lack of entertainment, and no ability to leave the campus.

"I'm hating this whole thing," said Ed Ratleff. "Everything is a mile away. All we do is walk up and down steps. Where is the air?"[49]

U.S. head coach Iba—who watched six players quit that first week—had reasons for implementing such a stringent regimen.

"Iba gave the coaches marching orders that were direct: He wanted a lot of discipline on the team," noted author John Feinstein. "He wanted tough kids who could deal with adversity. He wanted kids who would respond to being yelled at by getting things right sooner rather than later."[50]

Two exacting coaches, Indiana University's Bob Knight and University of Kentucky's Joe B. Hall, helped conduct practices. Kermit Washington, a top-notch college player at American University (and later a number-one draft pick of the Los Angeles Lakers), failed to make the squad. He was aghast at the coaches' demeanor.

"I couldn't take it," he said. "Those coaches were always grabbing you, putting their hands on you, shouting at you. I *never* had that done to me before. I guess when I was at American with Coach

[Tom] Young I had been sheltered. I hated being there. I was never so unhappy. They made you feel so stupid."[51]

Jim Brewer, a University of Minnesota star who made the team, was stunned at Iba's behavior.

"Iba couldn't remember anyone's name. He certainly didn't remember mine. The fifteen best basketball players in America and none of us seemed to have names. 'Young-uns,' he called us. I don't think he much liked the way we dressed, and he hated the stereos. A lot of blacks arrived with stereos."[52]

Amazingly enough, at this point, Iba was two years retired from coaching. Yet at age sixty-eight, he had been picked to lead the U.S. squad again, ahead of younger, successful rivals. Which prompts the question: Who, exactly, was Hank Iba?

4

TEAM BUILDING

NOT LONG AFTER BASKETBALL had been invented, Henry Payne Iba was born in 1904 in Easton, Missouri, a town of a few hundred people. As a boy, he was interested in baseball; he knew nothing of the sport that would eventually shape his life.

He found out about it at Easton High School, where an unorthodox court was created in the school basement. After graduating with nine others, he matriculated at Westminster College in Missouri, where he flourished in a variety of sports but was particularly adept at basketball, primarily because of his unquenchable fire. Noted Jim Pixlee, the college's basketball coach, "He became one hell of a basketball player. I have never seen a boy in any line who wanted to play as badly as he did nor any boy who wanted to win as badly. I have coached many boys with more ability but none willing to pay the price in mental and physical energy to the same degree as Hank. He had those virtues in abundance."[1]

Iba's flexibility on the court astounded others. At the end of his senior season, the *Kansas City Star* hailed his basketball acumen.

"If a one-man all-Missouri college union team was to be picked the selection of the first team would be an easy matter, for Iba, superstar of Westminster, undoubtedly would be elected by acclamation," the newspaper reported. "Iba appeared to be the unanimous choice of the entire group of coaches. The blond leader of the two-year champions was chosen for some position by every coach that saw him in action. Four chose him as their center, one as his forward, and three as one of their guards."[2]

After rejecting an offer to play baseball for the St. Louis Cardinals (whose farm system was being developed by one of the great twentieth-century general managers, Branch Rickey), Iba became a high school basketball coach, where he instilled his trademarks of tight defense and interminable practices. After coaching the University of Colorado for one year, Oklahoma A & M hired him as its head man in 1934.

While bringing discipline to the formerly lackluster squad in Stillwater, Iba's slow-paced, ball-control offensive philosophy—executed years before the shot clock was implemented—exasperated opposing coaches. Regardless, he ignited the program; in 1945 the Aggies beat a DePaul team featuring the great center George Mikan to capture a national title, and his squad finished 31-2 the following season and earned a second straight national crown.

As captured in a *Tulsa World* piece, no player could ignore Iba's tireless, animated coaching style.

"Once the game is under way, Iba works as hard as any player," the newspaper observed. "He is a roaring volcano and his voice becomes hoarse. But even though 9,000 fans may be creating bedlam, players say they can always hear Iba as he shouts directions, encouragement and criticism.

"Iba is a perfectionist. He is tolerant of mistakes of skill, but he is easily disturbed by mental mistakes, particularly by seniors. . . . Such mistakes as these sometimes cause Iba to leap off the bench in snarling disgust."[3]

By the time he retired from the school then called Oklahoma State, in 1970, he had compiled a 752-333 career mark. Impressive as that sounds, four out of his last five teams finished well below .500, and he hadn't led the Cowboys to the Final Four since 1951.

In fact, Iba was no shoo-in to coach another Olympics. UCLA's John Wooden had just won his sixth consecutive NCAA title; North Carolina's Dean Smith had recently helped lead three teams to top-five finishes, according to the end-of-season Associated Press polls (and would later end up guiding the 1976 Olympic team). Even aging Adolph Rupp of the University of Kentucky was promoted by the AAU as a solid choice.

Bill Wall, part of the Olympic Basketball Games Committee, said Wooden was rejected because of a power struggle between the burgeoning NCAA and the declining AAU.

"You have to understand the mentality of the AAU," he said. "They were not basketball people; they were money people. They were there simply because of the fact that they had the money and that's what drove everyone nuts. . . . They were just not going to give up control of the Olympic team."[4]

To dismiss so offhandedly perhaps the greatest basketball coach of the twentieth century boggles the mind. Maybe the NCAA and AAU expected Wooden to beg for the post. According to Wooden, he was offered a spot as an assistant on the team as long as he brought the country's best player, superstar UCLA center Bill Walton, with him, which he refused. The vaunted coach was unsure why he was never approached to run the team.

"There was a time when I would have been delighted to have been considered to be an Olympic coach, but as time went on, it was too late," he said. "I liked Mr. Iba very much, but I honestly feel that I'd like to see them change the coach every four years."[5]

Reluctantly taking the Olympic job one more time as he neared seventy, Iba tapped two assistant coaches (both jobs were unpaid) who embraced his conservative style. One, Don Haskins, breathed basketball. At Enid High School in Oklahoma, while the prom took place on one side of the curtain at the Convention Hall, Haskins shot baskets by himself for hours on his side.

"I thought everybody on the other side was nuts," he noted. "I was perfectly content. I had no desire whatsoever to be on the other side of the curtain."[6]

After high school, Haskins—a superior shooter—decided to play for Iba in the 1940s at Oklahoma A&M, even though Iba loathed shooters. Haskins recalled practices in Stillwater.

"Back then it wasn't supposed to be fun, see," he said. "Over Christmas break he'd have us go nine to noon, two to five, and seven to ten. And seven to ten would be three one-hour scrimmages. No water. No sitting. One night by the end the skin on the ball of my foot had come off. School president was at that practice, and he asked me if I was tired when I came off the floor.

"'No, sir,' I told him.

"'Sure shouldn't be,' he says back. 'Cause you haven't done a damn thing all day.'"[7]

Haskins coached University of Texas at El Paso (also known as Texas Western) for decades, including to a historic 1966 NCAA championship upset over Kentucky. Aside from it being the only year from 1964 to 1973 that UCLA did not capture the title, Haskins's team distinguished itself in college basketball history: he fielded an all-black squad when blacks were still being blasted by fire hoses and worse across the country for marching for civil rights. The victory prompted an avalanche of hate mail—thousands of pages of vitriolic scroll—directed at Haskins.

The coaching veteran had learned discipline from Iba—as the 1972 Olympians quickly found out. Thomas Henderson, a six-foot-three guard and the sole junior-college player to make the squad, couldn't believe Haskins's approach during workouts in San Francisco after the tryouts in Colorado Springs.

"Haskins cussed everyone out. I don't play well when I'm cussed out like that," he recalled. "For three days in San Francisco, he thought I wasn't getting around screens well enough, and I thought my middle name during those days was motherfucker."

Even years after the Olympics, Haskins was as punishing as ever:

It should be noted that the Miners have fashioned their 13-0 record mostly out of the same ornery defense and bushwhack rebounding that Haskins has been teaching for twenty-three seasons. And, oh yes, a raw tenacity and low estimation of themselves that Haskins vociferously encourages at the hint of a missed assignment. "Are we this God-awful sorry or what?" he keeps asking his friends.

"You're the biggest bunch of mess I ever did see," he keeps scream-
ing at his players.[8]

Iba's other assistant, Johnny Bach, matched Haskins's intensity
with a slightly more even-keeled manner. He served in World War
II and headed into Nagasaki after the atomic bomb was dropped
there, which essentially ended the war. At Fordham he played basketball before and after the conflict, earning MVP honors one year.
His freshman basketball coach was slightly better known for his
football prowess: Vince Lombardi.

After graduation, Bach played for the Boston Celtics even before
Red Auerbach joined the organization. Not planning on a lengthy
stay in the sport, Bach thought he'd play a few years before finding
a more lucrative profession. Though he only lasted a season—not
because of any ambitious business plans, but because he got cut—
Celtic coach Alvin "Doggie" Julian influenced the rookie. Recalled
Bach, "He was the type of guy who could scare the hell out of you. . . .
He used to tell us, 'You have to always play hard. You have to love the
game. If you don't, you'll find yourself out driving a cab somewhere.'
Well, a few years later, I was walking down a street in New York and
this taxi driver pulls over and starts beeping his horn at me. I look
over and it's my oldest Boston teammate, John Ezersky. First thing
he says to me is 'Tell that SOB Julian that his prediction came true.'"[9]

Tapped as head basketball coach of his alma mater, Bach guided
Fordham from 1950 to 1968 and became the Rams' all-time win-
ningest coach, recording a 263-193 mark. When Iba recruited him
for the Olympics, Bach was coaching the Penn State squad. He
had taken part in the U.S. Olympic Trials in 1964 and 1968. Highly
organized and gruff, he was a perfect fit among the trio of coaches,
whose characters had been etched during World War II and the
Great Depression.

The Colorado Springs camp where athletes battled ferociously for
twelve spots lacked some of the best collegiate players of the era, thanks
in part to the American Basketball Association (ABA). Inaugurated in
1967, the upstart league signed not only college seniors but also under-

classmen to contracts worth hundreds of thousands of dollars a year. In 1971 it landed George McGinnis, a bruising Indiana University sophomore who had averaged nearly 30 points a game and who had competed in the Pan American Games. Jim Chones signed with the New York Nets after graduating from Marquette University in 1972, nullifying his eligibility for the Olympic team (he didn't ponder the decision long, given he was offered a $1.5 million contract). Though not as well known in college as the other two, Julius Erving of the University of Massachusetts—who became one of the greatest players in ABA and NBA history—chose big money with the ABA's Virginia Squires over any chance to represent his country on the basketball court.

The ABA—which featured innovations later adopted by the NBA such as the three-point line and the Slam Dunk Contest—decimated the AAU, which had served as a bigger talent source for Olympic athletes than the NCAA for most years since 1936. Players who didn't turn pro could continue to play on AAU corporate teams, such as Goodyear and Marathon Oil. As former San Antonio Spurs general manager Bob Bass noted, "The ABA effectively put the AAU out of business by taking its best players, and the league had some pretty good ones, guys who just missed out on making the NBA."[10]

Of course, the NBA—hardly a factor in the 1950s and most of the 1960s in terms of offering big bucks—grabbed college players' attention as well. Recalled Tom McMillen, "What happened was the goal for a lot of kids wasn't to play in the Olympics; it was to go into the NBA for the dollars and the incentives."

Even Europe became a destination for college players wishing to turn pro. Clubs in Italy and elsewhere looked to American players to buoy their teams and bring publicity while paying them tens of thousands of dollars. About one hundred U.S. players competed over there by the end of the 1960s.[11]

One of the greatest players who ever lived—who had not eschewed college for a massive pro contract—did not try out for the Olympics: UCLA's Bill Walton.

The Bruins, led by the legendary Wooden, won a record eighty-eight games in a row at one point, the lion's share involving the six-foot-eleven redheaded center. Walton would end up capturing NCAA Player of the Year honors in three straight seasons.

But the antiwar protester had little interest in representing his country (and four years before, UCLA's towering Lew Alcindor also had turned down the chance). Walton's experience during the 1970 World Championships in Yugoslavia, when he was only seventeen, seared him. His wrath for U.S. coach Hal Fischer played a huge role in his decision not to try out in Colorado Springs in 1972.

"You could not invent a more miserable human being than Colonel Hal Fischer. He made Bob Knight look like Mother Teresa," Walton wrote in his autobiography *Back from the Dead*. "He was an arrogant, crude, vulgar, boorish bully of the lowest order."[12]

During a lengthy exhibition trip before the championships, Fischer refused to play Walton until an *opponent* needed an extra player. Walton responded with an outstanding performance, yet Fischer barely let him into the next contest. Walton averaged fewer than 4 points a game during the World Championships and was benched for the final three contests, all losses. The U.S. team finished a jaw-dropping fifth overall.

Still, one scenario unfolded that summer of 1972 that might have satisfied everyone:

Walton wanted to play. So he offered a compromise: let me join the team on the eve of training camp, and don't force me to play in any exhibitions. He promised he would show up in shape and represent his country. The USOC told him no. So instead of playing for Iba, Walton spent most of his summer hitchhiking with buddies across North America.[13]

Once the Olympics arrived, the Soviets were surprised by Walton's absence. Said Sergei Belov, "We realized one player who was missing. That was Bill Walton, the famous center. He wasn't coming. He was a hippie back then."[14]

Amazingly, the top two scorers in the country, Dwight "Bo" Lamar of Southwestern Louisiana and Richard Fuqua of Oral Roberts, failed to be invited. They didn't possess the attitude Iba wanted.

"Attitude is important, very important," the coach explained. "I'll take a player who has the right attitude and incentive over a more talented athlete."[15]

Befitting the military setting at the Air Force Academy in Colorado Springs, staff sergeants could be clearly seen, and players were not allowed to cross the quadrangle, unless they wanted to be stopped by police. Bach remembered the militaristic practices.

"We followed a strict regimen," he recalled. "Early practice, hard drills. I mean hard, long drills because Coach Iba was a fundamentalist. It was hard-ass, let's see what they can do. One of his principles was that two good men could stop anything. Do you know what the drill was? Five-on-two."[16]

Sensational talents who showed up to Colorado Springs were guaranteed nothing. Marvin Barnes of Providence College made the team as an alternate, even though he was the only player to average in double digits in rebounds per game (12.9) during the tryouts and also finished in the top five in assists (two years later, for good measure, he was selected second overall in the NBA draft).

Recalled Jim Brewer, "Marvin tore the camp apart. The best player in the entire place. He was quick and strong. They thought he was too physical in practice. . . . They did not like Marvin. He had all that ability and he knew he had all that ability and he didn't pay too much attention to giving the coaches a lot of *respect* and they were coaches who put a lot of value on getting *respect* from players."[17]

True, Barnes didn't exactly fit the mold of Iba, and perhaps an anecdote later in his career shows why. Shunning the NBA for the ABA, Barnes confounded the St. Louis Spirits, missing flights time and again—including one that, because of a time zone change, was scheduled to arrive one minute earlier than it departed. As reported in *Loose Balls*, "Why did Barnes miss the flight? Because, as the man nicknamed 'Bad News' explained, he 'didn't want to get in no time machine.'"[18]

One attendee, future San Antonio Spurs coach Gregg Popovich, seemed to exhibit the tenacity and possess the background to win a spot. He had played extremely well in the Soviet Union for the U.S.

Armed Forces team (he even spoke Russian), and in 1972 his squad won the AAU championship, a big deal back in the day.

Jack Herron Jr., a U.S. Air Force assistant, helped him secure the tryout. Herron attended the selection-committee meetings in Colorado Springs, where Popovich was always ranked highly. But then things turned odd: As the committee began to vote on the final roster, members who hadn't showed up at any of the previous meetings suddenly surfaced. When Herron asked why they were there, he says they told him, "We're here to get our guys on the team."

The process, Herron says, quickly dissolved into factions fighting for representation instead of choosing the top performers. When the final roster was announced, Popovich was left off.

"I've been aggravated about this for almost fifty years," Herron says. "Gregg belonged on that team."[19] (In recognition of his many NBA championships as head man of the Spurs, Popovich is slated to coach the 2020 U.S. Olympic team in Tokyo.)

One player who made the team, Bobby Jones, hadn't even been invited originally.

"As they were coming up that June, I was in the hospital," Jones recalled. "Coach [Dean] Smith stopped by. He said the tryouts were coming up and he could get me a spot.

"The Olympic team was run by a guy [Iba] who was all about defense, and I was all about defense. At tryouts the coach for my team was Bobby Knight, who was all about defense. All of a sudden, I had gone from the hospital bed to the Olympic team."

Dwight Jones overcame a tantrum on the court to make the team. In a foreshadowing of the gold medal game in Munich, he got into a fight during a Colorado Springs contest and was removed. Though he possessed international experience, he hadn't played well in the most recent Pan Am Games. Still, he was a brawny, tenacious center, and any flaws the committee saw were overlooked.

"When they called my name I took off running," he said. "I didn't know my name was going to be called out, because there had been so many good players at the tryouts. I just hoped and prayed that

I made it. I thought I was in contention because of the way I had played. I didn't back down to anyone."[20]

Kevin Joyce worked as hard as ever to gain a spot.

"The tryout for the Olympic team was war," he recalled. "It was probably one of the toughest things I've ever done because back then it added so much to your professional draft status, being an Olympian."[21]

As the trials wound down, Iba downplayed expectations of Olympic glory.

"We'll be playing against some players who were in the 1964 Olympics. We've sent coaches over there, we've sent players, we've done all we can to help them. Those other countries are hungry, and we better realize our task won't be easy."[22]

Once twelve players and twelve alternates were chosen that June, the next stop was Pearl Harbor—another military spot—in July for a three-week training camp. Save for Davis, an AAU player, the other eleven hailed from the NCAA, which was beginning to shake off the AAU and military to populate Olympic teams on its own. This meant players would be younger since NCAA athletes were, by definition, still in college (Davis, in fact, was the oldest player on the U.S. team at twenty-three).

The dozen who gathered in Hawaii—Bantom, Brewer, John Brown, Burleson, Collins, Davis, Henderson, Bobby Jones, Dwight Jones, Joyce, Nater, and Ratleff—were stunned at the conditions. Mosquitoes infested their sleeping quarters (where, for much of it, all cots were positioned in one room) and blood spotted the gym floor from dead bodies laid there on December 7, 1941.

"The base was the worst decision," Bobby Jones said. "When you walked to the bathroom in the middle of the night, and you were wondering how many rats you would encounter, it just didn't make a lot of sense."

Hailing from a small town in Illinois, Doug Collins was thrilled to go to Hawaii for the first time—until he saw what Hawaii meant to Iba.

"We should have been where there was no sunshine because we were in the gym probably about nine hours a day—practiced three times a day," Collins said. "I really don't know how we got through that. It seemed like it would never end. Hot. Mosquitoes. Practices were brutal. I mean, they were brutal! Guys just absolutely knocking the crap out of each other.

"The big night out was on my twenty-first birthday. Johnny Bach talked Coach Iba into giving us the afternoon off and dropped us off at the Polynesian Cultural Center, with matching Hawaiian shirts on and white shoes Sears gave us. It was like, 'Here guys, I'm picking you up at midnight, enjoy yourselves.' There was concern maybe some of us wouldn't come back."[23]

For Bach, who had known Pearl Harbor well when he served in World War II, the spot was appropriate for both basketball drills and instruction in life.

"We took the players over to look at the uss *Arizona*. I don't know if they appreciated Pearl Harbor and its history," he said. "My ship came in [there]. We saw the ships with, like, 400 caskets on deck. I mean, I've seen death and, you know, we didn't make fun of it. The players couldn't understand this ironclad discipline. Doug Collins said, 'They don't have toilet seats.' I said, 'Doug, this is something that you have to recognize: They're training thousands of men, and they're not going to worry about a toilet seat.'"[24]

One of the few prepared for the excruciating training at Pearl Harbor was Kenny Davis.

"I was used to running steps. My coach, Bob Davis, did training stuff I can't even talk to you about," he said. "It was the dream of a lifetime for me to be there. Anything they threw at me, I was going to take. Iba kept promising we'd have a day off but never gave us one."

Swen Nater, Walton's backup at center at UCLA, who enjoyed a much lighter practice load under Wooden, couldn't handle the strain. Worn out and demoralized, he was also famished, desperate to eat more food than the coaches would allow.

"The first day I was there I started to wonder about the whole situation," said Nater, who dropped twenty to twenty-five pounds in about a week. "I tried to stick it out. Maybe I'd get used to it. Instead, I got weaker and weaker. I couldn't rebound. I couldn't do anything."[25]

Said Bantom, "It started getting real physical in practice, and he became a target. Every day, Swen was elbowing somebody and he was hitting somebody and he was hitting them the wrong way. At first people complained about it and then it was like, okay, we're going to get you back. So every time we'd scrimmage, people were hitting him and he felt like he was getting the crap beat out of him every day."[26]

In Colorado Springs Nater had been a beast, averaging a tryout-best 21 points a game and etching a phenomenal 93 percent free-throw percentage. The privation at Pearl Harbor broke him. To the amazement of most of his teammates and coaches, Nater quit and flew home. One who understood Nater's decision was Bobby Jones, who had roomed with him in Colorado Springs.

"He was a calm guy there. Then, the conditions at Pearl Harbor made him leave the team. I understand why he left—it was the conditions, not the practices."

Tom McMillen, a star player under Lefty Driesell's guidance from Maryland, replaced Nater. Then, on the final day, Brown—a six-foot-eight forward from the University of Missouri—injured his ankle. He missed exhibition games back on the mainland against former Olympic stars and standout players such as Erving. Finally, Iba could not wait any longer to see if he would recover. The coach told Brown he was off the team, devastating him. Jim Forbes, an alternate from University of Texas at El Paso, who had not spent a second at the Hawaii training camp, filled Brown's spot.

Back on the continent, the Olympic team won its handful of exhibitions but did not exactly impress its opponents. Predicted Butch Beard, who faced the fledgling '72 squad, "They didn't have too much trouble with us. But they're going to have trouble with Russia."[27]

Though the team Iba, Haskins, and Bach assembled could easily have played a run-and-gun game, a highly popular strategy at the college level in the 1970s, Iba was determined to stick with his traditional style of play in all settings, whether they be in high school, college, or even the Olympics. On offense, players were ordered to pass the ball at least four or five times before shooting, a style that flourished in the days before the college shot clock. An uncompromising taskmaster, the coach threatened to bench players whose shots fell short of his high-percentage criteria and would often yell, "Cut that out!" at transgressors.

"I'm not against shooting," he once said. "I'm against bad shooting. I want my boys to shoot. I love my boys to shoot. But glory be, make it a good shot."[28]

Mike Bantom, who sported a sizable Afro like many of the players of the era, suggested that even seemingly good shots were frowned upon.

"We were all interchangeable, and Coach Iba made us feel that way. We were to run the ball up the floor, pass it to the baseline, pass it back out and pass it about three or four other times before we shot. It didn't matter if you were open, you could run up and down the floor and be wide open. Unless you had a layup, you better not shoot that ball."[29]

Tom Henderson lambasted the ineffectiveness of such a system.

"The shot you get in the first five seconds is different than the shot you get in the last five seconds," he said. "The defense is going to be set in the last five seconds, but he wanted us to pass it for the first 25 seconds of the [30-second Olympic] shot clock."

Closing in on three score and ten years, the silver-haired disciplinarian could have been the grandfather of his charges—none of them were even born when he captured his last national championship in 1946. Though the phrase "generation gap" became famous in the 1960s because of the rift between baby boomer children and their parents concerning values, politics, hair length, and more, the U.S. squad faced a *two*-generation gap between Iba's rigid system and the players' more freewheeling style. Defense was the key, the coach believed, even though he had recruited a team heavy with shooters. Iba said repeatedly that if the United States held the Soviets to fewer than 50 points when it faced them (as it was expected to in the gold medal game), the country would capture its eighth gold medal in a row.

"Iba was pretty regimented," Kenny Davis recalled. "He felt that the foreign teams had not progressed as far offensively as they had defensively, so he wanted us to focus on defense."

Before heading together to Munich on a Pan Am chartered jet (whose return date would be postponed because of terrorism), the team gathered in Washington DC, where Sears, Roebuck and Company measured them for their opening ceremony blazers and pants and where they visited the White House to meet President Richard Nixon. They all received a letter from him. Addressed "To The Members of the United States Olympic Team," the missive quoted miler Roger Bannister about "a need to feel our bodies have a skill and energy of their own" before continuing:

> The time is near when each of you—the finest athletes of this good land—will match these skills and energies against competitors from across the world. You have emerged from the fires of countless testings as champions in your own right. You have persevered and endured, not only to win but to excel. . . . You have proven the surpassing value of individual effort and determination. . . . You are America, and her traditions, aspirations, and indomitable spirit go with you on your journey.[30]

Once in Munich, rather than trek to, say, the Hofbräuhaus, like most college kids after arriving, players were escorted to Dachau, the Nazis' first concentration camp. They learned that political prisoners, from Communists to champions of democracy, began populating the camp before all types of others Hitler deemed menaces joined them behind the horror-filled walls.

Then the young men prepared for their first game. Despite the country's undefeated streak, newspapers gave Iba's charges little hope of continuing it.

"Raiding of collegiate talent by American professional leagues sliced deeply into the United States' Olympic resources, and Iba's group will be the least experienced in history," reported the *New York Times*. "Not a man has ever played in the Olympics and few have seen international competition, where rules allow a much rougher style of game."[31]

Iba's comments in the piece were equally pessimistic (or might be seen as a masterful exercise in lowering expectations). "All I'm saying is we can't hope to win when the players are together for only about a month before the Olympics start," he said. "Kids have to face the likes of Russia, Cuba, Yugoslavia, and Czechoslovakia, which are together four years and play 52 to 60 games.

"If we come through, it's only because the Big Guy upstairs has his hands on our heads."[32]

Iba's words proved unprophetic at first, even laughable, as the United States rolled past Czechoslovakia, 66–35. The U.S. defense led the way, as Czechoslovakia managed only 3 first-half field goals. Said Collins, in part explaining why he was held to a lone field goal, "I felt we had to put a clamp on the Czechs immediately on defense . . . and I stuck with my man like a leech."[33]

While acknowledging his team's successful showing on defense, Iba fretted about his offense.

"We didn't look good until our third game in Mexico City three years ago," he said (obviously meaning four years previous), "and it might take us that long to get our offense jelled this time, too.

"We've got to start playing forty minutes of basketball. Today, we only really competed for thirty-one minutes."[34]

Under the clever *Chicago Tribune* headline "U.S. Cagers Bounce Czechs 66–35," some of Iba's postgame comments needed to be translated:

Iba said he told his youthful team before the game that "I don't want nobody comin' down the middle unless he's got hairlips." Dwight Jones of Houston University, one of four men on the American squad who scored in double figures, translated Iba's remarks as follows:

"What coach meant," said Jones, "was that anybody that tries to get thru the middle of our defense is going to have to pick his lips up off the floor and throw them away."[35]

Scoring 15 points, Dwight Jones said he was inspired by something he couldn't translate. He told reporters he was furious when someone read him a story in another language that the U.S. basketball team should be kicked out of the Olympics. A West German correspondent on hand explained, "We in this country get tired of the United States basketball team winning all the time. It gets boring to us."[36]

About twenty-four hours later, the United States dominated Australia, 81–55, with Ratleff scoring 18 points.

"I think when Ratleff plays a couple of years of pro ball, he will be among the very best," said Iba of the athlete already considered to be one of the best college players in the United States in 1972. "He has a good disposition, and he knows when to lose his temper and what to do with the ball when he does.

"We didn't play as good as we wanted to play, but we handled the ball a little better in the second half," the coach added. "Every game from now on is going to be tough."[37]

Thoughts of revenge invaded the minds of U.S. players with Cuba scheduled next in the preliminary round. After all, the island nation of nine million had squashed a twenty-four-game American winning streak during the Pan American Games in 1971, prevailing 73–69. Unable to stop Pedro Chappe, who scored 25 points in that victory, the U.S. was forced to face the player—now twenty-seven and a veteran of the 1968 Olympics—again in Munich.

Aside from Dwight Jones, the Olympic squad was entirely different than the one who had faltered at the Pan Am Games. The new group played tenacious defense, and Cuba never enjoyed a lead. Motivated by the previous year's loss, Dwight Jones dropped in 18 points, and the United States rolled to victory. Next up: Brazil.

The United States harbored no illusions that the South American country resembled a typical Olympic pushover. During the preliminary round of the 1971 Pan Am Games, the U.S. squeaked by Brazil, 81–79, in overtime. (As noted, Brazil won the gold in part because of its stall tactics against Cuba, meaning it wouldn't have to face the U.S. team again in the championship.)

Down by 7 in the second half, and with Dwight Jones suffering from both an infected tooth and a bad cold, the United States recovered against the bruising opponent. Outmuscled under the boards by twenty-eight-year-old veteran Pereira Ubiratan Maciel—an eventual

FIBA Hall of Famer who grabbed 12 rebounds and ended up with 14 points—Brazil seemed in control. But Iba decided to send rugged rebounder Brewer—languishing on the bench with four fouls—back in the game. Despite knowing he'd be out for good with one more foul, Brewer played aggressively, taking rebounds away from Maciel and Brazil, helping to spark a scoring run led by Collins. Ratleff then scored 6 of the last 8 points, and the United States triumphed, 61–54.

"I tried to play as if I didn't have any fouls," Jim Brewer said. "I've played in games like this before when we've been behind, and I've found that if you don't panic and just remember to pay attention only to the game, you'll come out on top nine times out of 10."[38]

A stunned Brazil coach, Togo Soares, shared his disappointment.

"When we were seven ahead (43–36), I thought we would win. Even when we got three points behind, I thought we had a chance."[39] Despite their 4-0 mark in the preliminary round, the Americans seemed somewhat bewildered by the international rules. Often, they didn't throw the ball in quickly enough on inbounds plays; under international rules a player didn't have to "check" the ball with the referee. In addition, although goaltending wasn't allowed, it was rarely called in international competition. Brazil started swatting the Americans' shots away as they descended toward the basket. The U.S. players, on the other hand, never challenged Brazil's shots in this manner.[40]

But the less-than-thorough understanding of international rules wasn't enough to prod Egypt to threaten the Americans, with the United States running away, 96–31.

Against Spain, the final result of 72–56 didn't indicate the game's tightness. Spain's zone defense stifled Iba's team in the first half, and at one point the underdogs grabbed an 8-point lead. The United States held a slim advantage at halftime, but with just over nine minutes to go, the teams were locked in a 48–48 tie. A U.S. surge sparked by Brewer soon lifted the United States to a 9-point lead before the team coasted to victory.

"We were ankle deep in mud," complained Iba. "They were keyed higher than any team we played."[41]

Though a game against Japan still remained, the 6-0 U.S. team had clinched a spot in the semifinals, win or lose. Win they did, topping their World War II enemies, 99–33.

"We played probably our best game against Japan, but . . . well, they're not much better than Egypt," Davis said. "Our defense was much better; it had to be because Japan was so quick."[42]

Even after the 66-point victory, Iba's pessimistic comments continued.

"Americans need to go back to fundamentals. Look at our team. Sometimes we play what I call county fair or playground basketball. Then look at Russia. They do things the way they're supposed to be done."[43]

Though the contest may sound like a yawner, Joyce recalled sitting next to a vocal Bach on the bench.

"They were bad, but Johnny Bach was all worked up," Joyce said. "He was a little bitter, since he had been in World War II. He'd yell, 'You guys took four years of my life from me.'"

Bach and others could take solace that only one more win remained to reach the gold medal game. Though terrorism then shook the Olympics, that didn't disrupt the players' focus. Ratleff remembered practices afterward.

"Once you're on the floor, everything changes—you're playing basketball," he said. "Growing up, you went through a lot of stuff, too, but you still had to play. You still worked as hard as you could."

Recalled McMillen, "You put your blinders on. That's what athletes do."

Rather than let up, players suggested Iba may have made practices harder.

"He kept us under control and watched us like a hawk," Davis said.

In the semifinals Italy beckoned, with its 5-2 record. Italian coach Giancarlo Primo realized that despite advancing far, its next step would be the hardest.

"The United States is very tough defensively and in rebounding. Beating the Americans to the boards is going to be one of our problems," he said. "Somehow I get the impression that they only have played as hard as was necessary to win. Now I'm just hoping that they don't decide to really open up against us."[44]

His hopes were in vain, as the United States led by 17 at halftime and won handily, 68–38.

For the fourth time in the Olympics, the United States and the Union of Soviet Socialist Republics would meet for the gold medal (in 1960, though the Americans captured the gold and the Soviets the silver, their one meeting did not occur with the gold medal on the line). With no tanks rolling or missiles launched during the quarter-century Cold War between the nations, political points would be scored once again on the basketball court.

Before the Soviet players headed to Munich, according to team forward Alexander Boloshev, "The Communist Party Central Committee . . . gave us the instructions. This time it was reasonable to take only prize of second place."[45] But based on its play, the team seemed to have dismissed or forgotten the edict. The Soviet Union roared through its opponents, the only team in the Olympics to score in triple digits twice. Only its ally Cuba managed to somewhat contain the scoring juggernaut in the semifinals, giving up 67 points to the Soviets—the fewest number of points the squad had scored after eight Olympic games—in defeat.

Averaging shy of twenty-one years of age, the U.S. team was about five years younger per player than its biggest rival. At thirty-two, one Soviet player, Gennadi Volnov, was competing in his *fourth* Olympics with the squad. Yet a bit of hubris among the Americans was evident, as the coaches conducted little to no scouting of the Soviets during the games, perhaps counting on Bach's memories from facing them before. Asked about their opponent, Iba's response seemed a bit haughty.

"The Russians look a lot like us," he said. "We invented the game of basketball and I feel honored that teams throughout the world copy us."[46]

Given the way the Olympics had been progressing, Iba and his staff should have been worried that they might not face the Soviets on a level court. As the *Seattle Post-Intelligencer* reported regarding the Olympics, "Judges from the Eastern Bloc award unrealistically high marks to Soviet and East German athletes, and low marks to their Western rivals, especially to the Americans. The vaulting poles that Olympic favorites Bob Seagren and Steve Smith of the U.S. and Kjell Isaksson of Sweden had been using for a year were declared illegal on the eve of their competition. Wolfgang Nordwig of East Germany was allowed to keep his favorite pole and won the gold."[47]

Americans were hamstrung at the games in other ways. U.S. swimmer Rick DeMont, all of sixteen years old, set a world record in the 1500-meter freestyle but was disqualified for using a banned asthma medication. His gold was returned. Sprinter Eddie Hart—who shared a world record in the 100 meters—showed up a few seconds late for the dash and was disqualified. The IOC banned two U.S. medalists, Vince Matthews and Wayne Collett, from the remainder of the games for chatting on the podium during the "Star-Spangled Banner" after the runners finished first and second in the 400 meters.

And two other contests among athletes representing the world rivals provided eerie foreshadowing of the basketball game. In the super heavyweight wrestling matchup between Alexander Medved of Russia and the massive 434-pound Chris Taylor of the United States, Taylor dominated the action and seemed to have waged a clean enough battle. But the referee cautioned Taylor twice, once for fouling and once for passivity. The penalty points incurred by Taylor gave Medved the victory. The American coaches vigorously protested this decision, which the Olympic wrestling officials also found so egregiously flawed that they dismissed the referee for the rest of the games.[48]

In another surprise, Soviet athlete Mykola Avilov won the decathlon, the first time for the nation in an event long dominated by the United States.

And then came the long night of September 9, 1972.

5

GOING FOR GOLD

FAR FROM DREAMING ABOUT the Olympics as a boy, Thomas Edward Henderson focused more on survival.

Growing up in the Bronx—where streets teemed with junkies and desperation—eight Hendersons battled for space in two rooms. Attending college seemed impossible; finishing high school would be a major victory.

Around age twelve, Henderson picked up a basketball. He played with bigger kids in the neighborhood and shone under the street lights. But after his team won some games, the bigger boys tossed him off.

Enraged, Henderson vowed that would never happen again. He worked hard all summer, got in better shape.

A stint at trade school followed. He hated it. At one point he skipped school for forty straight days rather than face a teacher he described as a redneck, taking the subway from the Bronx to 42nd Street in Manhattan to watch movies. The phrase "truant officer" was not known to him, but he learned it one afternoon. Upon returning home, his mother asked him where he had been—after hosting a visit from a truant officer.

"At school," he replied.

She looked at him, a commanding presence at six feet two and 280 pounds. "Where have you been every day?" she demanded.

Knowing he was caught, he could only squeal—in full falsetto voice—"At the movies!"

Attending DeWitt Clinton High School in the Bronx followed, where one basketball game showed him the importance of fleeing the area for a better life. In a visiting gymnasium, about forty boys from the other team's baseball squad showed up wielding bats—and were prepared to use them. Frightened all game, Henderson only managed a handful of points.

Despite the threat of assault, DeWitt Clinton seemed poised to coast to victory, as it led by 7 with 3:29 to go in the days before the three-point line. But then a referee called a foul against the home team.

"A guy jumps out of the stands with a sword," Henderson recalled. "All of a sudden, the refs were blind. Our guards were mugged by the other players, but they called no more fouls against them. They came back to win."

In another high school game in Brooklyn, Henderson knocked down four straight jumpers. While feeling great about his performance, a man emerged from the stands with a knife and headed toward him. His message to the teenager: make another basket, and you will not be going back to the Bronx.

Despite such intimidation, Henderson helped lead DeWitt Clinton to a 20-1 mark his senior year, the only loss occurring in the championship game by 1 point. Soon he was off to San Jacinto College in Pasadena, Texas, where he quickly gained twenty-five pounds as he finally enjoyed access to three bountiful meals a day. There, he expressed amazement at the quality of basketball against players he called "dirt farmers" who never gave up. Averaging nearly 30 points a game, he attracted notice beyond the Houston area. By the time the Olympic tryouts were held in 1972, Henderson was invited to travel to Colorado Springs; he hoped to at least nail a spot on the alternates' list.

The announcement of who made the team arrived during a breakfast. When his name was called, Henderson's knees buckled. Armed with only one pick out of a dozen, Iba chose the powerful guard.

Though the duo never enjoyed a bond—perhaps asking an aging, set-in-his-ways white head coach ensconced in Oklahoma to embrace a self-willed black man from the Bronx (and vice versa) faced little chance from the get-go—Henderson always remembered the excitement and shock of being asked to join the Olympic squad. The boy with little hope for a positive future had made the national team.

Said Iba of picking Henderson, "Not many have heard about Henderson. At six feet two inches, he can rebound with the big boys. He can shoot and he can handle a strong, small forward on another team real well."[1]

Iba's faith paid off. Henderson had scored in double digits in a number of Olympic contests before the gold medal game. His 10 points in the semifinals against Italy trailed only Forbes, the leading U.S. scorer with 14.

In the finale, Henderson was tapped as a starter. Beyond the obvious motivation to win, he also was inspired by Boston Celtics basketball legend and ABC announcer Bill Russell.

"I wore the same number as he did in the NBA (6)," Henderson recalled. "At the Olympics he said, 'You know you're wearing my number.' I said, 'Yes sir, I know.' He said, 'You mess up, I'll make you a household word: garbage.'"

History favored the United States—the Americans had faced the Soviets in three gold medal games, most recently in 1964, and had triumphed in all by double-digit margins. But Iba downplayed expectations of another easy romp over the Soviets, pointing out they would be "the toughest thing we've faced in Munich by far. We'll have a tough time keeping them off the backboards. In most of our games, we have been able to dominate people, but that won't happen with the Russians."[2] In fact, the Soviet starting five possessed about 740 games of international experience among them, exponentially more than their opponents. And though the U.S. had steamrolled lesser rivals in the first eight contests, it entered the biggest game of the tournament without an intimidating force at center and without a player averaging double digits in scoring.

In addition to those weaknesses, think of the pressure on the

United States. Since 1936 its team had been nothing less than perfect. Always targets because of its success and—especially against the Soviet Union—for what the country stood for, even overmatched opponents fought their hardest against the Americans, hoping to make history by upending them.

Compared to basketball today, the differences in the look and behavior of the competitors was stunning. No tattoos were etched on players; shorts looked like the definition of the word, rather than drooping close to the knees. Dunks were few, and no chest bumps celebrated a big play.

Unlike a Wimbledon Finals between Roger Federer and Rafael Nadal—a duo completely familiar with the other's abilities, where surprises are few—the United States and the USSR were practically mysteries to one another. In truth, it wouldn't be a stretch to say that not only did the United States not know the strengths and weaknesses of all Soviet players; they probably didn't even know how to pronounce their names.

"We never scouted them and I hadn't seen them play, even though we were playing guys who had been together for years," Henderson recalled. "Some had played in the Olympics before. They were grown men."

Recalled Bobby Jones, "I knew nothing about them. I knew nothing about anyone we played. It was sort of unusual. I think there was an attitude that we're so much better."

"He [Iba] really didn't want us to know much about them," Joyce added. "He had his game plan, and that was enough."

Though heavyweight boxing matches in the 1970s began at crazy times to satisfy worldwide closed-circuit television audiences (such as at 4:00 a.m. for the Rumble in the Jungle in Zaire between Muhammad Ali and George Foreman), Olympic basketball games had always been played during waking hours. But the gold medal game of Saturday, September 9, shattered the norm. It would begin at 11:45 p.m. in Munich—5:45 p.m. on the East Coast of the United States.

ABC had paid a record $7.5 million for U.S. broadcast rights to the games—well above the $4.5 million it shelled out for Mexico

City.[3] The company originally planned to air the game live in the United States, necessitating the Munich start time beloved only by insomniacs. In the end, the network showed it on tape delay, just like the famous battle between the two countries' hockey teams eight years later. (In fact, ABC avoided televising nearly all of the basketball games before the gold medal battle, a far cry from today's Olympics.)

The interminable wait before the contest that Saturday was unprecedented. Both teams could enjoy breakfast, lunch, dinner—and practically a midnight snack—before playing the most important game of their lives. At the Olympic Village, Davis recalled, the team walked through some plays. No practice was scheduled, as Iba wanted players to have fresh legs. Many, as they had for previous games, dressed in their rooms, given the proximity of the arena.

Opinions vary on the mood inside the locker room before the game. "The same old stuff goes on—it's another game you want to win," Ed Ratleff said. "You don't get too hyped up about it." At the same time, the six-foot-six guard was brimming with optimism. "Before that last game Doug [Collins] and I talked about how we were going to accept the gold and even what we were going to say," Ratleff said.[4]

Joyce felt equally confident. "Going into it, I felt there was no way the Soviets would beat us," he said. "I thought it was just another game. I don't recall any pep talk or anything like that."

Jim Forbes, though, recalled a more anxious atmosphere. "Things felt a little different because of the tension. There are no more games left to play; this is it. . . . This is the game that everyone came to see. There is a lot of pressure—pressure on both teams, the coaching staff, the players and everybody. Plus, there's a lot of pent-up, nervous anticipation because you've been up all day."[5]

According to Doug Collins, Motown songs played in the locker room. The last song before he stepped onto the floor, he recalled, could have been an omen: "What Becomes of the Broken Hearted," a 1966 hit by Jimmy Ruffin, which laments shattered dreams and doleful endings.[6]

Before the game, the American players ran out together wearing blue warm-ups, and they waved at the crowd as they gathered near the foul line. Removing the practice wear, the U.S. players were bedecked in white uniforms with red numbers, a band of blue circling their midriff. USA graced the front of their jerseys.

Emblazoned on the Soviets' warm-ups was the familiar CCCP. Their team wore all red (though the red on the jerseys did not match that on the shorts) with white numbers; the Soviet jerseys offered no identification.

"I was surprised they let the Soviets wear red—I thought we were supposed to be in the darker color," Ratleff recalled. "But a lot of strange things happened in the Olympics, and it seemed like everything went Russia's way."

Olympische Basketballhalle in Munich sat a few miles from the Olympic Village. It featured 6,300 seats, of which 300 were reserved for journalists, meaning the attendance was almost akin to a big U.S. high school game (to cite only one example of those used to bigger crowds, Tom McMillen was already playing before 14,500 at the University of Maryland). The maple-wood court ran a bit over eighty-five feet in length and stretched nearly forty-six feet across. Two scoreboards informed fans of the names of the teams, player fouls, the score—and, as would soon became apparent, a number that would obscure the rest in its importance: the time remaining.

A packed house included people sitting cross-legged just beyond courtside. Soviet and American athletes from other sports gathered to cheer on their respective countries. Celebrities included King Constantine II of Greece—an IOC member and a one-time Olympic gold medalist in sailing—and Queen Anne-Marie. Not everyone got in: most notably, Soviet sports minister Sergei Pavlov was turned away because of the overflowing crowd and ended up watching the game on television.[7]

Before the tip-off, the Soviet and American players exchanged Olympic pins as gifts. Fans waved both Soviet and American flags and snapped pictures of the proceedings with their Kodak cameras. Then the USA team broke its huddle with the youngest team in its history. Starting were six-foot-eight forward Bobby Jones, six-foot-nine forward Jim Brewer, six-foot-ten center Dwight Jones (boasting the thick sideburns of the era), Tom Henderson, and Ed Ratleff. The latter was the old man among the starters at twenty-two; contrast that to the Soviets, where one starter, shooting guard Sergei Belov, was twenty-eight.

In fact, it is hard to overestimate the difference in age and experience between the squads. Even the best college basketball team then and now would be demolished by a mediocre NBA team. The repetition of skills, better understanding of systems, greater strength and full-time commitment to the game by professional players is nearly impossible for college teams to overcome. As University of Kentucky coach John Calipari tweeted in 2014, two years after guiding his team to a national title, "Let me be clear: If we played ANY NBA team we would get buried. ANY."[8]

McMillen summed up the gap. "The Soviets were grown men. They were big and strong. It was the American Kiddie Corps against the Soviet pros."

Having breezed through almost every game and having barely bothered to scout their opponents, the United States was surprised when the Soviets placed a speedy lineup on the floor. Soviet coaches and players had watched the Brazil game and noticed the Americans had trouble adapting to their opponent's quick pace. In response, Kondrashin inserted Zurab Sakandelidze and Mishako Korkia, both of whom had played sparingly in the games to that point.[9] Along with Sergei Belov, the other starters were Alexander Belov and Alshan Sharmukhamedov, the six-foot-nine center.

The ten players gathered near midcourt, opponents standing near each other without shaking hands. Winning the tip-off, the Soviets initiated their standard game full of passing and methodical movement. Brewer swatted away their first shot, and Bobby Jones picked up the loose ball. But on the other end, the U.S. committed a turnover.

With the game still scoreless, Brewer knocked away another shot, but this time the Soviets rebounded the ball. Brewer fouled Alexander Belov—who had scored 37 points against Puerto Rico earlier in the tournament—as he attempted to shoot near the basket.

"And that's one thing they can't let the Russians do—have that second and third shot," said Bill Russell, who added color commentary to Frank Gifford's call on ABC. "They are not great shooters."[10]

Alexander Belov made his first foul shot. With one hand, Dwight Jones leaped high to grab his errant second free throw and pulled it toward his body. The Americans hustled downcourt, executing five quick passes. With the ball back in Dwight Jones's hands, he gunned it to a streaking Bobby Jones entering the lane—but the Soviets intercepted the pass.

Neither team could sink a field goal early on. Ratleff fired a one-bounce pass to Bobby Jones at the basket; he missed an easy layup. Russell noted the tension.

"Both teams are a little tight right now," said the retired center, a crucial part of the U.S. Olympic gold medal team in 1956. "They're feeling each other out. And that'll happen in championship games. Even experienced pros will miss the first two shots most of the time, you know, in a game like this."[11]

Then, the quickness of Sakandelidze—reputed to be the fastest player in Europe—astonished the United States. He grabbed the ball from a U.S. player, was fouled by Henderson soon after dribbling right past him, and made two free throws. As the Americans brought the ball back, Sakandelidze batted down a soft pass from Dwight Jones and cruised down the court for an uncontested layup at the other end to make it 5–0 with about 17:50 to go in the half.

A shot by Henderson on the ensuing possession barely grazed the rim, and a tussle under the basket between Bobby Jones and Alexander Belov led to a jump ball. Moments later, Dwight Jones was fouled. He made one free throw to give the United States its first point of the game about three minutes into it.

Even this early in the contest, the ABC broadcasters were having as much trouble as the Americans. Frank Gifford—a former NFL star who mainly resided in the network's Monday Night Football booth—attempted to pronounce the name of the Soviet player who fouled Dwight Jones (Sharmukhamedov), and his valiant attempt prompted him and Russell to laugh.

"I tried," Gifford said.[12]

It pretty much exemplified the state of international basketball at the time (as did Gifford's misunderstanding of when foul shots could be taken under FIBA rules)—Americans seemed to consider teams outside their borders barely worth their time.

After trading a few baskets, a Sergei Belov jumper gave the Soviets an 11–5 lead. To this point, the United States mainly launched outside shots, as the Soviet defense allowed little penetration.

After a goaltending call against the Soviets made the score 11–7 with about 14:45 to go, Sharmukhamedov tossed an air ball from the outside. But at the other end, a pass from Collins deflected off of a U.S. player out of bounds. Bedeviled by turnovers, the United State negated any chance of gaining momentum. As if to emphasize that point, after a Sergei Belov jump shot at the foul line made it 13–7, another U.S. pass ended up out of bounds.

The Soviets hustled down the floor as U.S. fans chanted, "Block it!" Instead, Brewer was charged with a foul. Off the inbounds, the sharpshooting Sergei Belov swished a long shot for his seventh and eighth points—about as many as the U.S. leading scorer was averaging per *game*—and the Soviets led 15–7.

"Here's the guy they knew they had to be careful of because he's a great shooter, and especially he's using screens mostly, and he's got a good jump shot on the move," Russell pointed out. "So they're going to have to close him down."[13]

Said Gifford, "I'll keep repeating it . . . the United States [teams] have never lost an Olympic basketball game. But they're in trouble right now in the first half."[14] (The announcer, in fact, repeated the observation a number of other times during the game.)

Sergei Belov pumped his fist in the air after hitting another basket near the free-throw line, giving him 10 points. The Americans responded by turning the ball over yet again as a pass from Ratleff deflected off Joyce's hands near the basket and into the grip of a Soviet defender.

"You know they've made more offensive mistakes in this game than just about all of the other games put together," said Russell, who soon added after another U.S. turnover, "They don't show enough imagination on offense."[15]

With 8:39 remaining in the first half, the Soviets maintained an 8-point lead, 19–11. Then, from the corner, sharpshooter Sergei Belov sank another field goal. His dozen points were more than the entire American team combined. More than a quarter of the way through the game, the U.S. defense could not stop him. Defenders were unable to cut off passing lanes to him; his shots were mainly uncontested. They didn't try to double-team him to curtail his effectiveness. Meanwhile, the U.S. offense was shaky and turnover-prone, and it completely lacked any improvisation or creativity. Iba's strict passing mantra was hampering the players' natural abilities—and in a winner-take-all contest, no adjustments could be made for the next game. This was it.

Finally, the United States began to show life on offense. Bantom passed to Henderson as he ran toward the basket, and he banked in a one-handed layup while tightly defended. A few minutes later, Henderson controlled the ball near the top of the key. He raced past defenders and laid one in. By the time Henderson had hit another shot—this one a jumper off a pass from Bantom—the United States had sliced the Soviets' margin to 24–19.

With less than two minutes to go, Alexander Belov hit a turnaround jumper in the lane to make it 26–19. But those were the last Soviet points of the half. The U.S. defense had tightened up considerably—in fact, it only allowed 5 points in the eight minutes before the intermission. By halftime, the Americans cut the deficit to 5, 26–21.

Still, the overall numbers were grim. At the end of the first half, the United States had committed 10 turnovers, while the Soviets only tallied 6. Three fouls had been charged to Bantom, which would by necessity limit his second-half action as five would get him tossed from the game. And the U.S. shooting percentage embarrassed the team, ending at an anemic 29 percent versus 43 percent for the Soviets.

During the ten-minute halftime break, Davis said there were no rallying speeches or panic among the team.

"In the locker room, it was 'We have a game plan, and let's stick with it,'" he said. "But I knew even if we played as well as we could, we could lose to them."

Given they were facing the possibility of their first defeat in Olympic history, one might have expected the U.S. players to come out blazing in the second half. Far from it. Hobbled by more turnovers, the Americans could only manage 4 points in the first five minutes and trailed by 6.

Down 33–25, Collins banked in an off-balance shot. The Soviets failed to score on their next possession, but then Ratleff put up an air ball. With less than thirteen minutes to go, Collins fouled Sergei Belov, who made one free throw for his first points of the second half to give the Soviets a 34–27 advantage.

Coming into the game, Dwight Jones was the leading U.S. scorer. With about twelve minutes to go and the USSR holding a 34–28 advantage, Jones and Mishako Korkia battled for a rebound after a Sergei Belov miss. Jones, one of the youngest players on the court, threw an elbow at Korkia's face. They pushed each other. Though it would seem that neither deserved to be tossed, especially in such an important game, Jones deserved it more. Both were ejected.

"That was all Dwight's fault," said Ratleff. "I love the guy, but when you react like that, whether it's in a high school championship or in the Olympics, you can't let yourself get in a situation like that."[16]

Though Korkia had played a good chunk of the gold medal game, he was nowhere near the caliber of player as Jones, whose 51 rebounds in the Olympics was second best on the squad. "I think we lost on that exchange," noted Russell.[17]

Bantom, still with three fouls, replaced Jones. During the ensuing tip-off against Alexander Belov, after leaping to tap the ball, Brewer—the reigning MVP of the Big Ten—fell backward and struck the back of his head on the court. U.S. trainer Whitey Gwynne checked him out. Curled almost in a fetal position, his arms clinging to his head, Brewer played another possession, unsure where he was. He then departed from the game; though he eventually returned, his contributions were minimal.

"When I left the game," Brewer remembered, "I was so frustrated because I couldn't get a grip on the situation. I sat there trying to figure out where the hell I was."[18]

In a span of seconds, the U.S. had lost its top scorer and another starter, a big rebounder along with Jones, sat in a fog. About a minute later, with the U.S. down 36–28, Russell pointed out, "Offensively, we don't have anything going."[19]

After a Soviet miss, Sergei Belov got the ball back and nailed a jump shot. With a little over ten minutes remaining, the USSR extended its lead to 38–28, double the halftime differential. With a generous shot clock of 30 seconds per possession, as per FIBA rules, and with no three-point line yet implemented to buoy quick comebacks, the Soviets enjoyed a dominant position.

But thanks to a Soviet turnover and their players' inability to sink free throws, the United States roared back, netting 6 straight points, punctuated by a Ratleff tip-in. The Soviets withstood that rush, however, and protected a comfortable lead as time dwindled.

With roughly five minutes to go, the gold medal was slipping away. The United States had looked like a second-rate competitor. As Iba's self-proclaimed horse-and-buggy offense crawled, Kevin Joyce demanded during a time-out that the team change its conservative strategy.

"I told Johnny Bach, 'Get me into this game now,'" Joyce recalled. "I said we've got to press, we've got to go after it. We needed to take the reins ourselves."

Of all the players to take charge, Joyce was one of the least likely. After netting 12 points in the Olympic opener, he had not scored more than 6 in the other contests, and his overall shooting percentage was south of 35 percent. In the semifinal against Italy, he had managed only one bucket and no rebounds. Not only that, when he urged the coaches to let the players loose against the Soviets, his total number of points in the game was zero.

At the same time, his desire to compete in the games was unbounded, having been forged at a young age.

"I was enamored with the Olympics as a boy," he said. "I had read all about Jim Thorpe. Playing in the Olympics was a dream I held for a long time."

Joyce's pleading was backed up by other players, many of whom were running and gunning on their college teams and pressing on defense, the exact opposite of what Iba preached. The gravel-voiced martinet, along with assistants Bach and Haskins, did not fight the players' appeals. They could open up their game and go for broke.

Ignited by their newfound freedom, the Americans moved more quickly and gambled on steals, trying to fluster the plodding Soviets. All of a sudden, Joyce caught fire. With the United States down 44–38, he took a pass a few feet behind the top of the key and drove to the hoop uncontested, laying it in to make the score 44–40. Joyce then knocked the ball out of a Soviet player's hands on the ensuing possession, but the Soviets kept control.

With Henderson guarding Sergei Belov closely around midcourt, the Soviet star dribbled the ball off his foot and kicked it out of bounds. Joyce received the inbounds pass in the backcourt, dribbled to the foul line, pulled up and swished a jumper. He pumped his hands into the air. Only 2 points separated the rivals.

"They're coming to life," Russell said.[20]

"We went to our devices. We started to assert ourselves," McMillen explained. The sellout crowd, somnolent for the first thirty-five minutes in the late Munich night, began roaring.

With 3:21 to go, Forbes fouled Zurab Sakandelidze as he drove to the basket. He missed both free throws, and Joyce grabbed the rebound off the second. Given his hot hand, after taking a pass from Ratleff, Joyce attempted a wide-open jumper from about twelve feet to tie it. The pro-American crowd was ready to explode. But the ball bounced off the rim, and Modestas Paulauskas rebounded.

Down at the other end, with 2:58 to play, Paulauskas tried to dribble past Joyce and into the lane. Joyce tried to take a charge and, in fact, ended up on the floor. Though Paulauskas seemed not to touch him at all, Joyce was slapped with a foul.

According to international rules at the time, any foul with less than three minutes to play resulted in two free throws (unless the team chose to take the ball out of bounds, obviously the less preferable of the two options). The Soviet second-leading scorer coming into the game, averaging a little over 12 points a contest, Paulauskas made one of two, getting his first point—a testament to the Americans' tenacious defense.

Racing down the floor, the United States missed a jumper. The Soviets recovered and drove downcourt. As Paulauskas held the ball, Ratleff stripped it away from him but was called for the foul with 2:32 remaining. This time, Paulauskas made both free throws. The U.S. hopes were declining, as the Soviets seemed to be able to match any run they attempted. Collins entered the game in hopes of giving the United States a shooting threat.

Down 47–42—with Brewer and Bantom struggling with four fouls apiece, both one away from leaving the game—Collins and Joyce moved the ball quickly into the Soviet end. Forbes missed a jumper, but Bantom recovered and fired the ball to Joyce near the top of the key. Dribbling to his right, Joyce faced an outstretched arm as he shot. He sank a jumper—his third straight basket—to slice the lead to 3 points.

The Soviets worked the ball around in the American end. While dribbling, Edeshko ran into Collins with his left arm, knocking him backward. Edeshko was charged with a foul. With 1:50 left, Collins sank his first throw, and Edeshko was replaced by Sergei Belov, who had enjoyed a quick rest. Collins nailed his second, and the United States trailed by 1, 47–46.

After the Soviets calmly passed the ball around in the American end, Sakandelidze was fouled by Joyce, his third, far from the basket. The surprise Soviet starter shot his first and started walking backward. He jumped up and down with his hands in the air after it fell through the cylinder. The second one barely grazed the rim. It bounced off Forbes, who wasn't expecting the ball to move down after the free throw, and it looked to be headed out of bounds. But Forbes made a spectacular one-handed play to save the U.S. possession.

On the ensuing trip downcourt, Joyce launched a jumper from a tough angle (practically behind the net). It missed. Forbes tried to tap in a rebound unsuccessfully. The ball was swatted back beyond the key, where Ratleff gained control. He passed to Joyce. Collins began calling for the ball from his teammate. After Joyce's pass, Collins avoided his defender and attempted a running one-handed jumper. Not only did it miss, Bantom was called for a foul during the rebound attempt.

Down 48–46 with fifty-five seconds left, Bantom was out of the game. Though he had scored only 2 points, his game-high 9 rebounds were critical for the team with big man Dwight Jones ejected, Brewer hazy whenever he took the court, and the team's biggest player—the seven-foot-two Burleson—languishing on the bench, Iba's punishment for the player bringing his fiancée to his room in the Olympic Village. McMillen replaced Bantom.

"What a situation for this young team . . . they find themselves with their backs totally to the wall," Gifford said.[21]

On the line stood Sergei Belov, whose 19 points easily led the Soviets. Belov missed the first and made the second. On the follow-up trip downcourt, Forbes nailed a jump shot—which turned out to be the last U.S. field goal of the game—with under forty seconds to go: 49–48, USSR.

The Soviets brought the ball downcourt. Players passed and dribbled around as the 30-second shot clock wound down (in that prehistoric era, the device didn't even feature numbers—rather, a series of six lights under the basket supports slowly turned off, starting with three greens, followed by two yellows, and ending with red when time expired). While making sure to avoid fouling, the United States tried unsuccessfully to steal the ball.

Until this point of the game, Alexander Belov had been contained by the U.S. defense. His 6 points matched his Olympic low. Though six foot seven and around 220 pounds, he had failed to penetrate inside. That was about to change.

To the left of the basket, the Leningrad-born youngster took a pass. Forbes guarded him, and McMillen rushed over for the double-team. Alexander Belov faked a shot, which lifted both Forbes and McMillen from the court in hopes of a block. A half second later, the Soviet center attempted a four-footer for the win. He needed to shoot to avoid the 30-second clock expiring for the first time in the game, which would have handed the Americans the ball with plenty of time to score.

Somehow, McMillen—back on the court after being fooled by the fake—jumped slightly back into the air (almost like a pogo stick) to swat the shot away with his left hand. The ball bounced onto the court. Grabbing it with one hand, Alexander Belov pulled it toward him.

With the shot clock expired, and fewer than ten seconds remaining in the game, what were his choices? He could dribble the ball until fouled, though big men are not known for their dribbling prowess; with Forbes and McMillen surrounding him, dribbling was a poor option indeed. A teammate stood so close and open he could have handed him the ball, but Alexander Belov seemed not to notice him. He looked at the wide-open Sergei Belov, perhaps twelve feet away, in the eye. Instead of tossing the ball that way, he looked past Forbes and McMillen down the court and pumped once, faking an attempt to pass as he stood by the baseline.

When Alexander Belov had prepared to shoot a few seconds before, Collins stood at the free-throw line. He then strolled into the lane casually as the play developed to his left. Once McMillen blocked the ball, Collins moved closer to where Forbes and McMillen guarded the Soviet big man (at that point, in fact, about six players were all within a few feet of one another). Looking down-court, there was no way Alexander Belov could see Collins; even if he had, it's doubtful he would have considered him a threat to intercept a pass.

As Alexander Belov prepared to launch a wild, one-handed pass toward Sakandelidze near half court, Collins made a lightning-quick glance to his left, then began sprinting back toward the free-throw line as the ball was tossed. He nearly caught the ball like a wide receiver led perfectly by a quarterback, but as he tried to avoid a running Bantom, he dropped it, and the ball bounced to his side. Had Collins not been there, Bantom might have intercepted the pass, but Sakandelidze, rushing in, could have impeded his progress down the court. Even worse for the Americans, Sakandelidze might have retrieved Alexander Belov's toss (as Bantom's angle on the ball wasn't as good as Collins's), effectively ending the game, assuming he was fouled with perhaps five seconds remaining.

In this instance, Iba's persistent preaching about defense found its ultimate justification. What could be more important than a steal in that moment? Without it, the United States had no chance to win.

After rushing near half court to try to retrieve the pass, Sakandelidze stumbled as he tried to head backward, placing his right hand on the court to avoid falling. This gave Collins the slight opening he needed to make a legitimate run for the basket. After gathering the loose ball, Collins finally controlled it near half court, dribbling with his left hand before his more natural right hand held sway. He was charging ahead to the basket, coming in at an angle as Sakandelidze prepared to meet him near the foul line.

Just outside the lane, as Collins leaped off the floor and headed toward the basket for a layup, Sakandelidze moved low, not even attempting to block the shot. It resembled more of an open-field tackle in football. Sakandelidze fell first, and Collins toppled onto his back. The American's head skidded underneath the basketball stanchion. Sakandelidze was called for the foul.

Realizing the Soviets' best opportunity ever to win the gold medal may have slipped away because of an unnecessary, horrible pass, Sergei Belov was irate.

"It was catastrophic, like a nuclear bomb explosion," he said. "I hated Alexander at that moment. I was ready to kill him then. He had ruined the victory by his own hands. All the training, the dreams we had. The victory we had achieved. All of a sudden, it falls to the ground."[22]

Within seconds Joyce rushed to check the prone Collins, whose head lay in the lap of a photographer who had been sitting near the basket. He bent over his body.

"I said, 'Are you all right, man?'" Joyce recalled.

Collins stayed prostrate. About thirty seconds later, he was pulled up from the floor. He wandered, head down and feeling woozy, toward the U.S. bench at the other end of the court. He checked his left hand a few times. Suddenly, he turned around. Though the United States could have asked for a substitute to go to the foul line, Iba didn't consider it; he wanted Collins.

"I remember Coach Iba saying, "If Doug can walk, he's going to shoot them," Collins recalled. "And I just felt a bolt of confidence go through my body."[23]

His teammates were positive nothing would keep Collins—four for four on free throws for the night at that point—away from the foul line.

"I knew Doug would take those foul shots," Joyce said. "He's a great competitor. He wanted those free throws."

Noted Ratleff, "We played against each other all summer. I had seen Doug take harder hits than that."[24]

Never in Olympic history had two free throws meant more. Miss them both, and the United States loses for the first time ever. Miss one, and the team could fall during a five-minute overtime period. Miss none—and the U.S. players would be crossing the Atlantic Ocean wearing gold medals around their necks.

At least, it seemed that way at the time.

6

HORNSWOGGLED

IF ANYONE HAD TOLD a knowledgeable basketball coach at the 1968 games that Doug Collins would be the most memorable name to come out of the next Olympics, the coach would have laughed or, perhaps, looked perplexed—or even asked what country Collins played for.

Here's why: Paul Douglas Collins, the son of a county sheriff, didn't become a starter at Benton High School in southern Illinois until his final season; after all, he stood only five foot nine as a junior. The player rarely made his presence known with his voice.

"I used to be so bashful I couldn't hardly meet people in the face," Collins said.[1]

When he joined Illinois State after graduation, it wasn't even a Division I program. Early in his tenure there, his parents got divorced, devastating him. But he persevered.

There was plenty to like about Collins, whose height soared to six foot six while a Redbird, prompting the nickname "Toothpick Slim." Naturally tenacious, he could also shoot, becoming the third-leading scorer in the nation during the 1971–72 season. But given that he played at a little-known school, being chosen to try out in Colorado Springs in the summer of 1972 was far from guaranteed.

"I had to beg to get an invitation to the Olympic Trials," Collins recalled. "When I got my invitation, I was on cloud nine. My coach called me into his office and told me.

"To prepare for the tryouts, I spent three to four hours in the gym every day, running. We were going to Colorado Springs and I knew it was going to be in the altitude, so I was going to be in the best condition possible. I just prepared myself to go in and do the best that I could do. After a few days at the tryouts, I felt like I could play with anybody, even the cream of the crop, the players from the much bigger schools. The light went on for me that I could do it."[2]

Like the training camp that followed at Pearl Harbor, the disciplinarian Iba made sure tryouts in Colorado Springs—featuring constant, monotonous, grueling practices—were as miserable as possible. Said Collins in the midst of the torture, "When this is over, me and my partners are taking a van to the hills, opening up some Coors and turning on the stereo. And I ain't never, ever comin' back to this here Air Force Academy military fightin' place."[3]

In one game at the trials, he scored 30 points, and soon after Bach kidded him, saying he better play some defense, too, for Coach Iba. Replied Collins, whose growth spurt seemed to mitigate his bashfulness, "That's bull about my defense. . . . Iba will see. So will the Russians and all them others. We'll win it all. Talent always prevails."[4]

Hovering over the free-throw line in Munich, his jersey dangling outside his shorts, Collins stared at the basket five yards away. What seemingly stood between the United States and its eighth straight gold medal was whether a one-time high school benchwarmer from a town none of his teammates could find on a map could twice toss a basketball into a braided net under excruciating tension.

Soviet forward Alexander Boloshev studied Collins.

"I hoped he was through, but when I saw his eyes, his concentrated gaze, I thought that this guy would make his two foul shots."[5]

Collins examined the hoop, ten feet off the ground and nearly a foot and a half in diameter. Receiving the ball from the referee, he dribbled three times and spun the ball, his free-throw regimen from his days playing in his backyard.

He tossed up the first free throw. It was good. McMillen, standing at the lane for a possible rebound on the second free throw, pumped his fists, as did Forbes; the score was knotted at 49.

"This place goes insane," announced Gifford above the roar.[6]

Collins walked outside the arc of the free-throw area before returning. Again, he dribbled the ball three times. He looked at the basket. As he was poised to let go of the second free throw, a horn sounded.

Despite the unexpected blare, Collins followed through unperturbed. The ball swished through the net and, for the first time all game, the U.S. led, 50–49.

"I have not seen anything grittier or guttier," Haskins said years later. "I could not believe he swished the two free throws."[7]

Three seconds remained. Thanks to switching strategies—embracing a hurry-up offense and a relentless defense that forced turnovers—the United States scored 22 points in just over ten minutes to take the lead. Collins's steal and 2 points scored were as dramatic as the events more than a quarter century later, when Michael Jordan—a man Collins coached in his first stint as an NBA head coach—did the same to win an NBA Finals for the Chicago Bulls over the Utah Jazz on the road. But while Jordan represented one city, Collins played for an entire country, which counted on the U.S. team to prove once again that freedom and a bunch of college-aged amateurs could prove superior to the Soviet state and its machine-like sports complex.

Yet the sound of the horn during Collins's second free throw proved to be a harbinger of the most chaotic, controversial finish in the annals of the Olympics—and arguably in the history of sports.

In 1972, FIBA rules on time-outs during free throws were clear: one could be called before the shooter received the ball for the second shot, but a time-out was not allowed once the player touched the ball or after he shot. Two methods could be chosen to call time-out. Coaches could push a button that sparked a red light visible to the scorer's table or walk a few steps over to the table and signal for a time-out with one's hands (players were not allowed to call time-outs).

According to Soviet coach Kondrashin, he had signaled for a time-out via the electronic device before Collins ever stood at the free-throw line. He assumed it would be applied before the second free throw, while not asking as much.

"The idiots, they wanted to give me the time-out before the first free throw; of course I refused," he said.[8] Kondrashin's reasoning was simple; he would need to see if Collins made the first shot to figure out the proper strategy. But without letting the scorer's table know his intention, it correctly did not give a time-out before the second free throw.

After Collins swished his second shot, Sharmukhamedov quickly inbounded, with Bulgarian referee Artenik Arabadjian waving him on. Soviet assistant coach Bashkin rushed to the scorer's table to demand a time-out. Noticing the commotion, Brazilian referee Renato Righetto stopped play with one second left, positioning his hands into a T formation to signal an administrative time-out. The ball rested in the Soviets' backcourt in the hands of Sergei Belov who, despite his propensity for scoring in the game, was not even in the act of shooting.

The crowd chanted "USA! USA! USA!" Iba rushed to the scorer's table, demanding an explanation.

At that moment, a man dressed in a suit and sporting a bow tie (but foregoing his customary cigarillo) approached the scorer's table from a seat behind the end of the Soviet bench. He lifted his thumb, index finger and middle finger to signify the number three, meaning: Three seconds should be put back on the clock. The man was the secretary-general of FIBA, which ran the Olympic basketball tournament. His name was R. William Jones.

At sixty-five, the only person in the building who had been more involved in basketball than Jones was Iba. Jones was the most powerful man in international basketball, and he was heavily responsible for getting the sport included in the Olympics for the first time in Berlin in 1936. At the same time, the FIBA kingpin was tired of watching the Americans win every Olympic game.

Before the 1972 Olympics, in fact, Jones pushed an odd request that would boost one political bloc while harming another. He claimed that organizing a pre-Olympic basketball tournament in Munich in late June or early July would "provide the means of testing the [new] stadium and all technical facilities and equipment contained therein, as well as the personnel of the Scorer's Table."[9]

In the real world, anyone suggesting that a new basketball court—similar in rectangular size and wooden materials as others around the world—needs to be tested for nearly two weeks to assess its viability would be scoffed at. The agenda was obvious: teams within a reasonable flight of Munich (read: USSR) would be able to attend for special training and games, while the United States—whose team wouldn't even be finalized by the proposed start date—could not.

Cliff Buck, president of the U.S. Olympic Committee, denounced the idea. But the pre-Olympic basketball tournament occurred anyway, without the United States, as ordered by Jones. That added to the tension already swirling around the sport of basketball. Brundage, poised to retire, declared that basketball should be eliminated from the games, since semipros were "undermining the Olympic movement."[10]

Since two seconds had elapsed and no time-out had been granted to the Soviets before the ball was inbounded (or after, since no FIBA rule granted retroactive time-outs), the United States argued against rewinding the clock to three seconds. After all, two seconds had been played; how could they not count? Iba had to be pushed back toward the U.S. bench by one of the referees. The scorer's table and referees seemed unsure about the unprecedented move—and the fact that no one spoke a common language, such as English, confused matters greatly.

According to FIBA rules at the time, "The referee shall have power to make decisions on any point not specifically covered in the rules." Putting time on the clock was well outside Jones's purview. But considering he was the head of international basketball, Righetto, Arabadjian, and the timekeeper (who all owed their jobs to Jones) agreed to return to the three seconds that existed when Collins's second free throw dropped through the net.

After much confusion, the teams set up for the final moments. Though the scoreboard clock had not been properly reset, instead showing fifty seconds remaining (the operator could not change the old-time digital clock from one second up to three seconds; instead, he wound it down from one minute), Ivan Edeshko received the ball from referee Arabadjian behind the baseline. The fact that he had entered the game was surprising—and against the rules. According to the FIBA rulebook, a substitute needed to report to the scorer, who would then sound the horn so both teams and the referees knew what was happening. After the chaos of the inbounds play following Collins's free throws, no one was alerted that Edeshko would enter as a substitute (ironically enough, the one time a horn should have sounded). Further, no official time-out had been recorded where he could have entered the game after proper notification.

With McMillen guarding him closely, Edeshko bounced a pass to a nearby teammate to his left, who—as a horn again sounded unexpectedly—heaved a one-handed, eighty-foot shot that Alexander Belov tried to tip in. The ball bounced off the backboard. Three seconds had passed, and the game was over. Thanks to a remarkable comeback, the Americans had won their sixty-fourth game in a row—and their eighth straight gold medal.

Players jumped around, slapped hands, hugged and wept. Iba smiled, swept his fist through the air and was congratulated by Bach. Fans emptied out of the stands and stormed the court on the U.S. side.

"This place has gone crazy," Gifford announced. "The United States wins it, 50–49."[11]

Said Henderson, "I was hugging Tom McMillen, who I couldn't stand, so I was really happy. Someone from the stands was tapping me on my back and trying to get my shirt. He had it over my arms, and I was going to clock him. He hauled his ass away."

Recalled McMillen, "We were all jumping up and down. It was a feeling of exultation."

"We went through most of the game thinking we could lose, and then Doug makes those free throws and we've won this thing," Davis said. "We've kept the streak alive—that was a sense of relief."

"It was a great feeling. It was jubilation," Bobby Jones said. "My job the last few minutes had been telling Jim Brewer who he was and where he was. Then I told him we won."

Oddly, even as the celebration gathered steam, a horn kept sounding. Whistles began blowing. One of the referees approached Iba. Looking bewildered and angry, the sexagenarian walked to the scorer's table. There stood Secretary-General Jones, his back to Iba, his hand still positioned to form the number three as he watched the scoreboard slowly change the time. A pronouncement bellowed over the loudspeakers.

"There are another three seconds less [left]," emphasized the public-address announcer with a German accent.[12]

How could that be, when they had just played the final three seconds? Jones, with the referees' blessing, said the inaccurate scoreboard clock meant the play was nullified. Though the scoreboard clock had been set improperly, considering only three seconds remained—an amount of time a child could count to—it seemed almost irrelevant. Referees traditionally conduct their own count when only a few seconds remain in a game, in case there is a scoreboard problem, and there was no doubt three seconds had passed and then some once the ball bounced off the backboard and bounded around the court.

One of the referees waved his right arm more than half a dozen times at American players, trying to steer them to their bench. Iba was enraged. Bach confronted Jones.

"I was up at the table trying to speak to Dr. Jones. But he kept saying 'Three.' And I kept saying, 'You can't put time on the clock.' But his order to me was, 'Tell Mr. Iba to put the United States team on the floor or forfeit the gold medal.' And Coach Iba had to decide in that chaos what to do."[13]

According to the Games of the XXth Olympiad Munich 1972 Basketball Regulations, "Any team which without valid reason fails to appear to play a scheduled game or withdraws from the court before the end of the game, shall lose the game by forfeit." That would seem to be a good reason why Iba and others would be worried about departing the court, especially since the United States held the lead. But who could call a forfeit? FIBA rules at the time, under the header Duties and Powers of Referee, declared, "He shall have power to forfeit a game when conditions warrant." No one else is listed as possessing that power—including the secretary-general of FIBA, Jones.

At the same time, leaving the court seemed reasonable. After all, the team had more points at the end of the game, and thus had won it. It would take tremendous courage to hand the United States its first-ever loss via forfeit merely because it refused to keep playing the final three seconds yet one more time. Haskins demanded as much. But Iba said he wasn't going to lose the game sitting in the locker room.

Bach further pleaded the team's case futilely at the scorer's table, where neither the referees nor anyone in charge spoke English.

"It was the Tower of Babel," he recalled. "Who do I talk to? Who understands what I'm saying?"[14]

At some point Tommy Burleson—the tallest player on either team—tried to persuade Bach and Haskins that, despite his benching, he should defend Alexander Belov, who was hovering near the U.S. basket.

Iba refused.

"I was really mad—I was very upset," Burleson said, speaking passionately more than forty-five years after Iba's decision. "I said, 'We've got to be in their face when they go up to shoot the ball.'"

Beyond inserting Burleson, another way to achieve a similar result would have been to move McMillen away from the inbounder and have him guard Alexander Belov down the court, given that McMillen stood a few inches taller than the Soviet player. Even Kondrashin, in retrospect, said the United States should have done as much. But Iba wanted McMillen on Edeshko, especially since his defense had been successful on the previous play.

Though Iba made that decision, between his arguing with the refs and trying to talk with those at the scorer's table, he wasn't able to orchestrate the strongest defense. In fact, Bobby Jones—who was picked for the team because of his defensive prowess and ended up as one of the greatest defenders in NBA history—wasn't on the floor at all in the last three seconds.

The U.S. players matched up as best they could and awaited yet another inbounds play. On the Soviet side, though, Kondrashin really enjoyed two unofficial time-outs during the chaos. He had nothing to argue about at the scorers' table, so twice he gathered his players in front of their bench and explained what he wanted from them on the final play.

Remembered Edeshko, "Coach said that I must give pass to Belov. Only one moment was possible to win—a long pass."[15]

Kondrashin also tried to boost their morale as they faced their only deficit of the game.

"I said that three seconds is a lot of time," Kondrashin recalled. "Everything isn't lost."[16]

Known for his passing prowess from the end of the court, Edeshko had thrown lengthy strikes to Soviet players by the far basket in games before the Olympics. He set up out of bounds, seven or eight feet deep, as McMillen bounded to the baseline. Yet unlike the previous inbound pass, McMillen then moved far away from Edeshko, ending up near the free-throw line. Why? Referee Arabadjian motioned McMillen with his left hand to move away and then made an upward movement with his left arm near the end line, which the American player interpreted to mean: stay away from the inbounder.

"The Eastern European referee kept motioning me off the line," McMillen recalled. "The player had a lot of room to go back. Of course your arms are going to go over the line—that's fine, as long as my feet are behind the line.

"It's a stupid, made-up excuse that I was over the plane with my arms or couldn't go over with them. The referee shouldn't have been making any motions. Another problem was he didn't speak English—I thought he would give me a technical foul if I didn't move."

When McMillen guarded Edeshko's previous inbound pass, Arabadjian had made no gestures; McMillen stood right by the baseline, forcing a short pass in the backcourt.

With McMillen so far away as to be inconsequential, Edeshko moved closer to the baseline. Enjoying a clear and unimpeded view downcourt, he took one step and, with the motion of a shot putter, heaved the ball toward Alexander Belov at the other end of the court.

For the twenty-year-old Alexander Belov, the key was trying to outjump the equally tall six-foot-seven Forbes and the six-foot-three Joyce, who scurried away from Sergei Belov and began running toward the lane after Edeshko let go of the ball. Alexander Belov leaped up and clutched the ball. Forbes fell to the floor after knocking into Belov, and Joyce's momentum carried him out of bounds.

Alexander Belov stood alone in the lane, a few feet from the basket. Achieving the Soviet Union's first gold medal in basketball rested in his hands, only moments after he was prepared to go down in history as the nation's biggest goat. From the field during the game, he had shot miserably, making two baskets on eleven attempts, his 37 points in a previous Olympic game a mere memory.

He looked at the basket. After one fake (perhaps out of habit, as no one was guarding him), he released a soft bank shot—and it dropped in, likely the easiest 2 points of the whole Olympics. Then the horn sounded—for the last time. USSR 51, USA 50. In the dark late night of Munich, snapped was the U.S. streak of sixty-three wins in a row, along with its Olympic hegemony in basketball, which had started hundreds of miles to the north in Berlin on a rainy court during the reign of a German madman.

This time, at long last, the game was over. But the controversy was only beginning.

1. Players trying out for the 1972 U.S. Olympic basketball team gather with coaches and others in Colorado Springs, Colorado. Photo courtesy of Kenny Davis.

2. Head Coach Hank Iba. Courtesy of the U.S. Olympic Committee.

3. Assistant Coach Johnny Bach. Courtesy of the U.S. Olympic Committee.

4. Assistant Coach Don Haskins. Courtesy of the U.S. Olympic Committee.

5. Assistant Manager Herbert Mols. Courtesy of the U.S. Olympic Committee.

6. U.S. Olympic basketball chair
M. K. "Bill" Summers. Courtesy
of the U.S. Olympic Committee.

7. Members of the U.S. Olympic
basketball team preparing for
an exhibition game in Hawaii
before the Olympics. Photo
courtesy of Kenny Davis.

8. Michael Bantom. Courtesy of the U.S. Olympic Committee.

9. Jim Brewer. Courtesy of the U.S. Olympic Committee.

10. The U.S. basketball contingent posing for a photo in the Olympic Village in Munich. Crawford Family U.S. Olympic Archives, U.S. Olympic Committee.

11. Tommy Burleson. Courtesy of the U.S. Olympic Committee.

12. Kenny Davis. Courtesy of the U.S. Olympic Committee.

13. U.S. players, coaches, and others gather at one end of the Olympic basketball court. Crawford Family U.S. Olympic Archives, U.S. Olympic Committee.

14. Jim Forbes. Courtesy of the U.S. Olympic Committee.

15. Dwight Jones. Courtesy of the U.S. Olympic Committee.

16. Dwight Jones of the United States and Alexander Belov of the Soviet Union battling for the opening tip-off during the gold medal game. Photograph by Tony Duffy/Allsport Photographic, Ltd., Crawford Family U.S. Olympic Archives, U.S. Olympic Committee.

17. Tom Henderson. Courtesy of the U.S. Olympic Committee.

18. Kevin Joyce. Courtesy of the U.S. Olympic Committee.

19. Kevin Joyce, who helped spark a U.S. comeback late in the gold medal game, is stymied by a Soviet defender. Photograph by Duane Hopp, Crawford Family U.S. Olympic Archives, U.S. Olympic Committee.

20. Bobby Jones. Courtesy of the U.S. Olympic Committee.

21. Doug Collins. Courtesy of the U.S. Olympic Committee.

22. After being fouled and knocked under the basketball stanchion, Doug Collins shoots one of his two free throws with three seconds remaining to give the United States its first lead, 50–49, against the Soviet Union. Rich Clarkson/Clarkson Creative.

23. Ed Ratleff. Courtesy of the U.S. Olympic Committee.

24. Tom McMillen. Courtesy of the U.S. Olympic Committee.

25. Tom McMillen (13), Tom Henderson (6), and others join in the celebration after the apparent U.S. victory. Rich Clarkson/Clarkson Creative.

26. The Soviet Union's Alexander Belov puts in the final basket during the third time the last three seconds were played to give the Soviet Union the victory as U.S. player Jim Forbes lies on the court. Rich Clarkson/Clarkson Creative.

27. U.S. coach Hank Iba tries to plead the Americans' case while referee Artenik Arabadjian (who did not speak English) looks elsewhere. The final three seconds ended up taking eight seconds as time was twice ordered back on the clock. Rich Clarkson/Clarkson Creative.

28. Kenny and Rita Davis enjoying a welcome-home ceremony in Kentucky after Kenny returned from the 1972 Olympics. Photo courtesy of Kenny Davis.

29. Doug Collins embracing Kenny Davis
after giving a talk at the fortieth reunion
of the 1972 U.S. Olympic basketball team.
Photo courtesy of Kenny Davis.

7

"AND THIS TIME IT *IS* OVER"

DURING THE MOST IMPORTANT play in U.S. Olympic basketball history, James Ricardo Forbes seemed an unlikely choice to guard Alexander Belov.

On a team featuring a number of taller players, Forbes hardly stood out. But aside from McMillen, all of them—from Burleson to Bantom to Brewer to Dwight Jones—watched from the bench, having either angered Iba, fouled out, gotten knocked out, or been ejected.

Turning twenty only a few weeks before the games, Forbes was one of the least experienced U.S. players. Replacing the injured John Brown at the last minute, he didn't even train at Pearl Harbor and lacked time to prepare with his teammates and to get into ideal shape.

The fact that Haskins coached him at the University of Texas at El Paso, though, helped his transition. And in the semifinal game, Forbes scored 14 points to propel the Americans to another gold medal opportunity.

But now he lay sprawled on the floor in disbelief, having watched the U.S. victory streak disintegrate because of an uncontested basket only a few feet away. He jumped up, appealing to Righetto to change what had just happened. After handing the referee the ball, Forbes swept his flattened hands across his midsection, hoping that making a disallowed motion would somehow negate the improbable basket.

"All these years later, you ask yourself, maybe if I'd have fronted him, maybe if I had bumped him a little bit harder instead of getting knocked down," Forbes said. "I think about it every day of my life."[1]

Little did the one-time National High School All-American from Texas know that lying on the hardwood in Munich, unfortunately, served as a portent. During his junior year at UTEP that fall, he ended up strewn on the court again after coming down the wrong way following a layup. He severely injured his knee. Recalled Forbes, "I'd just come back from the Olympics and, even though we'd lost, I was really riding high. I figured a good junior year, a good senior year, and then I'd make me a little money in the NBA."[2]

The premature end of Forbes's career saddened Haskins.

"He was going in for a layup and he stopped to keep from running over a smaller guy. That was typical of Jim. He was an automatic first-rounder. From our first scrimmage, it was obvious he was an NBA player. It was just a tragedy.

"In fact, Mr. Iba told me after the Olympics that that kid would make a cellarful of money someday if I didn't mess him up."[3]

Even without the knee injury, being at school after the 1972 Olympic loss pained Forbes.

"I'd go in my room and close the door and not come out," he said. "I'd lie there and just think about it. My mind would play tricks and I'd start thinking, If someone else had been back there, would it have happened? But I never should've been put in that situation—those last three seconds never should've been played."[4]

To express their dismay, the vanquished Americans could choose from plenty of words. The dictionary groans with appropriate ones. Heartrending. Gut-wrenching. Stupefying. Galling. They all work. And there are others for them to champion—including unprecedented, both for the extraordinary chaotic ending and for the first U.S. defeat in Olympic history.

The way it finished, in fact, was almost akin to a pickup game, where a player yells, "That doesn't count," or "Redo," and that person's sentiments win the day. Nothing was typical about the last moments in Munich, nothing that dignified the game of basketball, nothing that felt like victory or defeat had been deserved.

That didn't stop Alexander Belov from chugging down the length of the court with unmitigated joy, his arms raised triumphantly and mouth in an open roar.

"We have an expression to go crazy from happiness," Sergei Belov said. "When Alexander Belov made the last basket, he was running without understanding anything."[5]

A number of years ago, Bobby Jones was approached by a woman after a talk he gave. She said her mother was a missionary in Germany and served as a housemother during the Olympics. Rather than stay in the Olympic Village, the Soviet basketball team rented the home.

"She shared Jesus each night with these athletes, and they looked at her blankly," said Bobby Jones, recalling her story. "Before the last game, she asked if any of them would accept Jesus as their savior. Alexander Belov said he would if she could promise through Jesus they would win the last game. She said she couldn't pray for them to win, but she could pray for God to do his will.

"After the game, Alexander Belov came back and said he would give his life to the Lord." Had the atheistic Soviet authorities known that, despite his newly heroic stature, he could have been ushered to Siberia.

Piling on top of each other in front of their bench, the Soviet players jettisoned their widespread perception as robotic zombies. They lifted their coach, Kondrashin, off the ground, tossing him into the air. Once standing on the court again, Kondrashin received a kiss on the cheek from a Soviet player (probably not from Alexander Belov, whom Kondrashin lambasted after the triumph for the wayward pass Collins stole). Sakandelidze—who had been spread on the floor moments before after fouling Collins—laid on the court by the baseline again, an ecstatic smile on his face. Bottles of vodka were raised triumphantly, and some threw their jerseys aside and celebrated shirtless.

Soviet television commentator Nina Eremina, a former player for the women's national team, was overcome.

"I yelled 'Victory!' Nothing but victory!" she recalled. "And I was jumping and dancing with complete joy."[6]

At home alone in Russia, a seven-year-old boy watched the game on a black-and-white television. His name was Mikhail Prokhorov. About forty years later, he would become well known in the United States as the owner of the NBA's Brooklyn Nets. But on this day, he was an excited, dumbfounded fan who listened to Eremina's historic call.

"As the game went on, she was so incredulous that she nearly lost her voice," recalled Prokhorov, whose father, Dmitri, attended the game as the head of the international department for the Soviet Sport Committee. "We had been leading for most of the game. I remember thinking as we got to the very end that we could lose this thing. I couldn't believe we won."

After witnessing the astonishing final basket, Gifford's words were more measured than those of his Soviet television counterpart. "And this time it *is* over," he said.[7]

After the Belov game-winner, U.S. players who hadn't participated in the last three seconds (which lasted more than five minutes in real time) were frozen on the bench. Some stared vacantly; others pressed their hands against their face and lowered their heads. Expressions were anguished—especially Forbes's, who was convulsed in tears while walking off the court.

Unlike today, no on-the-spot TV reporters grabbed U.S. players to ask how they felt. Bewildered and angry no doubt would have been their responses—along with cheated. Said Kevin Joyce in the aftermath, "They've been trying to rook the Americans in the Olympics and they've finally done it!"[8]

Long after the powerful, painful emotions had ebbed, U.S. players still offered strong visuals of their postgame suffering.

"It was sort of like being on top of the Sears Tower in Chicago celebrating and then being thrown off and falling one hundred floors to the ground," said Collins, more than thirty years later.[9]

Noted McMillen, "Never before or since have I plummeted from such heights to such depths so quickly."[10]

Think how angry you get if a referee or an umpire makes a bad call against your favorite team. Now magnify it a hundredfold— you're on the field, playing for a world championship, and a referee and an administrator make dumbfounding decisions to keep the gold medal from resting on your chest.

It might be easier to consider how unfathomable the situation was by comparing it to a similar scenario in another sport. Think if this happened in, say, baseball's World Series.

Your visiting team is up by one run, bottom of the ninth inning. Two outs, an 0-2 count with the tying run on first. The pitch . . . strike three looking! But wait . . . the batter says he had called time, and the home-plate umpire missed calling it. The umpires confer . . . one more pitch to go.

Reset. Another pitch . . . a swing and a miss! The celebration sprawls across the infield. But wait . . . the manager had been trying to get the umpire's attention to put in a pinch hitter. He argues his case. A few minutes later, the pinch hitter stands in the batter's box. Another pitch . . . it's a home run! Your team loses the World Series. And, if it's like the '72 Olympics for the U.S. players, none will get the chance to play in another one.

True, bad calls here and there have transformed outcomes— perhaps umpire Don Denkinger's safe call during the 1985 World Series that helped Kansas City come back to beat St. Louis is the most infamous among U.S. professional sports championships— but never before or since has a sequence of freakish events matched the ones that beset the 1972 gold medal game. In basketball, the only parallel (however slim) seems to be when a scoreboard malfunctioned near the end of a Harlem Globetrotters game in 1957. It showed the perennial winners enjoying a 61–57 lead over the Washington Generals. The Globetrotters performed their usual showboating, thinking they had pocketed another victory. But the scoreboard was wrong. At the end of the game, to the Globetrotters' astonishment, they had lost 67–63—though they refused to acknowledge it as a defeat in their official record for many decades.[11]

It comforts the U.S. team little, but other controversial competitions marred the 1972 games. Perhaps none matched the craziness of the field-hockey championship between longtime champion Pakistan and upstart West Germany. In a savage battle that included a brawl, West Germany—an obvious crowd favorite in Munich—won 1–0. Pakistan scored a goal, but it was disallowed.

What happened after didn't quite match Pierre de Coubertin's vision of the Olympics. "The players smashed the goal nets, while Pakistani fans raced onto the field and laid siege to the judge's table, pouring a pitcher of water over the head of Rene Frank, the Belgian president of the Internationale Hockey Federation," according to David Clay Large in *Munich 1972*. "Team members also physically assaulted a doctor who tried to administer the required postgame drug test."[12]

Other contentious Olympic finishes arose in later years. The 1988 gold medal bout between U.S. boxer Roy Jones and South Korea's Park Si-hun, representing the host country, featured Jones landing close to three times more punches than his opponent. Yet he was awarded the silver. And during the 2002 Winter Olympics in Salt Lake City, two French officials (including a judge) were suspended by the International Skating Union for fixing the figure-skating pairs gold medal event. In an unprecedented move, the IOC handed silver medalists Jamie Salé and David Pelletier duplicate gold medals.

In both instances, judges created the scores, meaning that results were based on subjective rankings and thus open to corruption. In the USSR-USA game, team points determined the outcome—something supposedly out of the realm of outsiders to influence. But that proved not to be true.

Protesting vociferously at the scorer's table once again, this time accompanied by a handful of players, Iba's objections yielded nothing (Jones stood placidly nearby, immune to Iba's barking and again displaying the number three, as if reiterating his belief that his intrusion had been justified). Even writer Gil Rogan of *Sports Illustrated* bounded down from the stands, giving up journalistic objectivity to argue the team's case with others at the table. When he became the magazine's editor, he recalled the moment.

"[I was] eloquently discoursing on the international rules of basketball, pointing out with devastating effect why the last Soviet basket should be disallowed, that the U.S. had won," he wrote. "I know as much about the international rules of basketball as I do about the rules of taekwondo. But I was in a zone and the ref was . . . hanging on every word I was saying. Or so I thought until I heard someone behind me saying, 'Give it up.'"[13]

His main takeaway: Learn the referees' language.

When it seemed nothing else could go awry, Iba suffered another indignity. Amid the mayhem of the final game of his coaching career, while exhorting that his team had been robbed, Iba, in fact, *was* robbed; a wallet containing nearly $400 was lifted from his tan-colored pants during the chaos on the court in Munich.

It's almost inconceivable that the United States—the best team by far in Olympic history—lost its first game ever on an uncontested layup during the most critical defensive play of its thirty-six-year run. And though the scoreboard clock finally read zero, the real-time minutes continued to tick on the still-crowded basketball floor.

"It was very surreal," McMillen said. "You don't have those moments in life very often. It was a real comedy of errors. The ending of the game was just unbelievable."

Joyce was flummoxed.

"I was very confused when they first put time on the clock. I thought, 'What do you mean? You can't do this.' Then they don't score again, and they put time on again?

"When it was all over, I evaluated what went on, and I said, 'This is bullshit.'"

Noted Kenny Davis, "It seems that everything was suspended in terms of legality. Our contention was you can't add time to the clock when the game is over. The whole thing was the Jones guy said the Russians were trying to call a time-out so they gave it to them. We were trying to score 100 points too, but no one was giving that to us."

Stunned at what he was watching, Dwight Chapin of the *Los Angeles Times* recalled the aftermath.

"No one seemed to have any idea what was going on. I opted

to go to the coaches' press conference rather than the U.S. locker room, looking for a few quotes and hopefully a little clarity, so I could make the bus back to the press center. The press conference was chaos, officials talking but saying nothing, and poor old Hank Iba looking as if he were having a stroke."

Iba complained bitterly to the reporters.

"There's no possible way that game could have been won by those guys. Even if the ball's out of bounds with three seconds I know this: They're not going to get the ball down there and score legally. I sent two guys back there and they both ended up on their cans. I don't think they could have got it down there in five seconds."[14]

Dejected, players wandered in a trance into their tiny white-brick locker room, featuring not much more than a long bench with angled hooks above it.

"You're kind of in shock," Ratleff recalled. "We knew the game had been taken away from us. How could we be losers if we won?"

Shooting for *Life* magazine, Rich Clarkson joined them in the tight quarters.

"The locker room was mostly quiet with much frustration," Clarkson recalled. "Mr. Iba paced and conferred with the other assistant coaches. No one ever called him Hank—it was always Mister. I think some thought his first name must have been Mister.

"After perhaps forty to fifty minutes we were told a decision would be announced later—later that day as it turned out. I have seen controversies at games' endings before, but never anything quite like this—for it resulted in no decision at the time."

Only one avenue remained for the United States to attempt to overturn the result: lodge a protest. According to the rules, the team had four hours to do so. The protest cost fifty dollars, to be paid to the Technical Committee.

Bill Summers, chair of the 1972 U.S. Olympic Basketball Committee and manager of the U.S. team, crafted the protest. Written on a typewriter whose *y* key seemed not to work—and typed so quickly that Summers spelled his last name as "Summer" (adding the final *s* by hand)—the protest emphasized eight points. A crucial detail concerned the score sheet, which did not list a time-out in the last three seconds, meaning that, truly, only one second was left during the last two attempts (and the Soviets didn't score in that amount of time during either play).

Summers handed the one-page protest to FIBA chief R. William Jones, who was also the president of the Technical Committee. Jones deferred the decision to the Jury of Appeal, the ultimate arbiter. According to FIBA rules of the time, five members and four alternates made up the committee, and all were required to represent a country taking part in the basketball tournament.

Problem was, the head of the committee for this novel case, Ferenc Hepp, hailed from Hungary—which hadn't competed in the Olympic basketball tournament. Hepp not only was absent from the original list of five; he wasn't even listed as one of the four alternates. Appointed by Jones, a fellow graduate of Springfield College, his biggest qualification seemed to be that he was one of the secretary-general's closest companions; as a caption for a photo of the duo notes in Jones's biography, "The two friends never turned down a drop of good vodka."[15]

Granted, Soviet and American representatives were obligated to recuse themselves, but the bylaws demanded that any representatives added needed to field a team in the tourney. Aside from Soviet-dominated Hungary, the five-member jury included Claudio Coccia of Italy (a NATO ally), Rafael Lopez of Puerto Rico (a U.S. unincorporated territory), Soviet-dominated Poland's Adam Baglajewski, and Andreas Keiser of Cuba (dominated in different ways by the Soviets). Available as an alternate, Spain and its representative for some reason were not chosen.

Neil Amdur of the *New York Times* stayed in the basketball arena until at least 4:00 a.m., and some players hung around as well, hoping to hear a decision on the protest. But others on the U.S. team, zombielike, shuffled out of the arena.

Recalled Henderson, "I got drunk that night. Went to the Hofbrau House after the game and drank the biggest beer I could find. Then I had another one. Had to crawl to my room. The cabbie driving me back was driving like a lunatic. I told him if he didn't slow down I'd knock him out."[16]

Davis returned to his room, changed out of his uniform, showered, and headed downtown with a few others. "We decided there wasn't anything to do in the Olympic Village except mope around," he recalled.

One player, Forbes, was forced to stick around the arena, having been picked for a random drug test.

"I couldn't go to the bathroom," he said. "I sat there in that nurse's office for 2½ hours, drinking umpteen glasses of water, thinking about what had just happened. It must have been 3:00 or 4:00 a.m. before I finally peed."[17]

Bantom was torn up.

"That was the first time I ever cried over a basketball game," he said. "My heart was broken."[18]

Dawn arrived in Munich. The morning slowly passed, as scores of people awaited a decision. Around noon on September 10, in a secret ballot, the verdict arrived: a 3–2 vote against the United States.

The Jury of Appeal statement released that day read, in part, as follows:

> In the early hours of 9/10/1972 the Jury of Appeal clarified the facts by hearing both the umpires of the game and the competent parties responsible at the scorer's table. In addition, the Jury of Appeal studied very carefully the televised versions of the last two minutes of the match, this being the version made by the German television (DOZ) and the American television network ABC.
>
> The Jury of Appeal confirms the final result on the score sheet which is 51:50 for the USSR Team.[19]

How was the United States team officially notified of the decision? A delivery boy showed up at Davis's room in the Olympic Village. He handed the team captain a torn story from the Associated Press wire that said the protest had been rejected.

Quickly word spread that Poland, Hungary, and Cuba had sided with the Soviets. Puerto Rico and Italy voted to overturn the 51–50 result. The decision mirrored Cold War politics. Cries of a kangaroo court were uttered to no avail.

The press conference to explain the decision that afternoon was as crazed as the end of the game—lacking only a horn blasting at inopportune moments. Doing his best to appear unflappable in a hot, crowded room, Hepp tried to justify the panel's decision, explaining the sequence of events. His reasoning was lambasted:

> Enraged, U.S. Assistant Manager Herb Mols asked, regarding the first stoppage with one second remaining, "We are asking you, who caused the referee to stop the play, and it was the Russian bench. You looked at the movies, and this is established. Why not credit this, and how can you penalize an American team for the Russian bench coming illegally on the floor with no technical foul called, which is in the book?"
>
> "I don't indeed see the point of the question," Hepp responded to uproarious laughter and a shout of "You're kidding!"[20]

Hans Tenschert of West Germany, the game's scorekeeper—a position of anonymity akin to a company's bookkeeper—voiced disbelief about the Jury of Appeal's decision during the news conference.

"It is true that when [referee] Righetto came to the scoring table," said Tenschert, "that he said only one second remained on the clock. But there was a sign of three seconds held up by a person not on the scoring table, by Mr. William Jones. Righetto had no choice but to rule the clock back to three seconds."

Declared the scorekeeper of the gold medal game, "Under FIBA rules . . . the United States won."[21]

The conference broke up. Bobby Jones, who had witnessed the theater of the absurd with teammate Collins and ABC broadcaster Howard Cosell, had had enough.

"It was another eye-opening experience for me," he said. "At that point I was thinking the Israeli tragedy, the farce of the game and the appeal, I had missed a lot of classes at school—just let me out of here."

To see if the United States' protest was justified, it is worth examining the happenings following Collins's second free throw, point by point.

> 1. Two seconds after the ball had been inbounded, referee Righetto stopped the game with one second left, with the Soviets having absolutely no chance to score (the player dribbling, Sergei Belov, was not in the act of shooting).

Manfred Ströher, part of the FIBA Technical Commission that sat behind the Soviet bench and coauthor of Jones's FIBA biography, says he saw Soviet assistant coach Bashkin attempt to call a time-out with the electric signal after Collins's first free throw.[22] The time-keeper told Mols he saw the light indicating a time-out request from the Soviets and, without checking the status of the ball, blew the horn to alert the referees. But the ball was already in Collins's hands, negating any time-out request.[23]

A technical foul on Bashkin should have been assessed for leaving the bench and yelling at the scorer's table that a time-out had been called. As FIBA rules stated at the time, "A Coach or a substitute shall not enter the court unless by permission of an Official to attend an injured player, nor leave his place to follow the action on the court from the boundary lines." The penalty: one free throw for the Americans.

Yet that didn't happen. R. William Jones, with no power to do so as per FIBA rules he helped craft, demanded the clock be reset to three seconds, though no time-out had been granted (a scoreboard shot before Collins's free throws and after the game ended shows the Soviets with one time-out left) and only one second remained after the Soviets had inbounded the ball and played two seconds. Those seconds cannot be undone—they were officially played. Further, Edmond Bigot served as FIBA's authority at the scorer's table, not his boss, Jones, making the secretary-general's imposition even more glaring.

> 2. Ivan Edeshko entered the game as a substitute without informing the scorer's table, which is a technical foul.

The penalty: one free throw for the Americans. That didn't happen.

3. After the ball was inbounded a second time and a USSR player missed a desperate heave from eighty feet that was tipped by Alexander Below off the backboard, three seconds clearly had elapsed.

Under FIBA rules at the time, referring to the Decision of Game, "a game shall be decided by the scoring of the greater number of points in the playing time." Thus, the United States won the game and the gold medal.

Critics of the U.S. protest would point out that a horn sounded during the play as the game clock had been erroneously set at fifty seconds. Mols talked with the Longines technician, who discussed the horn on the second play: "The technician confirmed that the horn to end the game had to be operated manually by the timekeeper since no automatic signal could operate while he was changing the clock. . . . He emphasized that there was nothing deficient in the clock operation and that 'one second was all that legally remained.'"[24]

In any case, why does it matter if the scoreboard showed three seconds or not? The public-address announcer had made clear to everyone more than once that three seconds remained. In the FIBA rulebook of that era, there is no mention of the scoreboard clock having to be accurately set for a play to count, just that the time-keeper will keep a record of playing time. He did, blowing the horn after the final second elapsed.

4. R. William Jones, once again with no power to do so as per the FIBA rules he had helped devise, demanded the clock be reset to three seconds yet again.

And then Alexander Belov scored.

In the game's aftermath and in ensuing years, many other claims were made. Some U.S. players and coaches said Edeshko stepped on the baseline during the final pass (he did after the pass had been tossed, which is fine) and that Alexander Belov should have been called for a three-second violation and/or traveling and/or a foul after grabbing the heave (all debatable). Whatever the case, the final three seconds were actually played over eight seconds—nearly triple the amount of allotted time.

None of that bothered Soviet coach Kondrashin.

"We deserved the victory no matter what the circumstances," he said after the game. "We had them puzzled from the start since we used a different lineup to confuse them at the beginning."[25]

(Beyond the game, according to FIBA rules, the United States could have lodged a different protest—about whether the Soviet Union's team was composed of amateurs. They were clearly organized paid professionals—but the chance of winning that protest was nil as well.)

What was the reaction to the controversy in the United States? Remember the game was played before the creation of ESPN, so no endless loop of the final three seconds was replayed. No outrage fomented on Twitter. About the only ones commenting consistently at a public level were newspaper columnists, both at large city dailies and in smaller locales across the land, and they were generally appalled at what had happened.

"I wonder how long the championship basketball game might have continued if Alexander Belov had blown that layup which 'won' the game for Russia, 51–50, over the U.S. Saturday night," mused Don Cronin of the *Anderson Daily Bulletin* in Anderson, Indiana. "It hardly seems possible that a R. William Jones, secretary-general of the Federation of International Basketball Associations, could do so much damage to the U.S."[26]

Over at the *Brainerd Daily Dispatch* in Minnesota, columnist Jim Wallace suggested if this was the way the sport was run, basketball might as well be dumped from the Olympics:

We've been covering basketball games for a great many years, but have never seen such a tampering with the clock. . . . How can an FIBA official, one Dr. R. William Jones, take it upon himself to rush down out of the stands to award the Russians three extra seconds of play when they created the disturbance asking for an

illegal time-out which helped run down the clock to one second?
. . . If the International Olympic Committee, which is to review
this game at its February meeting in Switzerland, rules the Russians won this game legally, then it's time a substitute be found for
basketball play in the Olympics.[27]

The impact of the game immediately resonated in political cir-
cles. On September 10, 1972, only hours after the controversial finish,
Soviet premier Leonid Brezhnev and U.S. secretary of state Henry
Kissinger talked in the Kremlin. Kissinger had just arrived from
Munich, where he'd met with West German chancellor Willy Brandt.

"We are hoping to finalize" plans for a conference on European
security, Brezhnev told him.

Kissinger didn't miss a beat. "You will defeat us in the last three
seconds," he replied.[28]

8

WAS THE FIX IN?

THE EXTRAORDINARY CIRCUMSTANCES—never seen before or since in any basketball game—spur a crucial question: Was the fix in? Or put another way: Had underhanded means been used to make sure the United States lost the game?

One man seemed to affect the outcome more than any other: R. William Jones.

Near the tail end of his forty-four-year run as the secretary-general of FIBA, the international governing body of basketball—which didn't even exist until he helped create it—the powerful executive touched every rule, decision, assignment, and job.

From age sixteen, when basketball sparked the Rome-born teen's passion at a YMCA in Turin, Italy, Jones dedicated his life to the sport. He traveled abroad to earn a bachelor of science degree from Springfield College, in the U.S. town where basketball was invented and which houses the Naismith Memorial Basketball Hall of Fame. Procuring another degree in Geneva, he received his diploma from none other than Pierre de Coubertin, founder of the modern Olympics.[1] He proceeded to teach courses in basketball in Germany.

In 1930 Jones spoke with the president of the Italian Basketball Federation, Aldo Nardi, regarding the possibility of a world federation. Rules were paramount during the discussion. "For Jones the issue of uniform rules was to remain a constant preoccupation throughout his life," noted Manfred Ströher and Hans-Dieter Krebs in their FIBA-backed biography, *Dr. h.c. R. William Jones.*[2] (Given his ultimatums during the USA-USSR game, he did not possess a matching desire to apply the rules.)

Though the 1932 Olympics in Los Angeles nixed basketball despite its U.S. origins, many who wanted to establish a world basketball body hoped to showcase the sport in Berlin. In Geneva that same year, a group of basketball leaders met, and by the end of the gathering, Jones was tapped as honorary secretary-general of what would become FIBA.

Despite FIBA's formation, the IOC hesitated to add basketball for one main reason: Coubertin believed in individual, not team, sports. Yet by 1934 the IOC was persuaded to unveil the game in Berlin. Noted Jones, "In less than three years from the day of its creation, the International Basketball Federation had achieved unity, full recognized independence, recognition by the International Olympic Committee, and had won its rightful place in the family of Olympic sports."[3] Not yet thirty, Jones was already becoming an international powerhouse in basketball.

During World War II, the role of Jones—an English citizen because of his father, though he rarely spent time on the island—was somewhat curious. Serving the British while still working in Switzerland on behalf of FIBA, he continued to reach out to countries such as France and Spain, a move which disturbed Swiss authorities. Despite good works on behalf of Polish soldiers who were interned in Switzerland, according to the Ströher and Krebs biography, "Jones made many contacts and also facilitated the exchange of information via various channels, some slightly less legal than others. From time to time these activities aroused the suspicions of the Swiss authorities and of observers from the warring countries. At one stage he was even suspected of being a British spy."[4]

In 1947 the Soviet Union not only joined FIBA but captured the men's European Championship in its inaugural try. The Soviets' first entry in the Olympics, in Helsinki in 1952, spurred a written complaint about Jones that seems prescient. In an August 11, 1953, letter from Jones to Daniel J. Ferris of the Amateur Athletic Union in New York City that was copied to Avery Brundage, head of the International Olympic Committee, Jones confronted accusations by U.S. Olympic basketball coach Forrest "Phog" Allen that he was a Communist: "As there is no truth in Mr. Allen's statement, and as his utterances were made in public, I suggest that Mr. Allen should prove what he has said or at least give substantial evidence of the data upon which his statement was made, or else, send me an apology. . . . I must perhaps add that I am not a Communist; I am a loyal subject of Her Majesty Queen Elizabeth II and do not belong to any political party.[5]

In a personal missive to Brundage within the same package, Jones added, "It seems that to be a General Secretary of an International Federation in which the Soviet Union is a member is enough to be considered a Communist. Mr. Phog Allen is guilty of loose talk of a damaging nature."[6]

Brundage replied to Jones on October 28, 1953, and noted, "Here in the United States we are more or less accustomed to explosions from Phog, but I can understand your concern."[7]

Brundage forwarded Jones's thoughts via mail to Allen. On November 6, 1953, responding on University of Kansas letterhead, Allen wrote a lengthy, biting rebuttal. After acknowledging he had received Brundage's letter, he immediately lit into the FIBA founder and organizer of international basketball tournaments, such as the Olympics:

> I am convinced in my mind that R. William Jones is a collaborator. And I assure you that I am guilty of no loose talk. I do not owe him an apology. . . . Jones sat with the Russians and was in high glee with them when the Russians were victoriously playing a stall game against the U.S.A. [in the gold medal game]. . . . If Jones belonged any place, it certainly was not with the Russians at that time during any contest. He should have maintained a neutral position and attitude and should have not been on their bench visiting.

Further, if you will look at his appointments on the Basketball Committee, you will find that the North Koreans, and not the South Koreans, received committee appointments.

I talked to a number of distinguished people, one of them highly outstanding, formerly in the Japanese Federation, and he complained bitterly of Jones' actions and attitudes in collaborating with Russia and the Communists.[8]

Allen also expressed outrage at the weakness of FIBA's response after Uruguay players—upset over the number of fouls called on their team—assaulted American referee Victor Farrell after a close loss to France in the 1952 Olympics. Two players involved were suspended, and when Uruguay won the bronze medal, those players did not receive medals. Allen said the team should have been kicked out of the games after players kneed Farrell in the groin, punched him in the face, and attacked him in other ways.[9]

On November 12, 1953, Brundage responded to Allen. He said FIBA had never been a strong federation and suggested he at first thought he might not send a copy of Allen's letter to Jones "because, if true, it will only put him on his guard."[10]

Nearly a year later, Jones wrote a to-the-point letter to Brundage, looking for some resolution regarding Allen's alleged comments. On September 7, 1954, Brundage responded by enclosing a copy of Allen's letter without judgment on its merits. But he did weigh in heavily on the Uruguay fracas, noting that "if there is a repetition of incidents of this kind, I would not be surprised if the IOC removed the sport involved from the Olympic program."[11] Nothing in the Avery Brundage Collection at the University of Illinois suggests Jones responded to Brundage about Allen's letter.

Despite that troublesome event, by the 1960s Jones was so respected in the basketball community that he became the first European elected to the Naismith Memorial Basketball Hall of Fame. His alma mater, Springfield College, bestowed upon him the title "Mr. World Basketball."

"He was able to listen to other people, analyze their views, and deduce arguments, as a way of identifying and implementing the correct course of action," noted Ströher and Krebs. "These skills enabled him to guide FIBA safely through the difficult years when the world was divided into political blocs."[12]

Yet it was his seeming favoritism toward one political bloc that provoked cries of crooked behavior in 1972. Given that the U.S. didn't procure a lead until three seconds remained in the forty-minute gold medal game, anyone who may have signed onto a theoretical fix had little to do. But the final moments offered plenty of opportunity for altering the outcome.

Though witnesses saw Jones demand that three seconds be put back on the clock twice—moves corroborated by videotape evidence—after the game he denied any involvement. Calling Jones "that little guy in the bow tie who ran on the court," Bach was stunned at the goings-on.

"At the appeals meeting the following day, Jones claimed he was never on the floor. He was sure surprised when ABC showed a film of the incident with Dr. Jones eminently involved.

"I knew our protest attempts were futile, though," Bach continued, "when I saw the Cuban member of the appeals committee flash the 'Okay' sign with his fingers to the Russians."[13]

Jones backtracked somewhat when FIBA's press release appeared a few days later, offering its explanation of events during the final three seconds. Jones confessed to his role in changing the clock as head of the Technical Committee—but only during the *second* time he did it:

Immediately following the second free throw, the Umpire caused the ball to be put in play from behind the end line by the Soviet team. However, at about the same time, the Referee gave the signal of "no play," thus stopping the game. At this time, the Referee was in front of the Scorer's table and very near to it. Upon interrogation, the Referee stated that he had stopped the game because of a signal from the Scorer's table. After consultation with the personnel of the Scorer's table, the Referee indicated that 3 seconds remained to be played . . . the Officials then caused the ball to be put in play again from behind the end line by the Soviet team, thus clearly indicating that this was a repetition of the first play. The ball was passed to a player on the court and immediately after (one second) the automatic signal for the end of the game was sounded. Quite rightly, the American players thought they had won the game. However, the Officials came to the Scorer's table to find out why the signal had sounded after one second of play, and also the Chairman of the Technical Committee went to the table to inquire why it had been announced in three languages (French, English and German) that 3 seconds remained to be played, and only one second had actually been played. They were informed that the Timekeeper had neglected to reset the game clock at 3 seconds before play had been resumed for the second time.

The Chairman of the Technical Committee then instructed the Longines operators to set the clock right, and this was done under his supervision while the Officials informed the two coaches that the 3 seconds still remained to be played.[14]

U.S. Assistant Manager Herb Mols offered a withering response about the FIBA explanation of the first repetition of play. "The referee denied, first at the time of the termination of the game, and again at noon of the next day, that he indicated 3 seconds remained to be played," he noted. "As shown on the film, he never spoke with personnel at the table, except to indicate 'One' for one second, which was the response from the table officials . . . it has been shown that only Mr. Jones has decried the extra three seconds."[15]

Also, just as the horn blaring during Collins's free throw didn't stop the action, the horn sounding after one second during the Soviets' unsuccessful attempt to score failed to alter anything. The players continued without hesitation, and the Soviets failed to score. Following FIBA's press-release logic, one second actually should have counted during that play, meaning two seconds should have remained (not three) on the final play when Alexander Belov scored. And whether Belov's shot occurred before two seconds expired is debatable.

The FIBA press release also pointed out that everyone save the U.S. captain Davis—including the timekeeper, scorekeeper, referees, and others—had signed the official score sheet. But it omitted the fact that Iba had signed "Protest" in Davis's spot. Immediately after the FIBA press release came out, the Statement of the Table Officials— coordinator Klaus Meyer, timer Horst Baumert, 30-second timer Manfred Meiser, and scorekeeper Hans Tenschert—appeared after they had been interviewed by the vice consul of the United States, Norman A. Singer, in Germany. Their sworn deposition said that a Soviet coach asked for a time-out only *after* the referee had placed the ball in Collins's hands for the second free throw, meaning it was too late. They added that *only* R. William Jones had asked for three seconds to be put on the clock the first time. At the same time, though, Baumert, the timer, said the horn sounded on the second inbounds after one second not to signal the end of the game, but to let the referees know that the ball had been put into play too early for the game to resume, according to him, since the clock had not been reset.[16] That contradicted Mols's assertion that he had been told by a Longines technician the horn signaled the end of the game.

In the biography by Ströher and Krebs—the only full-scale one dedicated to Jones—the final three seconds are whitewashed almost beyond belief. Though many in the world only knew of Jones because of the controversy in Munich, the coffee-table-sized book published in four languages dedicated fewer than one hundred words to it.

"Russian coach Vladimir Kondrashin called for time-out," it notes. "The clock continued to run, so it had to be reset. Jones was put to the test. The scoreboard was twice set at 0:03 before the ball was finally put into play."[17]

A speech given by Jones in 1977 seems to mock his actions five years earlier. "The decision of the official is final and cannot be contested or reversed," he said. "The floor officials must have authority."[18]

The bottom line: With no authority to do so, according to the FIBA rules he created and superintended, Jones twice put three seconds back on the clock—once after time had expired, and the United States had officially won the gold medal. Leaders in sports, from the National Football League to European soccer, possess vast powers and oversee owners whose teams are worth tens of billions of dollars combined; no commissioner, president, or other sports chief has the jurisdiction to put time back on a game clock. NBA commissioner Adam Silver can help force Donald Sterling to sell his longtime franchise and ban him for life after he makes numerous alleged racist remarks, but he can't add ticks at the end of a Clippers game.

Said scorekeeper Tenschert, "I can understand people in the United States who have feelings that they were robbed. No one of us four table officials understand this [putting three seconds back on clock]. The only person who indicated three seconds was Mr. Jones. Why?"[19]

Since then, during the Olympics, time being put back on the clock changed another outcome. During overtime in the women's épée during the 2012 London Games, a fencer named Shin A Lam from South Korea thought she had advanced to the finals—after all, the clock read zero and, though the score was tied, she was slated to win an overtime tie based on fencing rules. But the fifteen-year-old operating the clock had mistakenly let the final second elapse. The referee, conferring with officials, ruled one second remained. After the referee said "*Allez*," Lam's opponent recorded a hit in that short span and won. To add to her woes, Lam soon after lost the bronze medal match.

To those who knew him, Jones lived with unchecked power, and he expected to get his way. Said Willy Bestgen, a referee during the 1972 Olympics, "He said on Saturday, red is red, and on Sunday, red is blue. He told me always, 'The last I said is correct.'"[20]

Added Bill Wall of the U.S. Olympic Basketball Committee, "The entire life for those officials and everyone at the scorer's table was dependent on Dr. Jones, especially the Eastern Europeans. To come out from behind the Iron Curtain in those days was phenomenal, and if you ticked off Dr. Jones you never got out."[21]

The Soviet Union sports authorities had showered gifts upon Jones throughout the decades, one of many nations to try to influence him; whether they gave more or less than anyone else is uncertain. Purportedly an independent arbiter of international basketball, Jones sounded nearly gleeful when asked after the game about the U.S. defeat.

"They have to learn how to lose, once," Jones said. "[They] had reason to be sorry because they were leading by one point with three seconds left and could have won with a little bit of luck. But they have to know how to lose, even when they think they are right."[22]

What were the stakes of this game to Jones? Simply put, a Soviet win justified his life's work—not only did a basketball team aside from the United States capture the top medal on the world's biggest stage, but the Soviets had upended the powerhouse country that had created the sport. Basketball's popularity internationally could only increase knowing that more than one team could win the Olympics. And the nabob of the international game was Jones.

"I think Jones saw an opportunity to change the world basketball scene. And he did," Joyce said. "European teams and others started believing in themselves, and the game took off."

Under Jones's watch, no doubt the growth of FIBA soared, featuring 138 member federations when he retired in 1976 from an initial eight. (Soon after the surprise announcement before the 1980 Olympics in Moscow that he would receive the Silver Olympic Order for his worthy contributions to basketball, he suffered a stroke; he died the following year.)

Russia native Prokhorov (whose Nets franchise has enjoyed the contributions of many European players over the years, most notably Drazen Petrovic) cited the importance of the Soviet win to the spread of basketball in Europe.

"The Soviet Union had a very strong school of basketball that had brought top results for many years in all the European competitions, but the 1972 game lifted the whole of European basketball to another level of respect and engagement with fans," he said. "They were watching not just the best on the continent but the best in the world. What we see today with the NBA's international expansion and also with the global careers of players, both American and international, is a continuation of this desire to see the sport in a global context as much as a local or national one."

In Europe, nearly twenty teams compete in Turkish Airlines Euro-League. More than thirty-five years after Jones's demise, the continent's impact on the sport in the United States is powerful. From Toni Kukoc to Dirk Nowitzki to Marc Gasol and beyond, even the tallest European players who have joined the NBA have become proficient long-range shooters; big men in America had always been known for their close-to-the-basket shots (Shaquille O'Neal could barely even hit free throws from fifteen feet). Then there's six-foot-eleven Giannis Antetokounmpo of Greece, whose speed in the transition game and fierce attacks on the rim have brought a new element to the NBA. At the start of the 2017–18 season, more than one hundred international players competed in the NBA from a record forty-two countries.

Of course, for the Soviet Union, the Olympic win doubled as a propaganda coup. The Communist system had beaten the capitalist one where, according to the former, racism and inequality reigned. Led by *Pravda*, the state-owned media could trumpet the glories of Communism as displayed through sports. Across the Eastern Bloc, sports—especially when engaged in the winnings of Olympic medals—served as a means to prove the merits of countries' political systems.

Though Jones's actions broke the rules in an unprecedented manner, his moves weren't the only suspicious ones that night.

Referee Artenik Arabadjian from Bulgaria (essentially a Soviet satellite since the end of World War II, just like nearby East Germany) was working his first Olympic gold medal game. Well respected since he joined FIBA in 1967, he refereed the 1971 European Championship between the USSR and Yugoslavia. A former player, he had captured national titles for Bulgaria. Though a young man of forty-two in Munich, he had spent a lifetime playing and refereeing basketball.

Yet during the 1972 Olympic championship, Arabadjian did not question the validity of the final seconds, as fellow referee Righetto did, nor did his voice join the many—including the scorekeeper Tenschert—who believed the United States won under FIBA rules. In fact, well before the last ticks of the clock, his decisions clearly benefited the Soviet Union.

Starting at 3:21 remaining, when 2 points separated the teams (the closest differential since the opening seconds), Arabadjian called three fouls against the Americans and none against the Soviets in less than fifty seconds.

To begin, Forbes was charged with a foul as Sakandelidze drove to the right of the basket—yet it didn't look like Forbes touched him as the Soviet player forced an off-balanced shot as he headed out of bounds, one which Bantom grabbed off the bottom of the backboard. Three of four from the foul line to that point, Sakandelidze missed both free throws, and Joyce grabbed the rebound.

With less than three minutes to go, Arabadjian levied an unwarranted foul on Joyce—again one where a rushing Soviet player (Paulauskas) seemed not to be touched by an American, as he did not hesitate to continue driving toward the basket before making a pass. Though not in the act of shooting, and perhaps fifteen feet from the basket when the call was made, Paulauskas was awarded two free throws (all fouls in the last three minutes of the game prompted two foul shots according to FIBA rules in 1972). The Soviets' second-leading scorer coming into game with about 12 points a contest, Paulauskas made one of two, getting his first point of the gold medal game.

Less than thirty seconds later, Ratleff tried to wrestle the ball away from the six-foot-four Paulauskas. He succeeded, but Arabadjian called another foul on the United States, one that seemed appropriate. This time, the Lithuanian native made both shots with 2:32 to go.

Then, with 1:28 remaining and the Soviet lead sliced to 1, a ticky-tack foul was slapped on Joyce as he reached toward Sakandelidze, who was moving past him. It looks like Righetto likely called this one, as he was closer to the play. Regardless, there is doubt whether it was deserved. Sakandelidze made one of two free throws.

With fifty-five seconds to go, Bantom fouled a player in the Soviet backcourt during a rebound, knocking him out of the game with five. Arabadjian called the foul and, with a flourish worthy of flamboyant NBA referee Mendy Rudolph, bounded over toward Bantom, jumped up and pointed to the U.S. bench. The call looked legitimate, as Bantom hung over the back of Alshan Sharmukhamedov.

In less than two and a half minutes, Arabadjian definitely called four fouls on the United States—two of which looked completely unmerited. During this span, the Soviets were charged with one foul. The five U.S. fouls overall during that time led to ten Soviet free throws. In the previous thirty-six minutes, the Soviets had shot eighteen free throws, or one every other minute. In the roughly 150 seconds cited, they averaged about four a minute—a 700 percent jump. Granted, the U.S. players were defending more aggressively than before during this span. But there is no doubt that calling shooting fouls—especially debatable or even nonexistent ones—is the best way a referee can influence the outcome of a game. Consider the Soviets hadn't scored a field goal in the final seven minutes of the game until Alexander Belov's winning four-footer, and the importance of free throws as time waned became enormous.

During the game, in fact, the USSR enjoyed twenty-eight free throws, while the United States only shot eighteen. Yet the number of fouls were almost identical; twenty-six assessed on the United States, twenty-five on the Soviet Union. The difference: those called with three minutes or less in the second half, prompting free throws.

Looking more closely at that last foul called by Arabadjian on Bantom: slated to go to the line was Sharmukhamedov, having netted all of 4 points. Instead, after a time-out, Sergei Belov, the Soviet star boasting a game-high 19 points at the time, shot the free throws. He made one.

When Sharmukhamedov was fouled by Bantom, Sergei Belov stood unguarded perhaps five feet away. The Soviets should have been penalized for sending the wrong man to the line; how Arabadjian allowed this to happen is certainly suspect. Joyce kept yelling and pointing and waving his hands as Sharmukhamedov stood by him, set up for a rebound instead of shooting at the foul line. He was ignored. According to a lengthy report prepared by Mols after the game, "When Joyce called attention to this flagrant switch, the official Arabadjan [*sic*] . . . allowed Belov to shoot."[23]

Following the whistle after the Soviets inbounded the ball with three seconds to play for the first time, Arabadjian, who roamed near the Soviet bench during the chaos, allowed Edeshko to enter the game illegally. Arabadjian must have known Edeshko was not among the five Soviets previously playing. The scorer's table didn't alert anyone that a substitution had been made—because Edeshko had not checked in there, which is the rule for a substitution.

Arabadjian jogged toward Edeshko to give him the ball before the clock had wound down correctly. As he neared the player, McMillen stood around half court until a teammate motioned him to get on Edeshko. McMillen quickly bounded to the baseline to guard him.

And Arabadjian's hand gesture as McMillen prepared to guard Edeshko a second time (along with a hand motion just beforehand to push McMillen away from the line) on the final play is bizarre, if not unprecedented. Among FIBA referee signals of the time, it does not exist as an option. Under the rules, McMillen enjoyed every right to stand by the baseline, and no suggestion of an infraction or problem on the previous play existed. It is unlikely any similar motion by a referee toward a defender exists in the annals of Olympic basketball. Because of it, Edeshko could heave the pass he patented to Alexander Belov (with McMillen gone, his vision downcourt was unimpeded) rather than bounce a pass in the backcourt, as had occurred on the previous play. Not only could he guarantee a makeable shot, assuming a Soviet player grabbed it, but the clock didn't start until it was touched.

Decades later, Arabadjian—by then a FIBA Hall of Famer—defended his action.

"I remember I make a sign 'This is a line,'" he said, while lowering his hand slowly. "With that sign, I like to remind McMillen it's not possible to trespass with the hands that line. I think he knows that, but it's necessary that I remind him at that moment especially."[24]

Though Arabadjian's point on trespassing with the hands is true today, it did not exist in the 1972 FIBA rulebook. It did not specify how defenders should act or not act after free throws; the closest is the following reference under Playing Regulations as to how they should comport themselves after field goals: "Opponents of the player who is to put the ball in play shall not touch the ball. Allowance may be made for touching the ball accidentally or instinctively but if a player delays the game by interfering with the ball, it is a technical foul."[25]

Then, one must consider the remembrances of Jim Bain, an Olympic referee that year and eventual FIBA Hall of Famer who watched the game in the first row behind one of the baskets. He shared a room in a Munich hotel during the games with Arabadjian. The day after the gold medal game, Bain asked him how he and fellow referee Righetto could flaunt the rules by putting time back on the clock.

"He said through the interpreter, 'Jim, you cannot perhaps understand this, but had we permitted the Americans to win that game, I would have had to fear for the safety of my family prior to getting home,'" Bain recalled.[26]

Though Bain's recollection is damning evidence, a Sports on Earth piece cites similar concerns, though from an unnamed source. A man purporting to be retired from the CIA emailed columnist Brian Tuohy around 2011. Wrote Tuohy:

> According to my source, the CIA had viable information that the second official on the court that fateful night, Bulgarian referee Artenik Arabadjan [sic], was in on the fix. Not because he was an avowed Communist, or that he felt Soviet pride, or even a desire to end America's dominance in the sport. Arabadjan allegedly participated in rigging the game because the KGB had threatened to kidnap and murder his family if the Soviets lost.
>
> In an attempt to prove my source's claims, I went straight to the CIA by filing Freedom of Information Act (FOIA) requests seeking any files relating to this game. The initial response I received stated, in part, "The CIA can neither confirm nor deny the existence or nonexistence of records responsive to your request."[27]

Today, McMillen believes a fix most likely was in.

"The game was such an outlier in terms of behavior," he said. "I think the Soviets wanted the game so badly that they worked on Jones beforehand. And I would not be surprised if the Eastern Bloc referee [Arabadjian] did not feel pressure to bend over backward to help the Soviets win."

Added Jerry Colangelo, former chairman of USA Basketball, "If you want to talk about a conspiracy theory, all of the facts lead maybe to that conclusion in terms of what took place with the clock, the FIBA guy, all of the people who were involved in that drama.

"Usually there can be one play that's controversial at the end of the game. Two is remotely possible. But three? No way in the world does that happen. It wasn't about sour grapes—you were left with the idea that it was stolen."

Said Kenny Davis, "William Jones felt it was a detriment for the United States to keep winning because it hurt the international game. I don't know if the fix was in, but a lot of people were hoping we'd lose that game. We were always the favorites."

The Soviets, obviously, believe they won fairly.

"American basketball was stronger than ours, but we exploited their mistakes," Kondrashin said.[28]

"We'll never find out who was right and who was wrong," Sergei Belov said. "In all fairness, there's always two sides with completely different opinions."[29]

A clear difference exists between honest mistakes, dereliction of duty because of a poor job, and outright corruption. Given Jones's intrusion into the game against the FIBA rules he had crafted and his appointment of Hepp to the Jury of Appeal against FIBA rules, along with Arabadjian slapping highly questionable fouls on U.S. players while also looking the other way as Sergei Belov shot free throws illegally and as Edeshko entered the game illegally—combined with other improper factors cited—it seems clear the United States was cheated. The rules, ethics, and norms of the sport were undermined repeatedly with the game on the line.

And that means the twelve U.S. players should be holding gold medals.

In many ways, the game made a mockery of the Olympic Charter. The first words of the entire 1972 charter, under the section headlined "Fundamental Principles," read, "The Olympic Games are held every four years. They assemble amateurs of all nations in fair and equal competition. No discrimination is allowed against any country or person on grounds of colour, religion or politics."[30]

In the gold medal game, the "fair and equal competition" clause was jettisoned, along with the "no discrimination is allowed against any country" section. In the three sentences of a charter stretching across many thousands of words, two violations are already obvious.

Then let's jump to the eligibility code:

> To be eligible for participation in the Olympic Games, a competitor must observe the traditional Olympic spirit and ethic and have always participated in sport as an avocation without having received any remuneration for his participation.
>
> His livelihood must not be derived from or be dependent upon income from sport and he must be engaged in a basic occupation to provide for his present and future.
>
> He must not be, or have been, a professional, semi-professional or so-called "non-amateur" in any sport.[31]

Since the Soviet players were paid by their teams and by the state and were professionals by any definition, that should disqualify them from the gold—though admittedly, trying to apply that philosophy retroactively across the board to the Cold War–era is as likely as a citizen of the Bahamas winning the luge.

Further, a handful of the Soviet players worked in the Red Army. A month after the games, Ivan Edeshko and Sergei Belov were both promoted to lieutenant. Yet both had signed the Participant's Declaration that summer before the Olympic Games, which read in part, "For national aggrandizement, governments occasionally . . . give athletes positions in the Army, on the police force or in a government office. . . . Recipients of these special favors which are granted only because of athletic ability are not eligible to compete in the Olympic Games."[32]

Perhaps the Soviets could have made the case that these players' military skills were the reason they were in the army. At the same time, according to a rule in the IOC handbook, the Soviet national federation was responsible if Edeshko and Belov had been hired fraudulently. As the *New York Times* reported in 1973, "The rule also places the basketball team in jeopardy of disqualification and for-feiture of games won with its mischief-makers. On such substantial legal ground, the U.S.O.C. might still cast its traditional caution to the winds and undertake a legalistic protest."[33]

The USOC never pursued that path.

9

TAKING A STAND

A YOUNG AMERICAN JETS off to Europe for the first time, thrilled to meet Olympians from around the world and to compete in the most important basketball games he's ever played. But in little more than a week, fellow athletes are murdered steps from his bedroom. A few days later, anticipating the quadrennial basketball corona-tion, he believes he is victorious not once but twice in the same gold medal game—yet his team loses for the first time in sixty-four tries.

Expected to be a crowning achievement of his fledgling life, instead the trip to Munich leaves him prostrate. And then indignant.

Said Bobby Jones, "It wasn't until we got back to our dorms in the Olympic Village that night that collectively an anger built up at the injustice of what took place and how it took place. We had experi-enced a lot of strange things in basketball, but what took place there really kind of overshadowed anything we'd ever thought about so I think just the confusion of the end of the game turned into proba-bly anger at the way the whole thing played out."[1]

The afternoon after their astonishing loss, still incredulous, the Americans gathered in their Olympic Village rooms and waited to hear if they would win the appeal and thus the game. Eventually, they found out it had failed by one vote.

While much in the past week had transpired beyond their control, instigated by terrorists and a man they likely had never met or even heard of before, R. William Jones, they talked about taking a stand—and thus ruling their own destiny rather than continuing to be hurled about by vicissitudes.

For the first and only time, an Olympic team rejected its medals.

The players believed they did not deserve silver medals; they had rightfully earned golds. Soon after the momentous decision, they packed their bags and boarded a Pan Am charter jet to New York City before dispersing to their various homes and colleges. Forty years would pass before some of those teammates would see each other again.

Details are fuzzy on the decision to repudiate their awards. No one remembers who suggested it, though it was first broached in the locker room after the game.

"Someone said, 'I'm not taking the silver medal.' Someone else said, 'I'm not taking it either,'" Davis recalled. "The locker room was chaos. I'm sure things were thrown around. We never ever sat down and said 'Let's vote on it'—it was by acclamation."

Noted Joyce, "I'm sure I was loud and boisterous about not taking the silver medals."

Remembered Ratleff, "The players together, a collective hearing of all of us without coaches, said we would not accept the silver medals. At that time, you stood up for what you believed in. We believed the game was stolen."

Only one player openly disagreed with the idea—McMillen.

"I played the devil's advocate. I said, 'How will this make us look?'" he noted.

Recalled Henderson, "Eleven of us were unanimous. We forced him to say yes."

During the chaotic Hepp press conference, U.S. Olympic Basketball chair Summers announced the decision to the world.

"Our team will not be present for the silver medal. We do not feel like accepting the silver medal; we feel we are entitled to the gold medal," he said.[2]

Joyce explained the team's position to the press.

"Everybody knows that we are still Olympic champions . . . we legally and morally won the gold."[3]

Later on, Davis explained, "We felt like they just did something to us that was illegal and we didn't know any other way to protest than to say that you're not about to get us to show up to take that silver medal."[4]

Still, worries bedeviled the players. Said Ratleff, "You had the two U.S. athletes in Mexico City four years earlier who raised their fists up on the medal stand. People got mad at them. How would we be accepted?"

Eschewing an Olympic medal is anathema to any competitor; as children, most create dramatic scenarios where somehow they win the gold. It's hard to imagine athletes working harder for anything. All labor four years without pay in hopes of merely gaining a shot at contending against the best in the world. To be part of the first Olympic team to ever refuse a medal? The searing decision—which was tantamount to calling the Olympics corrupt—refuted the players' long-held dreams and added pain to a horrendous week.

But they did not relent, even as others decried their move.

"Even my own coach at Maryland, Lefty Driesell, lambasted us—he thought it was bush league," said McMillen of the man who ignored his fear of flying to watch the gold medal game in Munich. "Our coaches wanted us to accept them. The U.S. Olympic establishment was worried the IOC would come down on us big-time."

Recalled Bobby Jones, "I remember USA representatives who said we'll jeopardize the future of USA Basketball in the Olympics if we don't take the medals. I had never met these people before. We said, 'We need to do what's right.'"

It is worth considering the times. Demonstrators on college campuses and elsewhere protested the Vietnam War. A year before, young men and women aged eighteen and above had earned the right to vote thanks to a Constitutional amendment (the age previously had been twenty-one), and many were passionate about upturning social norms, asserting their rights, and shunning the idea of meekly accepting any wrongs or injustices. Said McMillen of the unanimous decision of the U.S. Olympians, "I think today the ultimate protest of any group against the establishment was the '72 team not accepting the medals."

The establishment condemned the American decision. In the FIBA biography of Jones, the authors opined, "The U.S. players were still so shocked and angry—and they were in no way checked or encouraged by their coaches to exhibit a sense of fair play—that they refused to accept their medals. This was a serious case of poor sportsmanship that actually deserved to be punished."[5]

The basketball medal ceremony—originally scheduled to take place immediately after the game and then, given the protest, planned at the 80,000-seat main stadium on September 10 before being rained out—ultimately featured a sparse crowd at an indoor arena. Most spectators assumed they would only see team handball medals handed out to Yugoslavia (gold), Czechoslovakia (silver), and Romania (bronze), given they had just watched the sport's championship.

Then basketball players appeared. The Soviets, dressed in dapper blue suits with buttons emblazoned, accepted their gold medals from none other than Jones. They clapped, pumped their fists in the air, and celebrated yet again. To the Soviets' left stood the Cubans, winners of the bronze medals. To their right, a blue podium dotted with the numeral 2 sat empty. Two young German women, bedecked in traditional Fräulein outfits, quietly held trays of silver medals before the podium for the Americans, in case at any point they might appear and accept them. Three smartly dressed men stood rigidly nearby.

Boos rained down as the United States was announced as winners of the silver medal. Though the American flag was raised, no U.S. players materialized to admire it. In fact, none of them even attended the closing ceremony (where, as if to emphasize the errors that tainted the games, the scoreboard saluting Brundage for his long reign spelled his name "Brandage"). Said McMillen, "We just wanted to get the hell out of there."

For the first time, U.S. basketball players had the chance to understand a maxim from a great in another sport, Hall of Fame baseball pitcher Christy Mathewson. "You can learn little from victory," he once said. "You can learn everything from defeat." But it would not happen immediately. Though they returned home fine physically, some were psychologically battered, almost like battle-worn soldiers. Noted Bobby Jones, "I was happy to be on that plane home from Munich. My faith in man was ruined—I'd been awakened to what human beings can do."[6]

As Davis shared, "When I came back from Munich I was changed. All of us were. . . . At no time in my life did going home feel better."[7]

McMillen returned to school and, like some teammates, the chemistry major was in demand for his observations on what happened in Munich.

"I was besieged by folks wanting to hear all about these fateful Olympics. I gave a number of speeches to local groups.

"I went to the Olympics with a very idealistic view of the games and came home sobered by the practical reality that the Olympics were a very human institution with all the attendant flaws and shortcomings."

The day after Collins arrived back in the United States, he was given a hero's welcome in Benton, Illinois, as about six hundred (roughly the town's population) turned out. He defended the team's style of play.

"Some people question Coach Iba—why did he not run and shoot? But we won this way. We held opponents to 40 points a game . . . if we would have played any other way we would have had to have twelve basketballs because everybody was a shooter."[8]

Many of his teammates disagreed. Looking back on the USSR game, even with the final seconds of chaos, players believed they could have won had they played to their strengths.

Reflecting decades later, Henderson—like many players—blasted Iba's 1940s-style game plan that he had perfected at Oklahoma State, emphasizing a slowdown motion offense and a fierce defense. But Henderson also was dumbfounded that the coaches never made the players watch the Soviets in Munich.

"I had never seen Sergei Belov play until that night," Henderson said. "You have to watch a player and study him to know how to guard him. You scout to take advantage of everything you can.

"They played for years and years together. They knew each other so well they knew when each other needed to go to the bathroom."

Recalled Burleson, "We knew the Russian players shot 1,500 shots per day. They took their three best shots and shot them 500 times a day. So when you don't pressure them on defense and they are shooting 17-to-20-foot shots, that is in the bank for them. Playing slow with them was a slow, methodical death."[9]

Said Bobby Jones, "It was the most physical of all the games we had played. The refs seemed to let more go, like in an NBA play-off game. I remember taking a charge and then coming out. I don't remember going back in."[10]

When assessing Iba's strategy, it's hard to understand why he didn't play Bobby Jones more. His .609 overall shooting percentage from the field (fourteen of twenty-three) during the Olympics was tops on the team, and his proficiency from the foul line (nine of ten free throws made) was unmatched. Yet aside from Davis, no one on the team took fewer shots in Munich. Not only that, Jones—who would become one of the best defensive players in NBA history—fit Iba's emphasis on defense perfectly.

Edeshko believes the U.S. team hadn't taken the Soviets seriously.

"The Americans badly underestimated the strength of our team, as did nearly everybody else . . . even our chiefs in Moscow planned for us to take second place," he said.[11]

Unlike his players, Iba had not waited for the Hepp committee's verdict; he flew back to Oklahoma and heard of the final result upon landing, which prompted an angry outpouring from the man who coached his final game of a legendary career in Munich.

"I've never seen anything like that in athletics," he began. "I hope to God I never see anything like it again. It's hard to take. I think it'll hurt basketball and I think it will hurt the Olympics until they get a stronger authority in operation. Our young boys worked so hard, and came so far. Russia didn't win it. They took it away from the United States. Our boys worked hard. There's no doubt in my mind. They won it, too."[12]

Poignant words about the pain of losing after so much winning were spoken by one not there: Bill Walton. In 1973 his UCLA squad won its seventh straight NCAA title, just as the Americans had won seven straight golds. Recounting the end of that dynasty—a double-overtime loss to North Carolina State in the Final Four in 1974 (where he was defended by Burleson)—still haunts him.

"The losses are what you remember," he said. "The failures, the mistakes, and how it could have been so different. . . . We could have, we should have won them all, and we didn't get it done. And when you're in that position, it's the worst feeling in the world. . . . That's the timelessness of pain and suffering: the agonizing, the reflection and the endless questioning of yourself. When you're right there and it's there for you and the whole world is watching, and it's recorded as history that can never be changed, that is a terribly heavy burden."[13]

Even though the United States averaged 77 points a contest and gave up 44, the team arrived home without any medals. Believe it or not, despite the massive scoring differential, no U.S player averaged even 10 points per game. Henderson and Jones both scored 83 points, an average of 9.2 per game, to lead the team. Its shooting percentage overall was just shy of 44 percent.

Players received a one-page letter of condolence from President Nixon, who wrote, "You may be certain your fellow citizens still think of you as champions . . . on behalf of all Americans, I want to congratulate you for a splendid come-from-behind performance."[14]

In a twist worthy of George Orwell's *Animal Farm*, the players of the Union of Soviet Socialist Republics—where supposedly no one was more equal than anyone else—were treated to fruits usually found in capitalist countries. According to Bloomberg.com, players were lavished with thousands of rubles in bonuses and could buy Russian luxury cars that the typical citizen would never have the chance to. In fact, Alshan Sharmukhamedov soon crashed his new Volga.

"A policeman appeared and asked for my documents," he said. "Then he recognized me and said, 'Sharmukhamedov, you've got to be careful. Who will replace you at the team if something happens?'"[15]

Alexander Belov became a celebrity in Russia. In 1975 the New Orleans Jazz chose him in the tenth round, making him the first Soviet player ever drafted for the NBA (he never played in the league and died a few years later). In 1980 Sergei Belov lit the cauldron to signal the start of the Moscow Olympics, a huge honor also bestowed on the likes of Olympians Rafer Johnson and Muhammad Ali in the United States.

Bobby Jones recognized that the importance of the win to the Soviets outweighed what it would have meant to the Americans.

"Their lives changed drastically for the better. Our lives wouldn't have changed that much."

Nets owner Prokhorov later recalled the impact of the Soviets finally beating the Americans at the game they had created.

"Of course it meant a lot. We were the total underdog," he noted. "Maybe it was something like, for the Americans, winning at hockey in Lake Placid in 1980 with the 'Miracle on Ice.'

"This is really what national teams are about—unabashed pride and patriotism for a brief moment in time. It unites people, and we did feel united that day. And, like with the 'Miracle on Ice,' the whole thing was playing out against the backdrop of the Cold War. It was a drama far beyond the drama of the game itself. It was also the first time in history that the Soviet Union won in the overall [Olympic] medal count, so it was a heady time."

Still, despite their fame and possessing their nation's first gold medals in basketball (the Soviet Union also won in 1988, three years before it dissolved), full satisfaction eluded the players. As noted in a book about sports in the USSR, "No one connected with the Soviet basketball program would ever claim, in the wake of the Munich victory, that the Americans had ceased to be anything but the leaders of world basketball. They knew they had not beaten professionals."[16]

The joy was tempered also by the Americans' reaction. Sergei

Belov stewed over the fact that the Americans continued to challenge the Soviets' gold medal triumph into the twenty-first century.

"I've always been terribly insulted that the Americans never accepted our victory," he said. "Maybe the time has come for the Americans to accept defeat and forget it."[17]

Edeshko also bristled for years over the Americans' snub of the final tally.

"The American team was offended, and it wasn't right," he said. "It was the Cold War. Americans, out of their own natural pride and love of country, didn't want to lose and admit loss. They didn't want to lose in anything, especially basketball."[18]

"Americans always want to be first," Edeshko added. "If they're not, they're always looking for a reason. That's their national problem."[19]

As 1973 arrived, the USOC had gathered an ample amount of evidence—much of it new—to file a protest to the IOC looking to overturn the gold medal game's result. A letter to recently instated IOC head Lord Killanin from USOC chief Clifford Buck, dated January 18, 1973, cited eight exhibits of evidence. A statement from the Longines clock operator during the game, Andre Chopard, taken about a week after its finish, read in part: "Mr. Bigot, the technical representative of the FIBA for this match, asked me, at the request of Mr. Jones, to set back the clock three seconds, although the clock indicated only one second. In view of the fact that Longines does its work in the service of the organization and of the FIBA, I complied with this order in good faith. . . . I would like to add that it is twelve years that I have been timekeeping for Longines and never once in my career as timekeeper keeping for Longines and never once in my career as timekeeper at basketball, did anyone ever ask me to extend the time."[20]

Nearly two months after the game, referee Righetto proffered a sworn statement in Brazil. Aside from pointing out that the ball should have been put in play from the sideline rather than the end line on the last two attempts and noting that by signing the "bulletin-sheet" (score sheet) he was not approving what had taken place at the contest's close, he said, "I consider what happened as completely illegal and an infraction to the rules of a Basketball game. . . . The right and fair . . . would be the playing of 'one second.'"[21] Adding that the Soviet win "was completely irregular and outside the rules of the game of basketball," Righetto emphasized he had not granted the Soviets a time-out.[22]

Armed with scads of evidence from important principals, Buck explained what it meant.

"Examination of the foregoing exhibits proves conclusively that *the length of the game was extended illegally after the game had actually officially ended.* They prove that this illegal extension of the game was ordered by an individual who by FIBA rules was not an official of the game, and who had no authority or legal right under the FIBA rules to preempt the duties and responsibilities of the officials who the FIBA rules clearly state are in complete charge of the game.

"We request the IOC Executive Board to reverse the ruling of the FIBA Jury of Appeal and to declare that the USA Basketball team, which had the larger score when the official playing time had elapsed, was the winner of the game. Only you can now, by so doing, correct this injustice and thus erase what otherwise would be forever a dark stain upon the integrity of the Olympic Games."[23]

Buck—on the eve of resigning as USOC chief—flew to Switzerland to find out the verdict at IOC headquarters. As the minutes of the IOC Executive Board meeting make clear, he may have been surprised by the less-than-welcome response.

"Lord Killanin firstly expressed the IOC's displeasure at the conduct of the U.S. team, which had refused to receive the silver medals even under technical protest and the IOC felt that this was very discourteous," the minutes note. "He reminded Mr. Buck that the protest must be on ethical grounds and not on technical grounds, as the latter was beyond the competence of the Executive Board to decide."[24]

After Buck left the room, little debate ensued. The Executive Board agreed the matter was outside its purview, and that was that.

If Buck had presented the case differently, the board's decision could have been made on ethical grounds. Given that the ethics of both Jones and Arabadjian were extremely suspect, especially when analyzed in detail, it would seemingly be hard for the Executive Board to justify rejecting an American appeal. After all, the ending of the gold medal contest shattered sports convention by usurping what was just and expected—the officials' ruling over and controlling a game. Did this herald a new era, where those in authority could saunter from the stands and change referees' decisions—and thus outcomes? The officials were trained for their jobs and had experience working in them—one without that background trying to assert control over a game is similar to a player walking in to one of Jones's FIBA board meetings after an issue was voted down and saying the issue has actually been approved.

It's hard to overestimate the moral clarity sports seemed to offer during the decades of the Cold War. Statesmen, intellectuals, and others debated the merits and drawbacks of the capitalist and Communist systems. Both nations engaged in propaganda efforts to tout their way of life. Soviet premier Nikita Khrushchev memorably said, "We will bury you," to Western ambassadors; American presidents in general were more circumspect in their utterances. In 1962 the Cuban Missile Crisis brought the nations close to nuclear war.

But when their athletes competed against each other, sports spawned lucidity and certainty. One team won, and one team lost; end of debate. The reason is because of the rules. Imagine sports without them. Chaos would reign, as it often does in the real world. There would be no sportsmanship. But with rules, structure exists: fairness triumphs; participants understand right and wrong. Do the latter, and penalties will be levied.

During games, rules are worth nothing without professional, trained, disinterested officials to apply them (golf is the rare exception, where golfers are expected to call penalties on themselves). Granted, officials make mistakes—in baseball a runner's foot may reach the bag before the tag, but that person is unfairly called out; in football, a player may fumble before hitting the ground, but a referee might say he was down, making the ball dead while enraging defenders. At the highest level of games in the twenty-first century, many of these bad calls can be overturned thanks to video replay. Grandchildren of today's athletes likely will be nonchalant watching robots monitor games.

But in 1972, humans—with all of their flaws—were fully in charge. That meant rules could be bent, flouted, ignored. This was the case during the gold medal basketball game in Munich on a variety of levels, yet somehow, nearly a half century later, those entrusted to uphold its own rules, such as the IOC and FIBA, are nowhere near acknowledging that problems occurred and that the final result was, according to the rules in place at the time, completely unjust. Ironically, those in charge acted as if they were on the side of righteousness—the Soviets tried to call a time-out; the clock was not set correctly—but these only disguised the larger issues of corrupt management of a championship game. When rules during games mean nothing, the results themselves suffer the same fate.

To this day, the 1972 gold medal game remains the only sports championship decided in violation of that sport's own rules.

10

PICKING UP THE PIECES

AS THE PLAYERS RECOVERED from the shattering loss, many were soon heartened by great news for their professional careers. Tapped by a Philadelphia squad whose 9-73 mark the previous season remains the worst in NBA history, Doug Collins was the first pick in the 1973 NBA draft, followed by Jim Brewer; in all, over the next two years, eleven of the twelve Olympic players joined the NBA. (Drafted by a strong Chicago team in 1974, Jim Forbes—still hobbled by his knee injury suffered soon after the Olympics—didn't make the squad. Kenny Davis, who had accepted a job offer at Converse, had previously rejected overtures from the NBA and ABA.)

Some on the '72 squad were given a chance to redress that painful defeat in Munich. In 1973 the Soviet team visited the United States and played games against American collegiate All-Stars. Labeled the Revenge Tour, *Sports Illustrated* summed up the stakes, reporting, "The Americans . . . embraced the series as if it were a chance to avenge Sputnik, the grain deal, and the travails of Terry and the Pirates as well as that embarrassing loss in Munich . . . when [Bob] Cousy announced his team would play quarter-horse basketball instead of the dragging style so favored by Olympic Coach Henry Iba, it was all anyone could do to keep from quivering with anticipation."[1]

Six games were slated in various parts of the country. The basketball court became a bruising, bloody forum for the United States to attempt to avenge Munich and for the Soviets to prove it was not a fluke. The first game, broadcast on national television, set the tone: "Coach Cousy described the action after the game, saying, 'It's mayhem out there, especially under the basket' . . . Cousy's impressions were certainly borne out on the trainer's table and in the locker room, which was described as a field hospital, with virtually every player bumped and bruised and several bandaged. 'Pound for pound,' said Tom Henderson, 'they'll beat you to death.'"[2]

Perhaps the biggest takeaway from the battle, an 83–65 U.S. victory at the Forum in Los Angeles, was the following: Had Bill Walton played in the Olympics, the final three seconds would have merely been the moments of another American coronation. Even though hobbled by knee and ankle injuries, knocked down a number of times by the Soviets and on the court for fewer than sixteen minutes, Walton's rebounding prowess (he pulled in nine) overwhelmed the Soviets. He also blocked three shots.

Game two, a Soviet victory in San Diego, ended up even more physical than the first one. Bobby Jones—befogged the year before after being knocked to the floor during the gold medal game—took a charge that could have killed him: "Jones offered the token resistance of a carnival dummy being knocked over with a ball. Only this time the ball was the 6'10", 240-pound [Ivan] Dvorni. 'I saw him coming,' recalls Jones, 'and you can't imagine the things that went through my mind. At UNC I would have stood there because we always take charges. Then I thought, "He's 6'10" and 240." And then at the last moment, I thought, "I'm going to do it for my country." That was the most terrifying moment I've had in my life.'"[3]

After splitting the first two games, Cousy added some bulk, including Len Elmore and Marvin Barnes, to play in Albuquerque. The United States won that one, as well as the next in Indianapolis, where nearly ninety fouls were called. The United States then prevailed in New York, where eight players fouled out.

In the finale before a capacity crowd in Baltimore, the Soviets triumphed. Eighty-one fouls were assessed. Swen Nater was ejected for elbowing a player in the head. Despite the détente between the two countries at the government level, the series could have been mistaken for a low-level war—or even a hockey game of the era, when players rarely wore helmets and often fought, bloodying each other's faces with their fists.

While a number of Olympic players headed to the pros that fall of 1973, some were poised to play their best college ball. Consider Tommy Burleson, the benched big man in Munich. In the semifinals of the NCAA Tournament, North Carolina State faced UCLA, the most dominant team in college basketball history. The Bruins had defeated the Wolfpack by 18 earlier in the season, and no one would have flinched had they dismantled North Carolina State again.

In fact, UCLA rolled and led by double digits with only eleven minutes remaining in the game. Burleson's assignment had been the toughest of anyone's: contain Walton. Though Walton's eventual tally of 29 points were 9 more than his adversary, Burleson swatted away a number of shots and stayed with him not just for two halves but for two overtimes as well. The Wolfpack inched past UCLA 80–77 and romped past Marquette 76–64 two nights later before practically a home crowd at Greensboro Coliseum in North Carolina to win its first NCAA crown.

In the fall of 1975, the Soviet team—including both Belovs—traveled around the United States for nearly a month to play fourteen exhibition games. Perhaps most importantly, they lost to the University of North Carolina and its coach, Dean Smith, who would lead the U.S. squad in Montreal the next year. And in typical Soviet-American fashion, controversy reigned. This time, Soviet coach Kondrashin encountered bizarre proceedings with the scoreboard after he called time-out during a 28–28 tie. When the game resumed, suddenly he was down 28–26.

"Earlier in the game one of the referees had signaled incorrectly that a Soviet basket was good; as a result, the board operator had the wrong score posted," reported *Sports Illustrated*. "The official scorer corrected the error during the time-out, and that set off Kondrashin, who was certain that he was being cheated. As in Indianapolis, he threatened to quit the game."[4]

Basketball tryouts for the 1976 Olympics were held in North Carolina. Persuaded by Smith, the selection committee put four Tar Heels and seven Atlantic Coast Conference players overall on the team, drawing the ire of other colleges and sportswriters. Smith felt familiar players would help him best get ready in the short time frame. Unlike at Colorado Springs and Pearl Harbor, four years earlier, players could do as they pleased off the court.

In Montreal the Americans survived a second-game scare from Puerto Rico, whom they nipped 95–94. They then coasted before beating Yugoslavia by 21 in the final behind 30 points from future NBA player Adrian Dantley. They scored 90 or more points in all but one game and did not face the Soviets who, despite boasting much of the same team that had captured the gold, settled for a bronze medal. Despite the pressure to win after Munich, U.S. players seemed unaffected and won the country's eighth gold medal in nine attempts.

One more set of Soviet heroes would thrive against their rivals in Olympic basketball. The United States boycotted the Olympics in Moscow in 1980 as retaliation for the Soviet invasion of Afghanistan; in 1984 the Soviet Union refused to send athletes to Los Angeles for the games as payback. So when the basketball teams met in 1988 in Seoul, South Korea, it had been sixteen years since the controversy in Munich, and the first time the two nations had met in the games since then.

John Thompson, who had turned around a laggard program at Georgetown University and captured an NCAA championship in 1984, led the U.S. team. As it had been since Berlin, only amateurs were eligible. Many would become prominent NBA names, such as center David Robinson, a standout at the Naval Academy who would win a number of championships with the San Antonio Spurs, and guard/forward Dan Majerle, who flourished for the Phoenix Suns. Forward Danny Manning had just captured an NCAA title with the University of Kansas.

Far from Iba's plodding offense, Thompson emphasized speed, just as coach Bob Knight had during the 1984 games, where the

United States handily captured the gold. Thompson also played a tenacious pressure defense. The average age of the team was older than the 1972 squad, and its average height was impressive. For the most part, the United States easily dispatched its first six opponents, winning by an average of more than 30 points a game (without using the newly implemented three-point shot often) and setting up a long-anticipated Olympic rematch.

Just like in 1972, the Soviets opened up wide leads, and the United States was forced to battle back repeatedly. And, as in Munich, the Americans mounted a furious rally in the second half, coming back from a 51–37 deficit to cut it to 2, 59–57.

But the Soviets, led by sharpshooting guard Rimas Kurtinaitis (28 points) and seven-foot-three center Arvidas Sabonis (13 points and 13 rebounds), held off their rivals. Manning, the collegiate wunderkind, finished with zero points in the 82–76 defeat after getting in foul trouble in the first half. For the first time in eleven Olympics, the Americans not only did not advance to the gold medal game (won by the Soviets over Yugoslavia); they earned (and accepted) the bronze medal. Given that the Soviet Union broke up before the next Olympics in Barcelona, the great rivalry was finished, punctuated by two straight Soviet wins—the only blemishes on the 85-2 record of the United States overall to that point.

Unlike in 1972, no R. William Jones emerged from the stands; no referee called an excess of fouls against U.S. players in the final minutes. Instead, it was an uncontroversial defeat to the Soviets—and the Americans heard about it back home. Said Majerle, "Everyone took a lot of heat when we lost. I took a lot of heat . . . my rookie year, coming into the league, that's all I heard. 'Good job bringing home the bronze.' Just brutal stuff from the fans."[5]

One silver lining for the U.S. twelve during the '72 defeat was they were generally spared the wrath of fans coming home. Plus, barely in their twenties at the time, they had entire lives to recover from the stunning upset. What they have accomplished in the forty-plus years since the Munich Games is as diverse as the players themselves.

Tommy Burleson's experience in Munich haunted him. After hearing the hostages crying as they walked to their deaths, only four days later he suffered the ignominy of being benched during his sole gold medal game. But after winning the NCAA title, he was selected by Seattle as a number-one pick in the 1974 draft (the third player chosen overall). He immediately became a millionaire (the Super Sonics, coached by former NBA center and '72 Olympics announcer Bill Russell, paid highly for a big man they needed to battle other Western Conference teams already amply supplied, such as the Los Angeles Lakers with Abdul-Jabbar). Despite his size and success at North Carolina State, Burleson's pro career sputtered. Twice during seven seasons he averaged double digits in scoring. His final two years, with the Kansas City Kings and the Atlanta Hawks, were anemic; in one, his field-goal percentage dropped below 35 percent, rare for a towering figure often shooting near the basket. But knee and leg injuries had hampered him, and the player who had led the Wolfpack to the NCAA title while battling the era's best college center (he also faced Walton during the 1970s Seattle-Portland rivalry) lacked the physical health necessary to continue in the NBA.

He returned to Seattle for a spell, where he raced hydroplanes (given his height, he would pay for specially crafted cockpits to make him more comfortable), and owned a tavern. But Burleson and cities did not mesh; he returned to Newland, North Carolina, in the 1980s to raise his family of three boys with his wife, Denise.

Back home, he's served as an electrician, run an eponymous basketball camp for decades, and worked as an Avery County public servant, where he keeps a modest office—so nondescript that visitors are somewhat surprised upon entering:

> Once in a while the rare local who has never heard of Burleson stops by his office and is stunned to encounter a man so giant that his desk rests upon six-inch stilts. "Sometimes they'll tell me, 'Gosh, you're so tall, you should've played basketball,'" Burleson says. "I tell them, 'Yeah, that would've been nice.'"[6]

Since 1989 Burleson has also farmed and sold Christmas trees, where some firs are even taller than he. But it would be inaccurate to say he is simply a country boy uninterested in the outside world. In fact, those Christmas trees are sold to aid the impoverished in Malawi, Africa. Buoyed by his Christian faith, he has conducted mission work annually in third world regions for many years. He has done electrical work at the main hospital, labored to help the local church, and more, often at personal peril:

> He sneaks across the border from Ethiopia, then folds his 48-inch legs into a minibus to take medical supplies—mostly aspirin and antibiotics—to the town of Nkhoma . . . (How does a giant who has towered head and shoulders over everyone he knows except Bill Walton his entire life *sneak* anywhere? Well, a bazooka and a crisp salute helps.) "It was a little rugged the first time we went," Burleson admits. "We had outhouses and mostly outside facilities. I got an intestinal virus the first time I went."
>
> There was also an outbreak of viral meningitis on that first trip, something that could be treated with the Amoxicillin Burleson and his resource team had packed.
>
> "We were saving lives within 15 minutes after we got there," Burleson says.[7]

From hearing hostages march to their deaths to saving lives is quite a journey. And despite being sidelined in the gold medal game, Burleson holds no grudges and appreciates what he learned from his Olympic coaches.

"They were great coaches. Coach Haskins and Bach worked diligently with me," he said. "Making that team gave me confidence. When I returned to North Carolina State, I was playing two levels above what I was playing as a sophomore. Using the backboard with the hook shot served me well in a lot of big games.

"Even though I later won a national championship, making the Olympic team and being designated an Olympian is my greatest athletic achievement. It was just really an awesome day when I was one of twelve chosen to compete in the Olympics."

Doug Collins has spent his entire life in basketball in one form or another. During an eight-year NBA career, in which he averaged nearly 18 points per season, he helped revivify the woeful 76ers; by his fourth season, the team reached the NBA Finals, only to fall to Walton's Trail Blazers, 4-2. That postseason, Collins averaged more than 22 points per game. During his career, he was named to the All-Star team four times.

But injuries weighed on Collins. He never completed a full NBA season and, by the end, torn ligaments in both knees restricted his movements. Despite being known for working hard through injuries, that was the end for the guard.

Barely in his thirties, Collins encountered the vexing question nearly all pro athletes face at a young age: Where do I go from here?

"It was hard. My career was taken away from me as a very, very young man," he said. "I love basketball. I took care of myself. There was nothing I could do about it. All of a sudden, you were thirty-one years old, and back then you didn't make enough money so that you wouldn't have to work again. What are you going to do in your life? Your family becomes the focal point."[8]

Hard to believe for a lauded former number-one draft pick, Collins became an unpaid assistant for the University of Pennsylvania basketball team. Eventually, that metamorphosed into a paid position, and then he moved to Tempe, Arizona, to join Arizona State as an assistant coach. The man who once was painfully shy also became a basketball analyst on CBS.

Amazingly enough, five years after retirement, he earned his first head coaching job. Not at the high school level, not in college, but straight to the NBA as head man for the Chicago Bulls—led by Michael Jordan.

One of the youngest coaches in the NBA, Collins lifted the Bulls into the NBA Eastern Conference Finals in his third season—and then, to the shock of fans, he was fired. The usual euphemism of "philosophical differences" was trotted out.

What really happened? Why did owner Jerry Reinsdorf dump the successful coach?

"Reinsdorf saw a developing disintegration of his team, with virtually every player angered and frustrated by playing for Collins and several even plotting to cause the coach an embarrassment that might get him fired," wrote Sam Smith, who covered the Bulls for the *Chicago Tribune* and eventually authored a best-selling book, *The Jordan Rules*. "Reinsdorf saw a driven, insecure Collins, grasping desperately to succeed while fighting madly not to fail. He saw his coach missing sleep and meals and breaking down in his office over the pressures of the job."[9]

Basically, the same fiery nature and competitive zeal that helped him on the court hurt him as a young head coach. After Collins, the Bulls famously won six NBA championships under Phil Jackson in the 1990s. Collins bounced back to coach the Detroit Pistons, Washington Wizards, and his old team, the 76ers. Though he rapidly improved each squad, he never lasted more than three seasons with any of them. In between those stints, he forged a successful career as a well-known television basketball analyst on ESPN and NBC (where he has, in fact, announced five Olympic basketball gold medal games). And, in almost perfect symmetry, at age sixty-six he was hired as senior adviser of basketball operations by the Bulls, who had fired him almost thirty years earlier. Still, amazingly, the talented, intelligent Collins has never won a championship as a player or coach.

Around age twelve, Jim Brewer began to get serious about basketball. Although of average height at that point, he shot up to six foot six when he joined the Proviso East High School team in Maywood, Illinois. By the time he graduated, he had led the Pirates to the state championship as its center and was named "Mr. Basketball" as the state's best player. Recruited by the University of Minnesota, the bruising forward's passion for the game was evident his freshman year. After scoring 20 points in his first game, he wrote "I ain't satisfied" on the blackboard in the locker room.[10]

After the Olympics, Brewer finished his vaunted college career at the University of Minnesota, where he ended up as the team captain, won three Most Valuable Player awards, and played to loud chants of "Brew-w-w-w" at his home arena. He scored more than 1,000 points overall as a Golden Gopher, which persuaded both the Cleveland Cavaliers of the NBA and the New York Nets of the ABA to draft him in 1973 and fight for his services. Cleveland won, in part because its coach, Bill Fitch, had persuaded him originally to go to Minnesota when he led the Golden Gophers.

After struggling his rookie year, shooting below 40 percent and averaging barely more than 6 points per game, Brewer shone by his third year, averaging double digits in both points and rebounds. But after five and a half solid seasons, he was traded to Detroit and then Portland before ending up in Los Angeles, where he earned a championship ring with the likes of Abdul-Jabbar, Magic Johnson, and others.

After playing in Italy, Brewer entered coaching, first as an assistant at Northwestern University. He then returned to the NBA with the Minnesota Timberwolves, where he served in a number of positions, including assistant general manager, before he headed to the Los Angeles Clippers, Orlando Magic, Toronto Raptors, and, finally, the Boston Celtics. Save for Orlando, where he was a scout, he was an assistant coach at his other stops.

Like Brewer, Jim Forbes also jumped into coaching, albeit on a smaller level. After serving as an assistant for Haskins at UTEP after graduation, he became the boys' basketball coach at Riverside High for twenty years before assuming the reins at Andress High in El Paso, where he has tallied more than three hundred wins.

Forbes's teams are driven and focused. Though he had hoped to play ten years in the NBA, and ended up not even playing a game, one goal he wrote down at UTEP was to coach high school basketball. He's done that for about thirty-five years.

Though he doesn't mention Munich specifically to his boys, he alludes to it when he talks about overcoming adversity.

"One thing I say to them is that they can work hard and do everything right and sometimes, things still go wrong," he said. "What are you going to do if something disappointing happens to you?"[11]

Of the twelve, Bobby Jones arguably enjoyed the best NBA career.

158

Given his lack of interest in the sport growing up, it's pretty amazing he excelled on the professional level above his Olympic teammates. His father and mother (well before Title IX) were both accomplished basketball players, but as a youth, he expressed little interest.

"I was fairly quiet and uncoordinated and didn't like sports," Jones said. "My dad made me go out in the backyard and do certain drills every day. I didn't really enjoy the drills."[12]

As a child he was forced to play on his church's league team. Even though he was not interested in the game, he still gave his all. "In the Bible, it says we're supposed to give 100 percent in whatever it is we do—and that's what I do," he explained.[13]

After playing for coach Smith, Jones graduated from the University of North Carolina in 1974. The rare Olympian who chose the ABA over the NBA, where he was a top-five pick, Jones enjoyed a lengthy career (eventually in the NBA after the leagues merged) thanks to his flexibility and tenaciousness. Though he never reached the 60 percent shooting mark etched in his rookie year with the Denver Nuggets, he consistently made well over 50 percent of his shots each season during his NBA career as a forward, and his final field goal percentage of 56 percent is among the top fifteen in league history.

Yet some of his best work never showed up in the box score; his hustle and dedication on defense prompted him to be named to eight consecutive All-Defensive First Teams. Not only that, the 1982–83 76ers team he played on captured the NBA title, and Jones earned the inaugural Sixth Man of the Year award, a selfless presence off the bench giving future Hall of Famers such as Julius Erving a rest. With barely an announcement, much less a farewell tour, he retired in 1986 in his mid-thirties, and his number 24 jersey was lifted to the rafters, never to be worn by another 76er.

Jones is given credit for starting pregame chapel services in the NBA. In fact, the active speaker for the Fellowship of Christian Athletes attributes his religious beliefs for helping his career.

"It was a great encouragement to me," he said. "As I look at my career in the NBA, I was a good player but not a great player. I lasted for twelve years, and I probably shouldn't have. So many guys fell by the wayside, whether it was alcohol, or drugs or something else. They didn't stay on course. My faith allowed me to stay on course."[14]

Like many of his teammates, Jones has made his mark beyond the arena. After retiring, he stayed committed to basketball and Christianity. He became a basketball coach and athletic director at Charlotte Christian High School, where his three children attended. He then joined the ministry 2xSalt to aid inner-city youth in Charlotte through sports, music, and more.

Considering that Christianity has been a linchpin of his life, Jones was asked if he forgave those whose actions impeded a U.S. gold medal.

"Yes. Absolutely," he responded. "As Romans 8:28 says, "And we know that in all things God works for the good of those who love him, who have been called according to his purpose." What it means is you won't have a perfect life—you'll have ups and downs. The Olympics was a trying experience but also an uplifting experience."

Like Bobby Jones, Tom Henderson—intense on the court—became a quiet champion of troubled youths off it.

After retiring from the NBA, where he earned a championship with the Washington Bullets, he said he spent about three years just lying on the couch. Then he adopted four children in the Houston area with his wife, Denolis, as they became foster parents.

"Growing up, my wife's mother in New York always took people in," said Henderson, who has known Denolis for more than half a century. "Her mom's grocery bill went up $150 a month with me there all of the time.

"I thought I'd become a foster parent for my wife. To be a foster parent was giving back like guys gave back to me in New York. It's a good feeling to watch the kids grow. We're making sure they get to the next level."

Beyond those four, the Hendersons have taken in other court-appointed boys who needed guidance. Tom takes them to Rockets games. Overall, they've provided a home environment for more than one hundred who desperately needed it.

"They'd come in the house and tell me about their day," the Olympian said. "You have some that come out decent and others that end up in the news for doing something stupid. It makes you feel good when one of them calls and says thank you. That makes it all worthwhile."

Said Larry Misiak, who served as the foster care coordinator for DePelchin Children's Center and who worked closely with the Hendersons, "We see the result of some rather poor home life and poor parenting, and in most cases there has been serious abuse and neglect, where these kids have been damaged emotionally and, in some cases, physically. Tom and Denolis have a pretty thick skin . . . when you bring them into your home and they're angry, aggressive kids, they're gonna be busting things up. They can put their fist through a wall. They can be destructive in other ways I'd rather not mention."[15]

Growing up, Henderson saw plenty of troubled juveniles on the streets of the Bronx. In fact, when he looks back, he credits the junkies for helping him find his way.

"The junkies kept me straight. They kept me in line because they saw something in me. I had the drive to be the best I wanted to be. I'd play basketball until three or four in the morning. The ones that are still alive, I tell them thank you."

Raised in Ohio, Ed Ratleff played baseball as a boy before being persuaded to join the school basketball team in seventh grade. Put in only when a game was out of hand, he likely could have ended up a baseball player but for observing what happened to teammate and star Vance Carr, the homecoming king whose girlfriend was the queen:

> Ratleff worked it out in his adolescent mind: if he became the best player he would be the homecoming king and if he became homecoming king he would get a girlfriend.
>
> So, he spent the entire summer before his eighth-grade year training, quickly becoming not just the best in the school but the best in the region. It didn't hurt that he also grew to 6-foot-4 that summer.[16]

In high school at Columbus East, Ratleff flourished on the court. He earned All-American honors while helping lead the team to two state titles and a 70-1 mark.

Ratleff had decided to attend college at Florida State before Jerry Tarkanian traveled to Ohio, stayed for days, and persuaded him to switch to Long Beach State. As a freshman not allowed to play on the varsity per NCAA rules, Ratleff was a man among boys, averaging about 40 points a game. Then he joined the loaded 49ers squad in the midst of a sixty-five-game home winning streak. The always controversial Tark the Shark counted on Ratleff to try to help vanquish the nearly unbeatable UCLA teams of that era. He almost came through in 1971, guiding the 49ers against the Bruins in the NCAA Tournament before fouling out; Long Beach lost, 57–55. The assignment during the 1972 NCAA Tournament seemed almost hopeless. Explained *Sports Illustrated*, "Though Ed Ratleff is the most complete college player in the country and the one man able to control a game against the Bruins, most of his ability stems from the backcourt, and UCLA's devastating pressure defense would make Ratleff work hard in bringing the ball up court, giving him little time to concentrate on points."[17]

The 49ers lost again to their intrastate rivals.

Despite his prowess in college—his 21.4-point-per-game scoring average is still a record at Long Beach State—Ratleff's NBA career (the sixth overall pick in 1973, he was selected by Houston) proved short-lived. A back injury limited him to five years with the Rockets where, like most of his Olympic teammates, his professional dreams never quite matched his excellence in college. He returned to Long Beach State as an assistant coach before enjoying a successful career with State Farm.

In 2015, during the NCAA Tournament at Lucas Oil Stadium in Indianapolis, his superb play in Long Beach was recognized. Joined by greats such as Rolando Blackman and John Havlicek, Ratleff was inducted into the National Collegiate Basketball Hall of Fame.

"It's like a huge step," said Ratleff. "You go through your whole career with all the accolades and people recognize you . . . but to move up to Hall of Fame is really nice, it's the pinnacle.

"I was shocked to get the call . . . I tell all my friends I didn't stay on the phone long enough because I was afraid he had the wrong person. I didn't want to ask too many questions and have him realize he was talking to the wrong person."[18]

Among the five remaining Olympians, Kenny Davis forged a successful career as a Converse salesman practically upon landing from Munich, while the four other players on the team all played in the NBA but only experienced limited success. Afterward, Kevin Joyce ended up as a salesman on the East Coast before working on lift operations at a ski resort in Vermont during winters. Before passing away in 2016, Dwight Jones sold cars in the Houston area. Mike Bantom is in charge of NBA Referee Operations. Tom McMillen made the biggest name for himself away from the sport, serving as a U.S. Congressman for three terms from Maryland.

For all, the loss in Munich still stings. Some players only think deeply about the Soviet game every four years during the Olympics, while others relive the pain more frequently.

Davis, the team captain, undergoes the agony more than most.

"If I go to a game in a gym, there's a winner and a loser," he said. "After what happened to us, I have an empty feeling every time I leave a gym."

Reflected McMillen, "That was the most bitter and painful experience of my life. What happened in Munich was the most controversial and tragic sports competition in modern times."[19]

Only a chance encounter with pictures in his basement helped Brewer alleviate the pain of the Olympic defeat.

"I was bitter for a long, long time," he said. "I remember one day, about three or four years after those Olympics. I was looking for my passport in some cardboard boxes in the basement because I had to leave the country. And I came upon some pictures of the guys on that team, and some letters from that time, and I just started crying. I sat there for a while, alone in the basement, and cried. I finally let it go that day."[20]

Children of the Olympians often knew little about the impact of the loss on their parents. At home, Collins did not speak or dwell on that defeat. As a teenager, his son Chris Collins—now the head coach for Northwestern University's basketball team—saw how the defeat pained his father.

Chris and his dad attended a summer-league basketball game. Also in the house were two players from the '72 Soviet squad. When told they'd like to speak with Collins, he angrily refused.

"That was the first memory I had of how much that hurt," Chris Collins said. "That's when I fully understood just how tough of a situation that was."[21]

Said Doug Collins, "I actually got more bitter about that game as the years went on. If my two free throws had stood up, they'd be etched in history. After the Olympics I would watch other people getting gold medals, and I'd feel teary-eyed, I'd feel jealous. I've played in NBA Finals and All-Star games. My wife has taken my Olympic ring to the jeweler and put a cluster of diamonds in it so it looks like a championship ring. But nothing comes close to the feeling of a twenty-one-year-old kid playing for his country and winning the gold, nothing comes close to the feeling I *should've* had if they hadn't taken it away from me."[22]

Before the Beijing Olympics in 2008, Colangelo asked Collins to address the U.S. team at its training camp in Las Vegas.

"He showed incredible emotion in recounting that gold medal game. His message was, 'You never know if you'll have the opportunity again,'" Colangelo said. "It has stayed with him his entire life. I just have to look into Doug Collins's eyes to know what it means to him. Multiply it by twelve, plus the coaches and others. Think about the impact it had on their lives."

Colangelo knows how a loss can torment someone years later.

"Since I've been involved in USA Basketball, we've gone 83-1. But I can't forget that one loss (in the 2006 World Championships). Despite the fact we had a lot of young stars, it happened. I refused to look at the replay of that game for one year. It hurt too much. Then I watched it, and all of the hurt came back.

"Once we had that loss, we built on that. You learn from the loss. But for the '72 team, they couldn't because they weren't together again."

Like Collins, Bantom—who cried on the bench after the gold medal game—reacted viscerally when encountering Soviet players later in life. While playing in Italy in 1984, the future NBA executive faced a Soviet team touring the country.

"The Russians brought their own ref, and they started roughing us up, and their ref wouldn't call anything," he remembered. "So for two hours I lost my mind.

"I elbowed guys in the mouth. I kneed guys. I shot two for twenty, but I wasn't interested in making shots. I was something to behold. The Russians' coach was the same guy who coached them in '72 [Kondrashin], and he confronted me at halftime.

"'Why are you doing this?' the coach asked me.

"I said, 'I know who you are and I know what you're doing. You, more than anybody, should know why I hate you sons of bitches.'"[23]

After the shocking defeat, Iba enjoyed attending Oklahoma State games. He would also visit pupils such as Haskins at least once a year, watch his practices and offer his insights:

One day, Iba asked Haskins why the Miners didn't run a player along the baseline when in transition against a zone defense. Lost for an answer, Haskins said to his mentor, "Well, *should* we be doing that?"

The next day Haskins, who won a national championship in 1966, had the first player down court sprinting to the baseline in transition against a zone.[24]

After his wife, Doyne, died in 1983, Iba was depressed and unsure of what to do. Coach Bob Knight invited him to be a consultant for the 1984 Olympic basketball team, starting with the trials. The octogenarian was far from a wallflower. Recalled Pat Knight, Bob's son and a ball boy on that '84 squad, "He told my dad who he should select, how they should play, who he should get on, who he shouldn't get on—because everybody has got different personalities. It was kind of neat just sitting back and watching my dad ask advice from Coach Iba."[25]

The biggest highlight for Iba was when the players in Los

Angeles—which featured future Hall of Famers such as Michael Jordan and Patrick Ewing—carried him off the floor under Knight's orders after winning the gold.

"Nobody was happier for him about the situation than I was, with his ability to go with us and the day-to-day opportunity to be involved with him," Bob Knight said. "There couldn't have been anybody happier about those circumstances than me."[26] Iba passed away in 1993.

Johnny Bach's basketball career spanned more than half a century before he died in 2016 at age ninety-one. After joining the Golden State Warriors as an assistant coach in 1979, he led the team from 1983 to 1986, a sorry bunch well after the Warriors had peaked with Rick Barry and captured an NBA championship in 1975. He worked on Collins's Chicago Bulls staff but was best known as an assistant under Phil Jackson during the Bulls' first threepeat from 1991 to 1993. He instituted an aggressive defense that thwarted opponents. He also served as an assistant coach in Charlotte, Detroit, and Washington before joining the Bulls again at the end of his career. Even in his late eighties, Bach volunteered to assist a high school basketball team in Chicago.

Collins talked about him after his death.

"He was brilliantly organized. That comes from his military background. Every *i* was dotted and every *t* crossed," Collins said. "He had such a great feel for people. He might give you a gruff exterior. But he had a heart of gold and a sensitive spirit.

"He would always call me Paul Douglas Collins, my full name. He would say to me, 'That mistake you're about to make, I've already made.'"[27]

Don Haskins ended up coaching UTEP for nearly forty years, even after the death of his son, Mark, which devastated him and his wife, Mary. He finished his career boasting a 719-353 record, which included participating in fourteen NCAA tournaments.

In 1997, a year after suffering a heart attack during halftime of a game, Haskins was voted into the Naismith Memorial Basketball Hall of Fame (something that eluded fellow Olympic assistant Bach in his lifetime) while he was still coaching, even though UTEP suffered from NCAA sanctions in the 1990s and Haskins's teams bore little resemblance to the successful squads of the 1960s and 1970s. As the twenty-first century beckoned, Haskins barely left his seat on the floor anymore:

> Yet he continues to show up faithfully at the Don Haskins Center—right across Mesa Avenue from where Mary works part time as a travel agent—not so much because there isn't enough money in the bank, but because there's so much of himself invested in the program. "They should almost have exit counseling for some of these guys," says [Rick] Majerus. "Tark [Fresno State coach Jerry Tarkanian] wants to win one more. [Former Dayton coach Don] Donoher hung on, and now he doesn't remember the Final Four he went to or the 437 wins—only the last few seasons when he lost. Don Haskins reminds me of the milk horse my grandpa had in Sheboygan. Once he'd hitched it up, that horse didn't want to do anything else its entire life."[28]

In 2008, Haskins passed away at age seventy-eight.

On the Soviet side, head coach Vladimir Kondrashin died at age seventy in 1999. Despite his anger at him for his late, errant pass in the gold medal game, Kondrashin always cherished Alexander Belov, whom he coached on Spartak Leningrad during Kondrashin's long stint with the team (1967–95). He kept a photo of him in his car, and he possessed Belov's gold medal after his early death, since Alexander had willed it to him. Was he confident with him taking the final shot?

"I knew him from childhood, so I was sure of him. Still now I would choose Belov," Kondrashin said in 1989. "Unfortunately, more people remember Belov in America than they do here."[29]

Many years on September 10, he met with players and coaches to celebrate the victory again (the game finished on September 10 in the Soviet Union, though September 9 in the United States). But often it was bittersweet.

"On the anniversary I recall Belov more than the game itself,"

Kondrashin said through a translator. "I am more sad than happy on that day."[30]

For Sergei Belov, the man whose 20 points lit up Munich, his list of career achievements is extraordinary beyond his gold medal. He also earned three bronze medals in the Olympics, and in 1992, he was the first international player elected to the Naismith Memorial Basketball Hall of Fame. He coached the Russian national team for six years.

He always remained disappointed the Soviets couldn't capitalize more on their 1972 win.

"Everybody was very inspired. Our victory should have raised the game on a national level. But our leaders didn't find a way to do it. They didn't want to plan for the future. They could only think of today."[31]

Still, whatever successes he had beyond 1972, Belov—who died in 2013—was constantly drawn back to Munich.

"The most terrifying thing . . . is that people remember only the past. People are always saying, 'You were, you were, you were.' And that can keep you in the past. But you must go on with your life."[32]

Ivan Edeshko—who served as assistant coach on the Central Army basketball team when Sergei Belov coached it—concurred.

"People always want to talk to me about them," said Edeshko, now in his seventies and one of only four Soviet players out of twelve on the team still living. "So much that I can't even speak about it anymore. But if I didn't have those three seconds, I would never be that popular. I know this. My life would be very different than it is now."[33]

Though citizens of the former Soviet Union still enjoy talking about their upset victory—and a movie released in 2017, *Going Vertical*, became the highest-grossing domestic film in Russian history because it helped them relive the glorious triumph (and forget about Russia's 2018 Winter Olympics ban)—in the United States the defeat is cited mainly whenever a controversial loss is marred by alleged meddling.

Just before a congressional recess in 2007, Representative Ted Poe, a Republican from Texas, claimed "the House of Representatives had a replay of the 1972 Summer Olympic Games in Munich."[34] At issue: A vote denying benefits to illegal immigrants. In Poe's telling, according to the electronic tally board, the vote had passed 215–213 and the words "Final Vote" graced the screen.

But then, somehow, more time appeared on the clock—and the actual final vote ended up 216–212 against the measure.

Given the game had happened thirty-five years before, perhaps not surprisingly Poe's recollection was a bit scattershot.

"The Soviets were declared the winners even though they cheated—Team USA refused their Silver Medals and walked off the stage in disgust," railed Poe, though the Soviets themselves weren't accused of cheating and Team USA never stood on said stage. "Both the Soviet Basketball Team and those that want illegals to receive taxpayer benefits will do just anything to win—by any means necessary, whether legal or not."[35]

11

JOYOUS REUNION

WALK AROUND DOWNSTAIRS IN Kenneth Bryan Davis's house in Paint Lick, Kentucky, and you wouldn't know he played in the Olympics. Nor would you have any idea that, one year, he led all high school scorers in the basketball-mad state of Kentucky. In fact, you wouldn't even see any evidence he ever *played* basketball. Sure, step outside the kitchen door and the requisite basketball hoop stands nearby, but the picnic table's in the way of a layup and the net has become so rigid over the years that a successful shot would stick inside it.

What exemplifies the mindset of the humble man—whose wife of forty-five years, the former Rita Renfro of Paint Lick, found out he was captain of the U.S. Olympic team only when he was interviewed after the gold medal controversy—is the wooden American flag hanging on the house. On it is etched the Pledge of Allegiance.

On this day, Davis has returned to his house from his father's funeral in Monticello, Kentucky. Clyde Davis passed away at age ninety-five. Among other accomplishments, he served in the U.S. Army in Pearl Harbor and Japan before being honorably discharged in 1946.

As befits a veteran of the Greatest Generation, the national anthem played at his funeral. Davis has made clear that perhaps the greatest robbery back in Munich involved "The Star-Spangled Banner."

"I never hear a national anthem being played without thinking that something was taken away from us," he said. "I couldn't imagine the cold chills that would have run down my neck on the podium as they played the anthem and the flag was raised. I look back and think that was one of the things we were cheated out of—hearing our national anthem."

One of six children raised in rural Kentucky by Clyde and his wife, Zula, Davis discovered basketball when he entered fifth grade at Walker Elementary School, where a gymnasium court also served as the school lunchroom. Thanks in part to a coach's encouragement during layup drills there, Davis wanted to play more. At home, his parents found a flat spot on their hillside farm to set up a hoop—but the out-of-bounds area, where thorn trees and sinkholes reigned, was slightly treacherous.

"It was by far the worst location for a basketball court in the county and probably the state," Davis recalled. "It was not advisable to dribble as punctures from the thorns would quickly bring an end to my Western Auto ball. . . . But the blessing was . . . I learned when the ball went through the basket it diminished the chances it would wind up in a sinkhole or sustain a puncture from a nearby thorn tree. It is amazing how your concentration increases knowing that if something happens to this ball, it might be some time before funds were available to replace it."[1]

Dribbling a basketball even when he rode his bike, Davis couldn't get enough of the sport. By the time he reached high school, he played on the freshman team before facing a rough sophomore year on the varsity, where he averaged fewer than 7 points and shot only 33 percent on a 4-20 team.[2]

His reaction: work even harder.

"I went home and practiced as much as I could," Davis noted. "You really learn to shoot on your own, and I worked on improving my form by first shooting against a wall with no basket. And then I moved to a telephone pole. If you don't hit the pole in the dead center you know what happens? You have to chase the ball right or left."[3]

Davis's unorthodox training paid off. In one of the greatest turn-arounds ever seen at the Kentucky high school level, he averaged 24 points a game the following season. Though he was well known by his senior year and heavily guarded, he averaged more than 30 points per game, punctuated by a 61-point performance in which he outscored the entire opposing team.[4]

Davis then attended Western Kentucky University in Bowling Green, but he departed hastily during his freshman year. Even though the school featured a well-regarded basketball program, Davis packed up and left because he was upset upon finding that his scholarship was guaranteed for only one year, not four. Embarrassed by his impulsive decision to leave, he didn't even head home. He checked in with the Air Force Academy (his choice for college had he not been accepted at Western), but the military establishment where he would try out for the Olympics a few years later didn't take second-semester students.[5]

Fortunately for Davis, he ended up at Georgetown College, a private Christian school in Georgetown, Kentucky. There he was reunited with Coach Bob Davis. As a youngster he had attended the coach's camps for two summers and thoroughly enjoyed them. Unwavering in his dedication to basketball at his new school, "I wore shorts under my jeans, and after class I went straight to the gym," he said.[6]

Joining the varsity team his sophomore year, Davis smashed the school's single-season scoring record. He then averaged nearly 30 points a game the following year for the Tigers. Buoyed by his success, he played in the 1970 World University Games—a large disappointment for the United States, which lost to the Soviet Union in the final. Abroad for the first time, Davis was also disappointed by the European food.

"It made the cafeteria at Georgetown look like a five-star restaurant," Davis said. "I lived on bread and jelly for several days."[7]

After a successful senior season at Georgetown, Davis tried out for the Pan Am team (with the Olympics forthcoming the following year, Iba helped select players). In South America, the results were even more disappointing than in the World Games, as the United States failed to capture a medal.

Both the New York Knicks and the Carolina Cougars of the ABA tried to lure Davis to the pros, but he was unimpressed with the no-guarantee contracts and wanted to play for his country once more. In April of 1972, a letter from Bill Summers, chair of the Olympic Basketball Committee, arrived at his house and read in part:

> Dear Kenny:
>
> Congratulations! As one of the outstanding amateur basketball players of the nation, you have been nominated as a candidate for the United States Olympic Basketball Team. . . . For your information, the Selection Committee, who will watch these games, will select the final twelve players, taking into consideration individual ability on the floor, dedication to team work, all-around attitude, coachability and willingness to cooperate.

At the bottom in his own handwriting, Summers wrote, "This is the year Kenny."[8]

The good news for Davis: he boasted more international experience than just about any player invited to the tryouts. With games in Colorado Springs being played under international rules, he enjoyed an advantage, thanks to the knowledge he had gained in South America and Europe. And at the end of the three-week torture session at Pearl Harbor, the U.S. team voted the Kentucky native as its captain.

"I think it was more out of respect than anything," said Davis, the last AAU player to ever represent the United States in the Olympics. "I felt a lot of pride, especially coming from a small school and realizing most of those guys were probably better players."

Of course, especially as the team captain in Munich, he was devastated by the loss. Talking about it years later, his words remained thunderous.

"The loss was the greatest miscarriage of justice in the history of sports," he said.[9]

When he got home from Munich—numbed by the trauma of terrorism and the injustice of the gold medal game—his energy was sapped. Said his wife, Rita, "It was total exhaustion. All of that was emotional, plus being physically tired."

Less than a week later, a Kenny Davis Day captivated his hometown of Monticello. Kenny and Rita rode on the back of a convertible during the parade, which ended in the Wayne County Football Stadium where a number of speakers (including Coach Davis) lauded him. A few days afterward, he received a telegram from the Osmond Brothers asking U.S. gold medal winners (apparently, the famous musical family turned the TV off with three seconds remaining) to join them as their all-expenses-paid guests at Caesars Palace in Las Vegas for a "Special Salute to Olympic Champions." Compared to the bright lights of Vegas, a fish fry in Davis's honor on September 23 in Paint Lick—where he received the key to the city—must have seemed quite subdued.

Hired as a sales rep with Converse in Kentucky, Davis began a successful career spanning more than forty years. He helped sell thousands of pairs of basketball and tennis shoes while finding himself in interesting situations, such as fitting the Soviet basketball players for their sneakers during the 1976 Olympics.

"The game never came up," Davis said. "Obviously there was a language barrier."

Twenty years later, he carried the Olympic torch in Kentucky for about an eighth of a mile before the Atlanta Games.

"That's kind of my medal," Davis said. "That was really, really special."

Though the twelve U.S. players had met up over the years, some while playing in the NBA, since flying back from Munich to New York City on a chartered jet they had not been all together at one time. That changed in 2012, when Davis helped gather them at Georgetown College, aided by former *Sports Illustrated* writer Billy Reed.

In a testament to his tenacity, the guy who didn't even play in the final game—the smallest, lightest guy on the team, the only one not to go pro—was organizing the Olympic team's first reunion. Davis pitched the idea to Converse, which earmarked $100,000 to put it on.

Entitled "Courage in Munich," the changes among players forty years later were obvious. Davis himself wore glasses, and his hair was practically a memory. Players' wives attended, many of whom hadn't even known their husbands when they'd played for their country in 1972. Collins talked about having all of $200 to his name during the games, as he and others had no time to get summer jobs.

"Now every player [in the Olympics] is a corporation," Collins said.[10]

Attendees lined up to ask players to sign basketballs, pictures, and more. Miss Kentucky 2012 sang the national anthem. Seminars addressed how the '72 game changed international basketball and discussed the ethical debate over not accepting the silver medal, among other topics. *New York Post* writer Mike Vaccaro chided the team.

"It's time to accept the medals," he said. "The team doesn't deserve to be looked upon the way the rest of the world looks at them . . . spoiled losers. End the boycott, call the IOC and accept the medals."[11]

Said Davis, "I know when we all left Munich we received over one hundred telegrams and only one said we should accept them. But I've gotten a little criticism over the years from a few, so I've made an attempt to change one of the Olympic rules that pertains to medals to teams. It says if one refuses medals no one else can receive theirs. So if the others want their medals, I would support their wish."[12]

The bond among the dozen—all of whom received rings with the letters *USA* etched upon them at the reunion—was immediately apparent. Teary-eyed to be together again, they shared stories and memories that few others knew.

Ratleff had spoken by phone with most players over the years and had seen Dwight Jones quite a bit during their days with the Houston Rockets. Seeing everyone in person was unforgettable.

"It was awesome," he said. "It was almost like time stopped. We were laughing and talking about the same things. It was the best time in the world."

The gathering included Assistant Coach Bach, at the time the last living of the three coaches. Nearing ninety, Bach by far was the oldest man in the room.

"This was not a happy team the last time I saw them," he said. "We were the most disappointed, angry, upset team in basketball. All of them have transcended that, done very well in their lives, been very successful, and I see they've improved in every way."[13]

Said Davis, "It was four of the most jovial days I've ever had—I wouldn't trade those four days for anything. The biggest surprise was how different everyone looked, especially Bantom and Brewer. I did a double take."

It was especially important for the twelve to finally gather again to gain a sense of closure. Over the years, some had hesitated to share their bitter memories with those closest to them, such as their wives and children. Keesha Jones, daughter of the late Dwight Jones, grew up primarily in Houston while her father played for the Rockets. Photos of his basketball games, including the Olympics, dotted her home. But little, if anything, was said about the gold medal game.

"The story was Daddy played, he traveled overseas, he had a great time—that was about it," she recalled. "I don't remember my parents talking about it more than that."

Then she watched a documentary of the game, which showed that her father had been ejected.

"I didn't know my daddy had gotten into a fight. That bothered me, so I called him at work," Keesha says. "He started laughing. He said, 'Yeah, Daddy got into a little tussle.'

"I know that being in the Olympics was one of the most important events that happened in his sixty-four years. Some of the best basketball players never get picked to play."

Davis is thankful all of the players could get together one last time before Dwight passed away in 2016.

"He was kind of the clown of the team. He wanted everyone to be his friend," Davis recalled. "In the gold medal game, when he got ejected, I think any one of us would have reacted like he did."

These days, players still get fiery during the Olympics, but the changes in the basketball world since Munich have been jaw-dropping. In Rio in 2016, Nike's swoosh adorned the U.S. team's jerseys and shorts; no company sponsored the '72 uniforms. Sweatbands encircled heads, while sleeves crawled down players' arms, from above their elbows to their wrists, sometimes covering the incessant tattoos crawling across their skin.

Instead of staying in the athletes' village, the U.S. basketball players (including the women's team, one that did not exist in Munich) relaxed aboard a luxury cruise ship docked at a Rio pier, where they were greeted by porters wearing white gloves. The amount of security surrounding that ship practically outdid Munich on its own, with scanners, a bullet-proof fence, and police boats roaming the waters. A pool, spa, and other amenities greeted the players, including perhaps the most important aspect: beds they could fit in.[14]

Not all of their NBA brethren were so fortunate. Andrew Bogut, a Dallas Mavericks center representing Australia, was forced to put together a shower curtain and sleep in an undersized bed in the athletes' village. Others there also faced a lack of hot water and shabby furniture.

The players enjoyed media opportunities never before imagined. Whereas Davis had given intermittent reports to a Kentucky newspaper in 1972, in 2016 in Rio Kevin Durant, Draymond Green, and others offered real-time updates via their Twitter feeds to millions of followers. Highlights of their play lived seconds after the fact on YouTube.

And unlike the one-and-done young men of the past, these players could compile medals; in fact, Carmelo Anthony, often an enigma in the NBA, captured an unprecedented third gold medal for the Americans at age thirty-two (to add to his one bronze). In fact, the average age of U.S. players in 2016 neared twenty-seven years old, far from the days when collegians barely out of their teens competed on the international stage. They more closely resembled the Soviet teams of yore in experience and prowess. Also in 2016, the USOC paid gold medal winners (such as the U.S. basketball players) $25,000 apiece, silver winners $15,000, and those who took home the bronze $10,000. That is far better than what the '72 team took home: no medals and no cash.

Different rules were in place in 2016. Aside from the three-point line, which had been instituted nearly thirty years before, the shot clock had been reduced to 24 seconds from 30; bonus free throws were awarded based on the number of opponent fouls rather than the time remaining. Further, the trapezoid lane had been eliminated, and a rectangle one adopted. All changes were seen as giving NBA players more familiarity when they arrived at the Olympics. Still, some differences remained for the pro players; the international game lasted forty minutes rather than forty-eight, five fouls bounced a player from a game rather than six, and only a coach could call time-out (though the pesky electronic method had been eliminated).

Despite the rise of international basketball over the years, no country is close to matching the winning percentage of the United States, a team which has suffered just five losses since 1936. The U.S. squad has earned medals in all eighteen Olympics since basketball was included. The tally: fifteen golds, two bronzes—and a lone silver.

12

SEARCHING FOR A SILVER LINING

NO U.S. PLAYER HAS tried harder to find a solution to the 1972 medal issue than Charles Thomas McMillen—who once looked like he'd never make a grade-school basketball team, much less play on the ultimate stage.

As a boy, McMillen was told (by an orthopedic surgeon, no less) that because of knee problems, he'd never be able to play basketball. For five years, he slept wearing leg braces, which strengthened his knees. Standing six feet tall at age twelve, the Pennsylvania native became the hottest recruit in the country by the time high school rolled around—beguiling college coaches in ways not seen since Lew Alcindor (known later as Kareem Abdul-Jabbar) sparked a wooing frenzy.

More than two hundred NCAA schools contacted McMillen. University of North Carolina's Dean Smith, who knew the young-ster through basketball camps, applied a full-court press. For the first time in two years, Adolph Rupp left Kentucky to watch a high school player: it was McMillen. Looking to impress, the West Vir-ginia coach introduced him to the president—not of the university, but of the entire country, Lyndon Johnson.

Relentless media coverage prompted even *Playboy* magazine to weigh in with an article. And like his Olympic teammates Burleson and Collins, McMillen, too, appeared on the cover of *Sports Illustrated*, a first for a high school basketball player (wunderkind LeBron James of St. Vincent–St. Mary High School was so highly thought of thirty-two years later, he knocked the 2002 Winter Olympics from the magazine's cover).

Averaging nearly 50 points a game his senior year at Mansfield High School, McMillen was tapped to play in the Dapper Dan Roundball Classic in 1970, which featured the best high school players in Pennsylvania against those from other states. More than thirteen thousand people attended each game, sellouts at Pittsburgh's Civic Arena. McMillen poured in 37 points during a loss against future Olympic teammates such as Tom Burleson and Dwight Jones.

In a battle against future college teammate Len Elmore, who represented Alcindor's old school—Power, in New York—McMillen outscored him 40–5. Not that he was a one-dimensional jock; off the court, McMillen served as president of the student council and played in the school band.

The University of Maryland won the sweepstakes—even after McMillen had signed a letter of intent with North Carolina. "It might have been the most difficult recruiting battle I was ever in to get Tom," said George Raveling, then an assistant to Terrapin head man Lefty Driesell who eventually became the head coach at Washington State, the University of Iowa, and the University of Southern California. "It was only by the grace of God that we got him. Tom really wanted to go to North Carolina, but his dad got very sick, and it looked like he would die. He told Tom, 'If you want to make your dad happy, go to Maryland.'"

When players signed with Maryland, Driesell asked them to write down their goals.

"A lot of them had crazy goals," Driesell recalled. "Tom just wrote, 'I want to be an All-American basketball player and a Rhodes Scholar.' He achieved both."

Since the campus in College Park was within driving distance for the elder McMillen, a mainstay at his son's high school games (along with the fact that Tom's older brother, Jay, had played basketball at the university), McMillen matriculated in the fall of 1970. Joining Elmore, Mark Cartwright, and two other highly touted newcomers, McMillen and the Terrapins' freshmen squad was ranked the best in the country going into the season, considered superior to even Bill Walton's freshman team out West. Raveling coached the youngsters and got to know McMillen well.

"It was a team of highly recruited players and, for all the fame Tom already had, he didn't fall into the trap of being demanding," Raveling said. "He was a great teammate. He was the epitome of a student-athlete. He had a high IQ academically and on the basketball court. He was always inquisitive and disciplined for a person that age."

While at Maryland, McMillen turned down a $1 million contract to turn pro early, wanting to represent his country in the Olympics. Yet despite his prowess and despite earning Coach Iba's praise during the tryouts in Colorado Springs, he initially failed to make the twelve-man squad; being selected as an alternate provided no gratification.

"I was devastated by my failure to make the cut and the lost opportunity to play for my country . . . ever," he noted.[1]

Then, Swen Nater stalked out of the Hawaiian training camp, changing McMillen's life. His roommate in Pearl Harbor, Davis, remembered McMillen's devotion to intellectual pursuits.

"He brought two suitcases of books and only one suitcase of clothes," Davis said. "Every spare moment, he had a nose in a book. He'd set his alarm at 4:15 a.m. to get the newspaper. He'd read it and go back to sleep."

Davis also remembered that in Hawaii, he answered the phone for McMillen. On the other end was Martha Mitchell, wife of Attorney General John Mitchell, who that summer had hoped McMillen would work on President Nixon's reelection campaign (he declined, occupied with the Olympics, though he later worked for President Jimmy Carter's reelection campaign in 1980). Even as a teenager, McMillen served on the President's Council on Physical Fitness and Sports.

Drafted first by the Buffalo Braves in 1974, the high hopes that accompanied him to that city fizzled; he stayed less than two years before plodding through an NBA career with four teams.

"I never was quick and wasn't a very good jumper," he said. "Besides having the white man's disease [inability to levitate], I have terrible feet. They've always given me trouble.

"There wasn't much I could do about that, but I could do something about being weak—which I was—and about my defense. I lifted weights. I watched people play defense, thought about it, practiced it. And I kept working on my shot, as I always have."[2]

Unlike many athletes, McMillen prospered beyond sports. His upbringing ensured his mind stayed engaged after his body could no longer compete. Noted McMillen, "Our parents bombarded us with questions about the meaning of words, forced us to recite passages from Shakespeare, and grilled us on current events."[3]

As his NBA career neared its end, McMillen began to think seriously about a political future. It marked quite an evolution: during his days at Maryland, he showed little interest in politics or even current events.

"I didn't really have much of a social conscience," McMillen said. "I can remember sitting in my dorm room when a Vietnam demonstration broke out on campus. I had to close the window because the tear gas interfered with studying."[4]

In 1986, during his final season on the Washington Bullets, McMillen became the first active athlete to ever run for Congress. A Democrat, he won by just over four hundred votes in Maryland's Fourth Congressional District. While serving in the U.S. House of Representatives, one of his first resolutions hearkened back to memories of Munich: he asked that professional players be allowed to compete in the Olympics. By 1992 the Dream Team—composed of Michael Jordan, Magic Johnson, and Larry Bird, among other NBA legends—reasserted American hegemony in Barcelona.

Since leaving Congress in 1993 (just a few years after the United States won the Cold War over the Soviet Union, a tectonic event without controversy or medals), McMillen has championed ideas to resolve the 1972 medal controversy. With the support of some of his teammates, he sent a letter to the IOC thirty years after the controversial defeat. Spurred by dual gold medals handed out during a figure-skating controversy at the 2002 Winter Games, McMillen proposed a duplicate gold medal idea to end the basketball dispute.

"The IOC decided that the pair came in second not because of their performance but because a judge had been unduly pressured by one of the sport's governing bodies. I argued that Jones's unauthorized intervention in our game brought similar pressure upon the officials," McMillen wrote.[5]

He never received a response. Despite the snub, a comment by IOC president Jacques Rogge during the controversy offered some hope for the Americans. Asked if awarding duplicate gold medals to the Canadian skaters might lead to revisiting previous Olympic controversies during those 2002 games, Rogge said the IOC would not reconsider past officiating errors—only cases in which there appeared to be "manipulation of the judgment."[6]

A decade later, McMillen tried again. If the IOC awarded dual gold medals, the U.S. players would donate theirs to raise millions of dollars for Russian orphanages. Despite the seemingly noble gesture, said McMillen, "That had as much chance as a snowball in Miami Beach."

McMillen's efforts illustrate the unique place the USA-USSR title game holds in American sports history. After all, when one thinks of iconic championship moments in this country, what jumps to mind? Hobbling pinch hitter Kirk Gibson blasting a home run to change the trajectory of a World Series. Bobby Orr flying through the air, a Stanley Cup his to raise upon landing. A run into the end zone during the Greatest Game Ever Played. Victories all. In the Olympics? The triumphs of Jesse Owens, Mark Spitz, and the Miracle on Ice still resonate.

Only one anguished defeat lives on.

In part it endures because none of the American players or coaches have ever acknowledged that the Soviets won the contest. The U.S. players believe the gold medals that were draped around the Soviets' necks are rightly theirs. It is called the gold medal game, after all, because that's what both teams want to win, not the silver medal.

Why are medals even important? Why do athletes cherish them, and even fight more than half their lives for a different-colored one? A nice explanation is presented on the website of the New Brunswick Sports Hall of Fame, a neutral venue in the gold medal controversy:

> For athletes, these awards are more than just souvenirs of past victories: rather, they commemorate their skill, hard work, and determination in competitions . . . when awards are given out, it seems an athlete's personal achievement will never be forgotten. But sadly, as the decades pass, the details of medal or trophy-winning events slip away . . . these awards often become the only remaining physical evidence of an athlete's record.[7]

To consider what medals mean to athletes, listen to '84 U.S. Olympic basketball coach Bob Knight explain how he motivated his crew:

> Doug Blubaugh, the Indiana wrestling coach at the time, won the 161-pound freestyle wrestling gold medal in 1960 at Rome, and he let me get a picture taken of his gold medal. That first day we had our players together as a team, I gave each of them a three-by-five photograph of it to show them what an Olympic gold medal looks like. I told them, "I want this picture in your pocket, whatever you have on, wherever you go, until the real thing is yours."
>
> I gave them an eight-by-ten copy of the same picture. "I want this over your bed wherever you sleep between now and then."[8]

Then Knight asked Alex Groza—who had won an Olympic basketball gold medal for the '48 U.S. team in London—to attend a practice and to make sure to bring his gold medal, which he had turned into a necklace for his wife.

"I'll never forget Alex passing that gold medal/necklace around among our players, and each kid looking at it, and each kid thinking about what he was going to do with his gold medal," Knight recalled. "I could see it in their faces: each kid held it, and was reluctant to pass it on to the next kid, but finally did, until all twelve of them had held the gold medal."[9]

Raveling, an assistant under Knight in '84, remembered the joy of simply being asked to help work toward the highest basketball award in the world.

"For the first time in my life, my country was coming to me saying, 'We need you to win a gold medal for us.' Usually it's the flip side, asking what your country can do for you," Raveling said. "It was a seminal moment for me to be part of a gold medal team and hear the national anthem. I still get emotional about it."

Designed by Gerhard Marcks, the 1972 medals can be considered among the oddest ones (if not the oddest) in Olympic history. The front, etched with the phrase XX. Olympiade München 1972, is perfectly fine, with the Greek goddess Nike—the representative of victory—perched above a stadium. But on the flip side, two boys are standing completely nude, with all body parts displayed, and their faces resemble visitors from a Martian landing. They are the mythological twins Castor and Pollux, youngsters who shared the same mother but different fathers and were known for their sports skills.

The silver medals weigh just shy of six ounces, while the gold are slightly heavier. Both were made of silver by the Bavarian Mint; the golds contain a small amount of plated gold (had they been pure gold, they would have been worth around $8,000 based on the per-ounce price at the beginning of the 2016 Olympics). For the first time, the 364 gold medals and 352 silver medals (364, had the U.S. basketball team accepted them) handed out during the 1972 games were bound to a chain rather than a ribbon. Engraved on the back were the full names of the winners, along with their nationality and the sport they played.

What would it mean if the American players accepted the silver medals now? What would change? Would the anger, the sense of being cheated, subside? Two-thirds of their lives have been encumbered by a sense of injustice. Some think about it often, and it gnaws at them; others reflect upon it intermittently. Receiving the silver medals would be a sign, a symbol that they would acknowledge and accept that the Soviet Union beat them nearly a half century ago. If they chose, they could forgive the late R. William Jones and others for stopping the game when it was about to end, putting time back on the clock, and rejecting their appeal. They are forever in the record books as finishing second, regardless of whether they accept their medals; by choosing not to, bitterness engendered by the final seconds lives on. The story continues because they still eschew their reward as runners-up.

The first appeal asking players to change their minds, sent by USA Basketball, appeared in their mailboxes in 1982. Gary Smith of *Sports Illustrated* described the moment:

> Are they ready to let go of the principle yet? Will they take the medals now? "It's up to the kids, and we support them in whatever they choose," says Bill Wall, USA Basketball's executive director. "We all know we got screwed. But I wish they would accept it and put it behind us."
>
> There is one catch, the letter explains. Either all of them get the medals—or none of them does. The International Olympic Committee doesn't want seven men accepting medals while five holdouts howl to the press, reviving all the bitterness. The vote, like a jury's determination of guilt, must be unanimous. The verdict comes back: no medals.[10]

Pleading letters continued to arrive every so often in the 1980s. Team captain Davis remembers four he received overall: one from the International Olympic Committee and three from the United States Olympic Committee.

"I wadded them up and threw them away," he said. "The USOC wanted us to take the medals back in 1972—that frustrated us. The USOC has never been supportive of us—they want it swept under the rug."

Said Bobby Jones, "It took some guts for us to say, 'We're not going to accept the silver medals.' We knew there would be consequences and it would look like we are bitter, but I didn't concern myself with that. I was angry that this rip-off had taken place."[11]

Over the decades, with rare exceptions, such as when Burleson told Smith of *Sports Illustrated* he *would* take the silver medal (today, he says vehemently, he would not), all American players have consistently voted not to accept them, most recently at the Georgetown College reunion in 2012; Davis and Henderson have even marked in their wills that none of their descendants can accept the silver medal after they die.

Said Davis, the only U.S. basketball player who was married at the time of the games, "Some of the guys' families would probably try to get it after they're gone. If they do, I have no problem with that. That medal would be really valuable.

"I asked my attorney to put that in [no descendants can accept silver] at the end of the will my wife and I put together. My two children are supportive of it. They know my feelings, and they honor my feelings. You have one medal with two kids, what do they do? Switch it every week? To have them accept something that didn't mean anything to me didn't make any sense."

(In fact, Davis's stand has become a game-show answer. Under the category "Silver," an answer on *Jeopardy!* referenced the captain's decision with the line. "Kenny Davis of the 1972 U.S. Olympic Team in this sport forbade his heirs from ever accepting a silver medal." The question: "What is basketball?")[12]

Since Munich, one player *has* received a gold medal—though not from the 1972 games. Collins's son, Chris, served as an assistant coach on the 2008 Olympic basketball team that captured a gold medal. Though coaches don't receive a real medal, Chris and the other coaches were given replicas. Chris put it around his father's neck the following year when he was inducted into the Naismith Memorial Basketball Hall of Fame for his broadcasting work.

Consider this irony: Had the U.S. players captured the gold, they'd be all but forgotten today, one in a long line of American victors. Collins's free throws would be lauded and applauded, but the team itself would have been as memorable as Iba's champions in 1964 or 1968—which is to say, little in terms of sports history.

Further, had the players accepted their silver medals, the memory of the loss surely would have lingered. But the controversy over the final seconds likely would have faded—unprecedented and unfair decisions happened to be sure, yet the athletes would have gotten on with their lives, and the game would have simply been a hiccup before a slew of future U.S. gold medals.

If the players now surprised the world and announced they wanted their silver medals, a major question would arise: From where would the IOC retrieve them?

Though numerous reports throughout the years maintained that the silver medals were stashed in a bank vault or at IOC headquarters in Lausanne, Switzerland, during a lengthy NBC investigation in 1992, IOC secretary-general Françoise Zweifel claimed the organizations never got the medals back—"They are still in Germany," she said.

After much searching, an NBC reporter finally found a former Olympic official in Munich who said they were stored in his basement—but he could only come up with seven silver medals and wasn't even sure they were the right ones.[13]

When asked about the silver medals in 2017, the press office of the IOC responded, "Seven medals are currently stored at the Olympic Museum. According to our information the other medals stayed at the time with the Organising Committee."

It's fair to assume these seven were retrieved from the former Olympic official in Munich. They are not engraved in any way to distinguish them. So five of the medals the U.S. players would receive—if they decided against all odds (and wills) that they wanted them—would not be originals.

In a few instances post-Munich, individual athletes have eschewed their medals. In the 1992 Olympics, an unprecedented three-way tie existed in weightlifting. Competing in the light-heavyweight division, Ibragim Samadov—formerly of the Soviet Union who lifted for what was then known as the Unified Team—finished with a bronze medal because of tiebreakers. Upon accepting the medal, he dropped it on the ground and stormed away. He was immediately banned from the Barcelona Games and stripped of his medal.

In 2008, in Beijing, a similar medal-stand reaction occurred, this time from a wrestler. Believing he deserved the gold and infuriated by what he believed was bad judging, Ara Abrahamian of Sweden dropped his bronze medal and walked away. The IOC announced the medal was no longer his.

Even when Olympic athletes do accept and possess medals, the stories throughout modern history of what happens to these momentous awards are often dispiriting.

For some reason, U.S. basketball players seem more prone than most athletes to put their medals up for auction. Walter Davis, Jerry Lucas, and Vin Baker all tried to part with their gold medals for cash with varying success.

Davis received more than $100,000 for his 1976 gold won in Montreal, far more than he expected to nab. Buoyed by Davis's success, Lucas tried to get at least $250,000 for his 1960 gold earned in Rome, but that bid never materialized, and he held on to it. Baker asked for much less and got it, receiving just under $68,000 for the gold captured in Sydney in 2000.[14]

Even Olga Korbut, the golden pixie of the 1972 games who now lives in the United States, sold three medals, including two golds, from Munich. She received more than $300,000 for the medals and other memorabilia in 2017.

Some stories are more moving. U.S. Olympic diver Greg Louganis befriended Ryan White, a child who contracted HIV through a blood transfusion. White eventually died of AIDS. In 1995, during a benefit, Louganis—HIV positive himself—gave one of his five gold medals to Ryan's mother, Jeanne White-Ginder.

"He reached in his suit pocket and pulled out his gold medal and put it around my neck," White-Ginder said. "And he said, 'I want you to have this. Ryan just meant everything to me and saved my life.'"[15]

Other times, athletes simply lose them, especially if they possess more than one. As reported by the *Wall Street Journal*, "Snowboarder Shaun White once found one of his gold medals, which he has admitted to misplacing a few times, in a seat pocket of his mother's car. Another time, his mom had taken the medal to the dry cleaner—the ribbon was dirty—and had forgotten about it."[16]

The quickest recorded instance of a lost medal occurred in 1988. Having won the gold, Italian rower Davide Tizzano jumped into the Han River holding his medal. As he headed into the water, a teammate fell into him, and the medal sank. A diver eventually recovered it.

On occasion, medals aren't as sturdy as athletes expect. Less than a year after the Rio Olympics, more than one hundred medals were falling apart or rusting. An Olympics communication official blamed the problem on temperature differentials along with misuse by athletes.

During the Tokyo Games in 2020, medals are expected to be created from recyclable materials such as old cell phones. For the 2024 games in Paris, a new development is being considered. A design suggested provides the chance to share one's medal(s). Created by Philippe Starck, the thick medal has four pieces—three that can be removed and given to others.

"Today more than ever, the truth is that you're not winning alone," Starck said. "So I wanted this medal to reflect that. If the winner wants to share it, he can share it."[17]

Sometimes, athletes who should receive a medal based on the final standings do not—and then they eventually procure one. In 1952 in Helsinki, Swedish boxer Ingemar Johansson was disqualified by the referee for holding onto American boxer Ed Sanders too much rather than fighting him. The disqualification also negated the silver medal Johansson would have won for finishing second. But in the 1980s, after Johansson had finished an extraordinary career (which included beating Floyd Patterson for the world heavyweight crown), the IOC changed course and awarded him his silver medal.

A similar situation occurred during the 1968 games, also in boxing. Featherweight Al Robinson of the United States was beating handily Mexican opponent Antonio Roldan, whose blood flowed on his face, in the final in Mexico City. In the second round, the referee disqualified Robinson, claiming he had head-butted Roldan. The American denied the charge and, in fact, replays showed him merely landing punches to Roldan's head.

Regardless, Robinson finished second despite the belief that he was on his way to gold and, under the rules of disqualification, would not receive his silver medal. But the United States protested the withholding of his silver medal, and soon after Robinson arrived in Oakland (where he served in the U.S. Navy), he received it.

At the 1992 Olympics in Barcelona, Canadian Sylvie Fréchette— though recovering from her fiancé's suicide just before the games— was considered the woman to beat in synchronized swimming. During a preliminary round, a Brazilian judge, by pushing the wrong button, gave Fréchette an 8.7 score instead of a 9.7 (the other scores had ranged from 9.2 to 9.6) during the technical section. The body running international swimming, Fédération internationale de natation (FINA), said the judge's score could not be changed. This caused Fréchette to lose the gold, as the next day she started far behind the eventual winner, American Kristen Babb-Sprague; she was forced to accept the silver instead. But the International Olympic Committee, urged on by Canadian IOC member and erstwhile swimmer Dick Pound, persuaded FINA to change its decision. Fréchette received a co–gold medal about sixteen months later.

Even when they didn't finish in the top three, athletes can find out years after the fact that they've won a medal. Consider Chaunté Lowe, a U.S. high jumper who finished sixth in the Beijing Olympics. Eight years later, in 2016, she was told she had captured a bronze medal, as the three athletes who received medals were disqualified for doping.

But like U.S. player Davis, she also lamented what was taken away from her: Even as Lowe danced about her house, calling friends, another realization dawned. She had missed her Olympic moment. She watched in 2008 as a cheater stood on the podium with a national flag and accepted a medal that rightfully was Lowe's.

"Man, I wanted to get that feeling of being on a podium and the world is applauding your achievement," she says. "I was robbed of that moment, and I am surprised to find myself feeling joy and struggling to keep my faith."[18]

Once in Olympic history, gold medals were handed out, revoked, and handed out again—to the same person. It involved Jim Thorpe, perhaps the greatest athlete of the twentieth century. Months after winning two gold medals in the pentathlon and decathlon during the 1912 Olympics in Stockholm, it was discovered that Thorpe had been paid a small amount to play semipro baseball a few years before the games, a violation of the amateur code. The IOC stripped the medals from Thorpe and awarded them to the runners-up in both events.

Yet seventy years later, replacement gold medals were in the hands of Thorpe's widow. Bob Wheeler and his wife, Florence Ridlon, were entranced by Thorpe's life and interviewed people around the country about him. They had heard that the IOC's decision to remove Thorpe's medals violated its own rules; any challenge had to be made within thirty days of the closing ceremony.

The IOC, though, claimed not to have any proof of its own rules back in 1912. Florence Ridlon headed to the one spot in the United States that might have a copy: the Library of Congress in Washington DC:

> Ms. Ridlon searched the Library of Congress' card catalog. Nothing. A librarian let her browse the library's metal bookcases. Hours later, she had found rules for every Olympics except 1912.
>
> Discouraged, Ms. Ridlon headed for the exit. Something made her pause. She went back to the stacks, reaching her hand between two bookcases. She felt a piece of paper.
>
> "I opened it up," she said. "It was the rules and regulations for the 1912 Olympics. There was Rule 13—a challenge [to amateur status] had to be done within 30 days [of the closing ceremony] to take away someone's medals."[19]

Despite its lofty aims and ideals, as shown in part by its medal imbroglios, the IOC is far from a perfect body. In fact, it has been awash in scandal during its recent history.

During the 2002 Winter Games in Salt Lake City, reports years before the torch was lit revealed that the host Organizing Committee bribed IOC members by paying for their plastic surgery, Super Bowl tickets, and much more to secure the votes and win the right to host the Olympics. As projects were being built for the 2008 games in Beijing, construction firms gave millions of dollars in bribes to the vice mayor of Beijing, Liu Zhihua. Corruption also afflicted the 1976 games in Montreal, a financial disaster that almost ended the Olympic movement itself.

Said Bobby Jones, "They [the IOC] use the cover of world harmony and peace to promote their business agenda. I don't have a lot of faith in that organization."

If the U.S. team or its representative decided to appeal one last time for a gold medal, decades after its attempts were rejected by FIBA and the IOC, it would go the Court of Arbitration for Sport (CAS), the body to adjudicate an Olympic sports–related dispute. Created in the 1980s by the IOC (though now independent of it), it has decided scores of Olympic cases throughout the years, including a number involving those who believed they deserved a medal or a better medal, along with cases where it stripped medals from athletes.

In 2004, for example, South Korean gymnast Yang Tae Young protested judging mistakes during the Athens Olympics and believed he should have been awarded a gold medal rather than a bronze (he had more points had the judge not erred). The CAS panel ruled U.S. gymnast Paul Hamm could keep the gold. According to the *Los Angeles Times*, "To rule otherwise, to rip the gold from Hamm, would be to lurch down an untenable course, one that would invite legal scrutiny of every umpire's call or referee's whistle, the three-member arbitration panel made plain." An appeal for duplicate gold medals was rejected by IOC president Rogge.

Said Hamm, "There's been a lot of fighting for this medal. I felt like I won it three times already: in the competition, with the media, and, finally, in the court."[20]

A case for gold medals could be brought by the 1972 U.S. bas-

ketball players, USA Basketball, the USOC, or even other organizations. An appeal would be sent to CAS, and three arbitrators
would hear it. Though the IOC has been disappointed by some of
CAS's past decisions on Olympic medals, it does not possess the
power to overturn them. Essentially, CAS today is the final word
on Olympic disputes.

Jerry Colangelo said discussions have occurred at USA Basketball regarding making a case for the '72 players, but nothing has
ever been formalized.

"On a personal note, I'd like to see these players honored in a way
that recognizes that they had something stolen from them," he said.

Added Lefty Driesell, who originally was upset when the U.S.
players—including his Maryland star McMillen—rejected the silver medals, "I was wrong, and they were right. They were robbed.
I think the government should have some gold medals made and
give them to the players."

Of course, not only would it be extraordinary for CAS to reverse
course and say the Americans deserve the gold, retrieving the Soviets' scattered gold medals would be impossible (and those attempting to do so would likely be harmed). It would also suggest that
no team's victory or defeat is set in stone, even more than forty-
five years after the final horn—though exceptions have been made
in the past, almost always associated with doping. For instance,
the 2004 U.S. Olympic equestrian show-jumping team won gold
after a German rider and horse were both disqualified for doping.
But no Soviet basketball players were ever alleged to have violated
any doping rules.

At the same time, according to the rules of international basketball, the United States won the game. Time ran out, and the Americans were ahead. How great would it feel for the twelve who lived
through such anguish to hold the gold medal? No doubt the tears
would be even stronger so many years later, those with far more yes-
terdays than tomorrows finally accepting the award for what they
had accomplished as young men, much like an overlooked military
battalion being honored long after the war.

Yet even if the gold failed to materialize, the duplicate gold medal idea seems to have merit; after all, the U.S. players would receive the gold medal they desire. In reality, though, by definition a game cannot feature two winners. And while some U.S. players have said they would accept a duplicate gold, one has been adamantly against it: team captain Davis.

"I have no interest in a duplicate gold medal," he said. "If the other eleven want that, that's fine. For forty-five years we've said we won and they lost. To say we both won the game doesn't make sense. The only way I would take anything is if it was reviewed and they said the Soviets lost and the Americans won."

So that leaves the most controversial medals in the long history of the Olympics, the silvers. Over the years, the U.S. players have been asked the same variation of this question: Will you or any of your descendants ever accept the silver medal? Despite an occasional opinion to the contrary, their thoughts over the decades since that controversial night in Munich have been almost unwavering:

Mike Bantom: Each time I get that letter about taking the medal, I look at it for a minute, I think about it for a minute, and then I say, "The hell with it."[21]

Jim Brewer: I remember some official walking in after we'd voted not to take the medals, and I told him what we'd decided. He said, "Jim, you're not speaking for everybody." I said, "*Yes, I am*," and I looked at all the other players with this wild-eyed look, and nobody was going to argue.[22]

Kenny Davis: The reason I will not accept it is, according to the rules, we won the gold. Why would we sell out under those circumstances? The medal is just a symbol. The German federation paid twelve dollars for it. I have no desire to see it. The IOC sent me a silver pin. I sent it back.

Jim Forbes: The older you get, the anger begins to mellow, the stubbornness isn't quite as strong. It *is* an Olympic medal, after all, and not many people get one. I watch the Olympics and I imagine the feeling of getting that gold. But my first instinct is still the same. We earned the gold.[23]

Tom Henderson: I've been telling my kids for years we're not accepting that. If we accept it, we're saying that it was right. It wasn't right. Being cheated on worldwide TV didn't sit right. Don't tell us we didn't win.

Dwight Jones: My wife says, "Why don't you go get that medal? So your son can have it." Hell, no. He can wear my Olympic ring. I want *my* medal. Not no silver. I want my *gold*. It's probably sitting around some Russian's neck right now. That thing should be in my trophy case in my game room, dead center.[24]

Bobby Jones: I'll get cards from people in Europe addressed to Bobby Jones, Silver Medalist. They want me to sign and send it back to them. I will not sign. I did not finish second.

Kevin Joyce: Will I ever accept the silver medal? No. Wrong medal. I know we won the gold. I don't want the silver as a memento, but my will would not say that my descendants can't get the silver.

Today, the U.S. players are all eligible to receive Social Security. Paunches weigh down some; decades of running up and down the hardwood have left a number of them with wounded knees and joints. All childless at the time of the Olympics, a handful are now grandfathers. One of the dozen is dead.

Time is running out for any final decision on golds, duplicate golds, or silvers. In 2022 the fiftieth anniversary of the game will be marked. By then, and even beyond, it's highly unlikely anything will have changed since the stunning rebuke of a dozen silver medals forged amid the championship chaos in Munich.

If that's the case, players can at least take heart that since then they've experienced much of the grandeur of life—the ability to marry their loves, play with their children, and take pleasure in bountiful careers. Encountering the evil of terrorism and suffering an excruciating, unjust championship loss in only a four-day span—a sad and searing way for innocence to be shorn—shaped them then and continues to influence them today. They are men who refuse to give in—even when the stakes involve attaining their boyhood dreams of wearing an Olympic medal.

And though that enduring, principled stand unifies them, it cannot protect them from haunting thoughts that still invade their minds from a lifetime ago.

"Sometimes in my sleep," said Davis, now in his seventies, "I hear the announcer saying, 'Three more seconds.'"

NOTES

Introduction

1. Deford, *Over Time*, 88.

1. The Guns of September

1. Peeler, *Legends of N.C. State Basketball*, 78.

2. Peeler, *Legends of N.C. State Basketball*, 79

3. Peeler, *Legends of N.C. State Basketball*, 80.

4. William F. Reed, "An Ugly Affair in Minneapolis," *Sports Illustrated*, February 7, 1972.

5. Peeler, *Legends of N.C. State Basketball*, 76.

6. Brewster and Gallagher, *Stolen Glory*, 161.

7. "Tom Burleson Recounts His 1972 Munich Experience," Olympic Reunion 2012, Lexington KY, December 26, 2012, YouTube, https://www.youtube.com/watch?v=7N1Nd5au-60.

2. A Noble History

1. David Stuttard, "The Strange Rites of the Ancient Olympics," *Wall Street Journal*, July 30, 2016.

2. Coubertin et al., *Olympic Games*, 2.

3. Coubertin, *Olympic Memoirs*, 14.

4. Coubertin, *Olympic Memoirs*, 16–22.

5. Coubertin et al., *Olympic Games*, 1.

6. "Nazi Olympics: Berlin, 1936," exhibit at the Illinois Holocaust Museum and Education Center, Summer 2016.

7. "Nazi Olympics: Berlin, 1936," exhibit at the Illinois Holocaust Museum and Education Center, Summer 2016.

8. "Nazi Olympics: Berlin, 1936," exhibit at the Illinois Holocaust Museum and Education Center, Summer 2016.

9. Large, *Munich 1972*, 57.

10. Alexander Woolf, "When the Terror Began," *Sports Illustrated*, August 15, 2002.

11. Moore, *Bowerman and the Men of Oregon*, 284.

12. Organisationskomitee, *Die Spiele: Official Report of the Organizing Committee for the Games of the XXth Olympiad Munich 1972*, 1:81.

13. Large, *Munich 1972*, 202–4.

14. Groussard, *Blood of Israel*, 14–15.

15. Groussard, *Blood of Israel*, 35.

16. Groussard, *Blood of Israel*, 35.

17. Large, *Munich 1972*, 202–4.

18. Gary Smith, "A Few Pieces of Silver," *Sports Illustrated*, June 15, 1992.

19. McMillen, *Out of Bounds*, 142–43.

20. "Attack on 1972 Games Shadows Olympics," NPR's *Morning Edition*, February 21, 2006, https://www.npr.org/programs/morning-edition/2006/02/21/12956973/.

21. E. J. Kahn, "Letter from Munich," *New Yorker*, September 16, 1972.

22. Large, *Munich 1972*, 217.

23. Groussard, *Blood of Israel*, 142.

24. Groussard, *Blood of Israel*, 207.

25. Groussard, *Blood of Israel*, 236.

26. Groussard, *Blood of Israel*, 256.

27. Robert Markus, "Avery Brundage at the Finish Line," *Chicago Tribune*, November 19, 1972.

28. Woolf, "When the Terror Began," *Sports Illustrated*, August 15, 2002.

29. Michael Sokolove, "The Unexpected Anchor," *New York Times*, December 24, 2008.

3. "The Games Must Go On"

1. Brewster and Gallagher, *Stolen Glory*, 162.

2. Jim Murray, "It Was the Costliest Day in Olympic History," *Los Angeles Times*, September 6, 1972.

3. Red Smith, "Murder in Munich," *New York Times*, September 6, 1972.

4. Brewster and Gallagher, *Stolen Glory*, 122.

5. Don Yaeger, "How Safe Will It Be? The 2004 Games Seem Fated to Begin under a Cloud of Fear," *Sports Illustrated*, August 2, 2004.

6. Large, *Munich 1972*, 194.

7. Groussard, *Blood of Israel*, 437.

8. Organisationskomitee, *Die Spiele: Official Report of the Organizing Committee for the Games of the XXth Olympiad Munich 1972*, 1:39.

9. E. J. Kahn, "Letter from Munich," *New Yorker*, September 16, 1972.

10. Jack Ellis, "'Games Must Go On,' Says Brundage," *Stars and Stripes*, September 7, 1972.

11. Robert Markus, "Avery Brundage at the Finish Line," *Chicago Tribune*, November 19, 1972.

12. Brewster and Gallagher, *Stolen Glory*, 123–24.

13. Neil Amdur, "Munich 1972: Tragic Blur on Olympic Family Memory," *New York Times*, September 9, 1992.

14. McMillen, *Out of Bounds*, 144–45.

15. Aubrey, *New Dimension of International Terrorism*, 35–36.

16. Brokhin, *Big Red Machine*, 118.

17. Guttmann, "The Cold War and the Olympics."

18. Guttmann, *Olympics*, 89.

19. Brokhin, *Big Red Machine,* 123.

20. David Foster Wallace, "Roger Federer as Religious Experience," *New York Times*, August 25, 2006.

21. Stern, dir., *:03 from Gold*.

22. "The Battle of Melbourne," *Sports Illustrated*, December 17, 1956.

23. "In Full View of the World," *Sports Illustrated*, December 17, 1956.

24. Maraniss, *Rome 1960*, 9.

25. Turrini, "'It Was Communism Versus the Free World.'"

26. Arthur Daley, "The Protection of a Perfect Record," *New York Times*, June 13, 1972.

27. "FIBA legend looks back on life-long involvement in basketball," FIBA .com, January 28, 2010, http://www.fiba.basketball/news/FIBA-FIBA-legend -looks-back-on-life-long-involvement-in-basketball--part2-.

28. Dichter and Johns, eds., *Diplomatic Games*, 302.

29. Steve Rushin, "The Titan of Television," *Sports Illustrated*, August 16, 1994.

30. West, *Better Than Gold*, 139.

31. Brewster and Gallagher, *Stolen Glory*, 12.

32. Brewster and Gallagher, *Stolen Glory*, 12.

33. Pat Putnam, "Marathon Si, Basketball No!," *Sports Illustrated*, August 16, 1971.

34. Neil Amdur, "The Three Seconds That Never Seem to Run Out," *New York Times*, July 28, 2012.

35. United States Olympic Committee, *United States Olympic Book, Munich, Sapporo*, 282–83.

36. Stern, dir., *:03 from Gold*.

37. Daniel Golden and Stepan Kravchenko, "Miracle on Wood Humiliating U.S. Presaged by Levi's Theft," Bloomberg.com, July 23, 2012.

38. Vladimir Stankovic, "Aleksandar Gomelskiy, the basketball general," Euroleague .net, October 25, 2015.

39. John Underwood, "An Exuberant Finish in Tokyo," *Sports Illustrated*, November 2, 1964.

40. Underwood, "An Exuberant Finish in Tokyo."

41. Roy Tomizawa, "Coach Hank Iba: The Iron Duke of Defense Who Led the Men's Basketball Team to Gold in 1964," TheOlympians.co, August 7, 2015, https://

theolympians.co/2015/08/07/coach-hank-iba-the-iron-duke-of-defense-who-led
-the-mens-basketball-team-to-gold-in-1964/.

42. Tomizawa, "Coach Hank Iba."

43. Curry Kirkpatrick, "The Team That Went Over the Hill," *Sports Illustrated*,
April 15, 1968.

44. Cunningham, *American Hoops*, 191.

45. Cunningham, *American Hoops*, 201.

46. Peter Curry, "Only Ornery Recruits for This Boot Camp," *Sports Illustrated*,
July 20, 1970.

47. Jerry Kirshenbaum, "The Russians, Thanks Be, Are Leaving," *Sports Illustrated*, June 7, 1971.

48. Stern, dir., *:03 from Gold*.

49. Curry Kirkpatrick, "Babes Who Are Going Gunning," *Sports Illustrated*,
July 3, 1972.

50. Feinstein, *The Punch*, 148.

51. Halberstam, *Breaks of the Game*, 114–15.

52. Halberstam, *Breaks of the Game*, 115.

4. Team Building

1. Bischoff, *Mr. Iba*, 23.

2. Bischoff, *Mr. Iba*, 44.

3. Bischoff, *Mr. Iba*, 242.

4. Brewster and Gallagher, *Stolen Glory*, 33.

5. Davis, *Wooden*, 384.

6. Haskins and Sanchez, *Haskins*, 21.

7. Alexander Wolff, "The Bear in Winter," *Sports Illustrated*, March 1, 1999.

8. Curry Kirkpatrick, "The Miners Are Still Going at It Pick and Shovel," *Sports Illustrated*, January 16, 1984.

9. Carey and McClellan, *Boston Celtics*, 31.

10. Pluto, *Loose Balls*, 59.

11. Cunningham, *American Hoops*, 209.

12. Walton, *Back from the Dead*, 58.

13. Davis, Wooden, 383.

14. Stern, dir., *:03 from Gold*.

15. Paul Attner, "Olympic Coach Frets Over Cage Chances," *Salt Lake Tribune*,
June 25, 1972.

16. Brewster and Gallagher, *Stolen Glory*, 152.

17. Halberstam, *Breaks of the Game*, 116.

18. Pluto, introduction to *Loose Balls*.

19. Jackie MacMullan, "Gregg Popovich Will Lead the Team He Was Left Off of Four Decades Ago," ABCNews.com, August 21, 2016, https://abcnews.go.com/Sports
/gregg-popovich-lead-team-left-off-decades-ago/story?id=41558901.

20. Brewster and Gallagher, *Stolen Glory*, 181.

21. Brewster and Gallagher, *Stolen Glory*, 183.

22. Attner, "Olympic Coach Frets Over Cage Chances," *Salt Lake Tribune*.

23. Mark Heisler, "A Matter of Perspective: The '72 U.S. Team Made Do Without Some Top Players, but Dynasty Ended," *Los Angeles Times*, July 5, 1992.

24. Brewster and Gallagher, *Stolen Glory*, 153.

25. Cunningham, *American Hoops*, 215.

26. Brewster and Gallagher, *Stolen Glory*, 153.

27. Cunningham, *American Hoops*, 216.

28. Richard O'Brien, "Mr. Iba," *Sports Illustrated*, January 25, 1993.

29. Brewster and Gallagher, *Stolen Glory*, 4.

30. President Richard Nixon, "To the Members of the United States Olympic Team," 1972, courtesy of Kenny Davis.

31. "U.S. Five Risking 36-Year Streak," *New York Times*, August 27, 1972.

32. "U.S. Five Risking 36-Year Streak," *New York Times*.

33. Cooper Rollow, "U.S. Cagers Bounce Czechs 66–35," *Chicago Tribune*, August 28, 1972.

34. Rollow, "U.S. Cagers Bounce Czechs 66–35."

35. Rollow, "U.S. Cagers Bounce Czechs 66–35."

36. Rollow, "U.S. Cagers Bounce Czechs 66–35."

37. "U.S. Cagers Romp 81–55; Three Boxers Advance," *Chicago Tribune*, August 29, 1972.

38. Robert Markus, "U.S. Avoids Basket Upset," *Chicago Tribune*, August 31, 1972.

39. Markus, "U.S. Avoids Basket Upset."

40. Brewster and Gallagher, *Stolen Glory*, 109.

41. "'Sluggish' U.S. Cagers Still Stay Perfect 72–56," *Chicago Tribune*, September 3, 1972.

42. Earl Cox, "U.S. Played Best against Japan, Says Davis," *Louisville Courier-Journal*, September 4, 1972.

43. Earl Cox, "Iba Fears U.S. Reign Near End," *Louisville Courier-Journal*, September 4, 1972.

44. "Two Yank Boxers Move into Semi-final Bouts," *Monroe Evening Times*, September 7, 1972.

45. Stern, dir., *:03 from Gold*.

46. "Calamity Strikes U.S. in Munich," *Oakland Tribune*, September 8, 1972.

47. John Owen, "Olympics Flashback: 1972: Terror and Turmoil," *Seattle Post-Intelligencer*, July 24, 2008.

48. Large, *Munich 1972*, 159.

5. Going for Gold

1. Cunningham, *American Hoops*, 214.

2. "It's Yank Cagers vs. Russ," *Chicago Tribune*, September. 8, 1972.

3. Lenskyj and Wagg, eds., *Palgrave Handbook of Olympic Studies*, 136.

4. West, *Better Than Gold*, 285.

5. Brewster and Gallagher, *Stolen Glory*, 172.

6. "1972 Olympic Gold Medal Basketball Issues and What Happened to the Medals," hosted by Bob Costas, (1992; NBC), https://www.youtube.com/watch?v=RwZuPi4cbyg.

7. Stern, dir., *:03 from Gold*.

8. Kami Mattioli, "Calipari: If We Played Any NBA Team We'd Get Buried." SportingNews.com, Nov. 10, 2014.

9. Daniel Golden and Stepan Kravchenko, "Miracle on Wood Humiliating U.S. Presaged by Levi's Theft," Bloomberg.com, July 23, 2012.

10. "1972 Olympic Gold-Medal Basketball Game," 1972, ABC.

11. "1972 Olympic Gold-Medal Basketball Game," 1972, ABC.

12. "1972 Olympic Gold-Medal Basketball Game," 1972, ABC.

13. "1972 Olympic Gold-Medal Game," 1972, ABC.

14. "1972 Olympic Gold-Medal Game," 1972, ABC.

15. "1972 Olympic Gold-Medal Basketball Game," 1972, ABC.

16. Tom Hennessy, "U.S. 1972 Olympic Team Still Won't Concede," *Long Beach Press-Telegram*, August 8, 2008.

17. "1972 Olympic Gold-Medal Game," 1972, ABC.

18. Brewster and Gallagher, *Stolen Glory*, 127.

19. "1972 Olympic Gold-Medal Game," 1972, ABC.

20. "1972 Olympic Gold-Medal Game," 1972, ABC.

21. "1972 Olympic Gold-Medal Game," 1972, ABC.

22. Stern, dir., *:03 from Gold*.

23. "1972 Olympic Basketball Final USA vs. USSR," hosted by Chris Fowler, 2002, ESPN SportsCentury, https://youtu.be/SqUZ6dleduM.

24. "1972 Olympic Basketball Final USA vs. USSR," hosted by Chris Fowler, 2002, ESPN SportsCentury, https://youtu.be/SqUZ6dleduM.

6. Hornswoggled

1. Curry Kirkpatrick, "Ol' Pick and a Lot of Slick Comin' On," *Sports Illustrated*, January 15, 1973.

2. Brewster and Gallagher, *Stolen Glory*, 164.

3. Curry Kirkpatrick, "Babes Who Are Going Gunning," *Sports Illustrated*, July 3, 1972.

4. Kirkpatrick, "Babes Who Are Going Gunning."

5. "Where Are They Now?," hosted by Bob Costas, 1992, NBC Sports.

6. "1972 Olympic Gold-Medal Basketball Game," 1972, ABC.

7. "Three Seconds of Chaos," (ESPN Classic SportsCentury), https://youtu.be/6oIMdwuLe_o.

8. Brokhin, *Big Red Machine*, 133.

9. Avery Brundage Collection, Record Series 26/20/37, Box 232, University of Illinois at Champaign-Urbana.

10. Ströher and Krebs, *Dr. h.c. R. William Jones*, 132.

11. "1972 Olympic Gold-Medal Basketball Game," 1972, ABC.

12. "1972 Olympic Gold-Medal Basketball Game," 1972, ABC.

13. "1972 Olympic Basketball Final USA vs. USSR," hosted by Dave Revsine, 2004, ESPN Classic Big Ticket.

14. Stern, dir., *:03 from Gold*.

15. "Where Are They Now?," hosted by Bob Costas, 1992, NBC Sports.

16. "Where Are They Now?," hosted by Bob Costas, 1992, NBC Sports.

7. "And This Time It *Is* Over"

1. Brewster and Gallagher, *Stolen Glory*, 171.

2. Bill Knight, "Forbes Experienced Bittersweet Season in 1972," *El Paso Times*, November 8, 1985.

3. Knight, "Forbes Experienced Bittersweet Season in 1972."

4. Gary Smith, "A Few Pieces of Silver," *Sports Illustrated*, June 15, 1992.

5. "Where Are They Now?" hosted by Bob Costas during 1992 Summer Olympics, NBC Sports.

6. Stern, dir., *:03 from Gold*.

7. "1972 Olympic Gold-Medal Basketball Game," 1972, ABC.

8. Associated Press, "U.S. Cagers Won't Take Silver Medal for Losers," *Dubuque Telegraph-Herald*, September 11, 1972.

9. "1972 Olympic Basketball Final USA vs. USSR," hosted by Dave Revsine, 2004, ESPN Classic Big Ticket.

10. McMillen, *Out of Bounds*, 146.

11. "The Washington Generals Infamous 1971 Win," *Washington Generals Fan Blog*, June 11, 2011.

12. Large, *Munich 1972*, 272.

13. Gil Rogin, "A Patriot at the Games," *Sports Illustrated*, June 15, 1992.

14. Robert Markus, "Cagers Lose By 1—Protest," *Chicago Tribune*, September 10, 2016.

15. Ströher and Krebs, *Dr. h.c. R. William Jones*, 28.

16. Gary Smith, "A Few Pieces of Silver."

17. Gary Smith, "A Few Pieces of Silver."

18. Marc Narducci, "Losing Gold Medal in 1972 Was Life-Altering for Philly's Mike Bantom," *Philadelphia Inquirer*, August 29, 2012.

19. Jury of Appeal Statement, last3seconds.com, domain expired in 2018.

20. "1972 US Olympic Basketball Appeal Featured in NBC Report by Utley and Hager," 1972, NBC News.

21. Jack Ellis, "'Games Must Go On,' Says Brundage," *Stars and Stripes*, September 7, 1972.

22. Stern, dir., *:03 from Gold*.

23. "A Report of the USA vs. USSR Basketball Game at the Munich Olympics–1972," herbmols.com, http://www.herbmols.com/1972-usa-olympic-basketball/89.html.

24. "A Report of the USA vs. USSR Basketball Game at the Munich Olympics–1972," herbmols.com.

25. Jack Ellis, "Russian Cage Gold Upheld; U.S. Turns Down Silver," *Stars and Stripes*, September 11, 1972.

26. Don Cronin, "Let's Talk Sports," *Anderson Daily Bulletin*, September 11, 1972.

27. Jim Wallace, "Tech, Mesabi FBS Star," *Brainerd Daily Dispatch*, September 13, 1972.

28. Daniel Golden, "Three Seconds at 1972 Olympics Haunt U.S. Basketball," Bloomberg.com, July 23, 2012.

8. Was the Fix In?

1. Ströher and Krebs, *Dr. h.c. R. William Jones*, 28.

2. Ströher and Krebs, *Dr. h.c. R. William Jones*, 32.

3. Ströher and Krebs, *Dr. h.c. R. William Jones*, 34.

4. Ströher and Krebs, *Dr. h.c. R. William Jones*, 72–74.

5. Avery Brundage Collection, Record Series 26/20/37, Box 232, University of Illinois at Champaign-Urbana.

6. Avery Brundage Collection, Record Series 26/20/37, Box 232, University of Illinois at Champaign-Urbana.

7. Avery Brundage Collection, Record Series 26/20/37, Box 232, University of Illinois at Champaign-Urbana.

8. Avery Brundage Collection, Record Series 26/20/37, Box 232, University of Illinois at Champaign-Urbana.

9. Avery Brundage Collection, Record Series 26/20/37, Box 232, University of Illinois at Champaign-Urbana.

10. Avery Brundage Collection, Record Series 26/20/37, Box 232, University of Illinois at Champaign-Urbana.

11. Avery Brundage Collection, Record Series 26/20/37, Box 232, University of Illinois at Champaign-Urbana.

12. Ströher and Krebs *Dr. h.c. R. William Jones*, 12.

13. Associated Press, "Bach Recalls 'that bow tie,' Cuban's 'Okay,'" *Anderson Daily Bulletin*, September 15, 1972.

14. FIBA Press Release, September 15, 1972, last3seconds.com, domain expired in 2018.

15. Herbert Mols, "Three Seconds—To Be or Not to Be," herbmols.com.

16. Norman A. Singer, "Statement of the Table Officials," last3seconds.com, domain expired in 2018.

17. Ströher and Krebs, *Dr. h.c. R. William Jones*, 132.

18. Ströher and Krebs, *Dr. h.c. R. William Jones*, 198.

19. Stern, dir., *:03 from Gold*.

20. Daniel Golden, "Three Seconds at 1972 Olympics Haunt U.S. Basketball," Bloomberg.com, July 23, 2012.

21. Brewster and Gallagher, *Stolen Glory*, 131.

22. "U.S. Cagers Won't Take Silver Medal for Losers," *Dubuque Telegraph-Herald*, September 11, 1972.

23. "A Report of the USA vs. USSR Basketball Game at the Munich Olympics–1972," herbmols.com, http://www.herbmols.com/1972-usa-olympic-basketball/89.html.

24. Stern, dir., *:03 from Gold*.

25. FIBA Rules 1972, last3seconds.com, domain expired in 2018.

26. Rick Dawson, "Retired NCAA Referee Bain Recalls Enjoyable Career," *Journal Gazette & Times-Courier*, March 18, 2004, https://jg-tc.com/sports/retired-ncaa-referee -bain-recalls-enjoyable-career/article_7d902d53-c807-5403-ace2-c2dad9c431eb.html.

27. Brian Tuohy, "An Olympic Cover-Up?," Sports On Earth, October 22, 2013, http://www.sportsonearth.com/article/63232866/.

28. "Where Are They Now?," hosted by Bob Costas, 1992, NBC Sports.

29. "Where Are They Now?," hosted by Bob Costas, 1992, NBC Sports.

30. 1972 Olympic Charter Olympic Rules and Regulations, olympic.org, https://www .olympic.org/olympic-studies-centre/collections/official-publications/olympic-charters.

31. 1972 Olympic Charter Olympic Rules and Regulations.

32. Dr. J. Nelson Washburn, "Blowing the Whistle," *New York Times*, April 22, 1973.

33. Washburn, "Blowing the Whistle."

9. Taking a Stand

1. "Above the Rim," Sirius XM Radio, August 11, 2016.

2. "1972 US Olympic Basketball Appeal Featured in NBC Report by Utley and Hager," 1972, NBC News.

3. Tribune Wire Services, "U.S. Cagers Turn Down Silver Medal," *Chicago Tribune*, September 11, 1972.

4. Stradling, *More Than a Game*.

5. Ströher and Krebs, *Dr. h.c. R. William Jones*, 136–38.

6. Gary Smith, "A Few Pieces of Silver," *Sports Illustrated*, June 15, 1992.

7. West, *Better Than Gold*, 265.

8. UPI, "Collins Home; Says Iba 'Coached Right,'" *Chicago Tribune*, September 13, 1972.

9. Brewster and Gallagher, *Stolen Glory*, 161.

10. Brewster and Gallagher, *Stolen Glory*, 179.

11. Randy Harvey and Sergei Loiko, "Untarnished Gold: Controversy? What Controversy? Soviets Still Feel They Deserved Basketball Victory in 1972," *Los Angeles Times*, July 18, 1992.

12. "Iba Returns Home, Still Convinced U.S. Won," *Bloomington IL Pantagraph*, September 12, 1972.

13. Mike Lopresti, "40 Years Later, Bill Walton Still Aches," NCAA.com, February 16, 2015.

14. President Richard Nixon, "To the Members of the United States Olympic Team," 1972, courtesy of Kenny Davis.

15. Daniel Golden and Stepan Kravchenko, "Miracle on Wood Humiliating U.S. Presaged by Levi's Theft," Bloomberg.com, July 23, 2012.

16. Edelman, *Serious Fun*, 148.

17. Stern, dir., *:03 from Gold*.

18. Stradling, *More Than a Game*, 134.

19. Daniel Golden, "Three Seconds at 1972 Olympics Haunt U.S. Basketball," Bloomberg.com, July 23, 2012.

20. "USOC Appeal to the IOC, January 18, 1973," last3seconds.com, domain expired in 2018.

21. "USOC Appeal to the IOC, January 18, 1973," last3seconds.com, domain expired in 2018.

22. "Olympic Referee Rips U.S. Cage Loss," *Ellensburg Daily Record*, October 24, 1972.

23. "USOC Appeal to the IOC, January 18, 1973," last3seconds.com, domain expired in 2018.

24. "Discussion of Executive Board of IOC, Feb. 2–5, 1973," last3seconds.com, domain expired in 2018.

10. Picking Up the Pieces

1. Barry McDermott, "It Was a New Game All Down the Line," *Sports Illustrated*, May 14, 1973.

2. Dichter and Johns, eds., *Diplomatic Games*, 309–10.

3. McDermott, "It Was a New Game All Down the Line."

4. Joe Jares, "Their Goal Is Gold in '76," *Sports Illustrated*, November 24, 1975.

5. Bickley, *Return of the Gold*, 79.

6. Tim Crothers, "Tom Burleson, Towering Center," *Sports Illustrated*, November 13, 2000.

7. Tim Peeler, "Down from the Mountains, Above the Treetops," *One Brick Back Blog*, December 5, 2014.

8. Jason Wolf, "Coaching Is 'All in the Family for the Collinses,'" USATODAY.com, March 24, 2013.

9. Sam Smith, "The Doug Collins Case: Anatomy of a Firing," *Chicago Tribune*, July 9, 1989.

10. "A Champion in Many Ways," Bigten.com, February 19, 2009.

11. Roy Bragg, "El Paso Coach Learned from Olympic Disappointment," *San Antonio Express-News*, March 12, 2015.

12. Brewster and Gallagher, *Stolen Glory*, 44.

13. "Bobby Jones—The Gentleman of the NBA," NBA.com.

14. J. J. Smith, "FCA Welcomes Former Carolina, Philadelphia Great Bobby Jones," *Cateret County News-Times*, March 24, 2010.

15. "Henderson Devotes Life to Troubled Youths," *Washington Times*, May 6, 2003.

16. Chris Trevino, "Former Long Beach State Basketball Great Ed Ratleff to Be Honored during NCAA Final Four," *Long Beach Press-Telegram*, April 3, 2015.

17. Curry Kirkpatrick, "It's the Tip-Off for UCLA's Big Invitation," *Sports Illustrated*, March 20, 1972.

18. Trevino, "Former Long Beach State Basketball Great Ed Ratleff to Be Honored during NCAA Final Four."

19. Stephen Moore, "A Bitter Lesson in Basketball and Terrorism," *Wall Street Journal*, March 16, 2012.

20. Gary Smith, "A Few Pieces of Silver," *Sports Illustrated*, June 15, 1992.

21. Steve Wiseman, "Chris and Doug Collins Reflect on 1972, Look Toward 2012 Olympic Title Game," *Durham Herald-Sun*, August 13, 2012.

22. Gary Smith, "A Few Pieces of Silver."

23. Gary Smith, "A Few Pieces of Silver."

24. Steve Campbell, "Iba's 'Coaching Tree' Casts a Shadow over UH's Dickey," *Houston Chronicle*, January 22, 2011.

25. Jimmie Trammel, "Bob Knight and Henry Iba Forged a Special Friendship," *Tulsa World*, February 23, 2011.

26. Trammel, "Bob Knight and Henry Iba Forged a Special Friendship."

27. K. C. Johnson, "Johnny Bach Dies at 91; Michael Jordan: 'He Was More than a Coach to Me,'" *Chicago Tribune*, January 18, 2016.

28. Alexander Wolff, "The Bear in Winter," *Sports Illustrated*, March 1, 1999.

29. Rob Gloster, "Soviet Coach Marks the Anniversary of Olympic Triumph with Sadness," *Los Angeles Times*, September 24, 1989.

30. Gloster, "Soviet Coach Marks the Anniversary of Olympic Triumph with Sadness."

31. Glenn Nelson, "Three-Second Edeshko—The Thrill and Agony of Victory—3 Unforgettable Seconds Changed Edeshko's Life," *Seattle Times*, June 10, 1990.

32. Nelson, "Three-Second Edeshko—The Thrill and Agony of Victory."

33. Nelson, "Three-Second Edeshko—The Thrill and Agony of Victory."

34. U.S. Congressman Ted Poe, "The Soviet Basketball Team of 1972 and the Vote to Allow Illegals Federal Benefits," poe.house.gov.

35. U.S. Congressman Ted Poe, "The Soviet Basketball Team of 1972 and the Vote to Allow Illegals Federal Benefits," poe.house.gov.

11. Joyous Reunion

1. West, *Better Than Gold*, 17–18.

2. West, *Better Than Gold*, 30–32.

3. West, *Better Than Gold*, 31.

4. West, *Better Than Gold*, 33–34.

5. West, *Better Than Gold*, 41–42, 50.

6. West, *Better Than Gold*, 62.

7. West, *Better Than Gold*, 138.

8. Bill Summers, letter to Kenny Davis, 1972.

9. West, *Better Than Gold*, 260.

10. West, *Better Than Gold*, 284.

11. West, *Better Than Gold*, 285.

12. West, *Better Than Gold*, 287.

13. Eric Crawford, "They Don't Want Silver, but '72 Joops Olympic Legacy Is Sterling," WDRB.com, September 10, 2012.

14. Cindy Boren, "Team USA's Basketball Players Pass Up Olympic Village for Luxury Cruise Ship," *Washington Post*, August 3, 2016.

12. Searching for a Silver Lining

1. McMillen, *Out of Bounds*, 138.

2. Bil Gilbert, "Aspiring to Higher Things," *Sports Illustrated*, April 5, 1982.

3. McMillen, *Out of Bounds*, 32.

4. Gilbert, "Aspiring to Higher Things."

5. Tom McMillen, "An Olympic Détente for the 1972 Men's Basketball Team," thedailybeast.com, August 5, 2012.

6. David Wharton, "Second-Hand Smoke," *Los Angeles Times*, September 10, 2002.

7. New Brunswick Sports Hall of Fame Federation, "Medals, Trophies, and Ribbons! Oh My!!!," http://www.virtualmuseum.ca/sgc-cms/histoires_de_chez_nous -community_memories/pm_v2.php?id=thumbnail_gallery&fl=0&lg=English&ex =00000844&pos=1.

8. Knight with Hammel, *Knight: My Story*, 217.

9. Knight with Hammel, *Knight: My Story*, 217.

10. Gary Smith, "A Few Pieces of Silver," *Sports Illustrated*, June 15, 1992.

11. Brewster and Gallagher, *Stolen Glory*, 177.

12. *Jeopardy!*, episode no. 6730, NBC, 2013.

13. "1972 Olympic Gold Medal Basketball Issues and What happened to the Medals," NBC Sports, 1992, https://www.youtube.com/watch?v=RwZuPi4cbyg.

14. Dan Arritt, "What Athletes Do with Their Medals After the Olympics," ABC News.com, August 5, 2016, https://abcnews.go.com/Sports/athletes-medals-olympics /story?id=41140561.

15. Doug Williams, "What Athletes Do with Their Medals After the Olympics," ABC News.com, August 5, 2016, https://abcnews.go.com/Sports/athletes-medals -olympics/story?id=41140561.

16. Stu Woo and Geoffrey A. Fowler, "For Olympic Winners, Losing Track of a Medal Is a Personal Bust," *Wall Street Journal*, July 24, 2012.

17. Nick Zaccardi, "Paris 2024 Olympic Medals Could Be Separated into Four Pieces," NBC Sports.com. July 12, 2017.

18. Michael Powell, "Olympic Medal, Earned; Glory, Denied; Future, Uncertain," *New York Times*, July 7, 2017.

19. Patrick Hruby, "Jim Thorpe: Oral History Project in 1960s Becomes Quest to Right Wrong," *Washington Times*, August 16, 2012.

20. Alan Abrahamson, "Court Rules Paul Hamm Can Keep Olympic Gold," *Los Angeles Times*, October 21, 2004.

21. Gary Smith, "A Few Pieces of Silver."

22. Gary Smith, "A Few Pieces of Silver."

23. Gary Smith, "A Few Pieces of Silver."

24. Gary Smith, "A Few Pieces of Silver."

BIBLIOGRAPHY

Aubrey, Stefan M. *The New Dimension of International Terrorism*. Zurich: vdf Hochschulverlag AG an der ETH Zürich, 2004.

Bickley, Dan. *Return of the Gold: The Journey of Jerry Colangelo and the Redeem Team*. New York: Morgan James, 2009.

Bischoff, John Paul. *Mr. Iba: Basketball's Aggie Iron Duke*. Mishawaka IN: Western Heritage Books, 1980.

Brewster, Mike, and Taps Gallagher. *Stolen Glory: The U.S., The Soviet Union, and the Olympic Basketball Game That Never Ended*. Los Angeles: GM Books, 2012.

Brokhin, Yuri. *The Big Red Machine: The Rise and Fall of Soviet Olympic Champions*. New York: Oxford University Press, 1993.

Carey, Mike, and Michael D. McClellan. *Boston Celtics: Where Have You Gone?* Champaign IL: Sports Publishing, 2005.

Coubertin, Pierre de. *Olympic Memoirs*. Lausanne, Switzerland: International Olympic Committee, 1997.

Coubertin, Pierre de, Timoleon J. Philemon, N. G. Politis, and Charalambos Anninos. *The Olympic Games: B.C. 776–A.D. 1896*. Athens: Charles Beck; London: H. Grevel, 1897.

Cunningham, Carson. *American Hoops: U.S. Men's Olympic Basketball from Berlin to Beijing*. Lincoln: University of Nebraska Press, 2012.

Davis, Seth. *Wooden: A Coach's Life*. New York: Times Books, 2014.

Deford, Frank. *Over Time*. New York: Atlantic Monthly Press, 2012.

Dichter, Heather L., and Andrew L. Johns, eds. *Diplomatic Games: Sport, Statecraft, and International Relations Since 1945*. Lexington: University Press of Kentucky, 2014.

Edelman, Robert. *Serious Fun: A History of Spectator Sports in the U.S.S.R.* New York: Oxford University Press, 1993.

Elzey, Chris. "Cold War on the Court: The 1973 American-Soviet Basketball Series." *North American Society for Sport History Proceedings* (2000): 17–19.

Feinstein, John. *The Punch: One Night, Two Lives, and the Fight That Changed Basketball Forever*. Boston: Little, Brown, 2002.

Groussard, Serge. *The Blood of Israel: The Massacre of the Israeli Athletes, the Olympics, 1972*. New York: William Morrow, 1975.

Guttmann, Allen. "The Cold War and the Olympics." *International Journal* 43, no. 4 (1988): 554–68.

———. *The Olympics: A History of the Modern Games*. Urbana: University of Illinois Press, 2002.

Halberstam, David. *The Breaks of the Game*. New York: Hachette Books, 1980.

Hart, Eddie. *Disqualified: Eddie Hart, Munich 1972, and the Voices of the Most Tragic Olympics*. Kent OH: Kent State University Press/Black Squirrel Books, 2017.

Haskins, Don, and Ray Sanchez. *Haskins: The Bear Facts*. El Paso TX: Mangan Books and *El Paso Herald-Post*, 1987.

Hughes, Rich. *Netting Out Basketball 1936: The Remarkable Story of the McPherson Refiners, the First Team to Dunk, Zone Press, and Win the Olympic Gold Medal*. Victoria, British Columbia: Friesen Press, 2011.

Knight, Bob, with Bob Hammel. *Knight: My Story*. New York: Thomas Dunne Books, 2002.

Large, David Clay. *Munich 1972: Tragedy, Terror, and Triumph at the Olympic Games*. Lanham MD: Rowman and Littlefield, 2012.

Lenskyj, Helen Jefferson, and Stephen Wagg, eds. *The Palgrave Handbook of Olympic Studies*. Hampshire, England: Palgrave Macmillan, 2012.

Maraniss, David. *Rome 1960: The Olympics That Changed the World*. New York: Simon and Schuster, 2008.

McMillen, Tom. *Out of Bounds: How the American Sports Establishment Is Being Driven by Greed and Hypocrisy—and What Needs to be Done About It*. New York: Simon and Schuster, 1992.

Moore, Kenny. *Bowerman and the Men of Oregon*. Emmaus PA: Rodale Books, 2007.

Organisationskomitee für die Spiele der XX. Olympiade. *Die Spiele: The Official Report of the Organizing Committee for the Games of the XXth Olympiad Munich 1972*. München: pro Sport, 1974.

Peeler, Tim. *Legends of N.C. State Basketball: Dick Dickey, Tommy Burleson, David Thompson, Jim Valvano, and Other Wolfpack Stars*. New York: Sports Publishing, 2015.

Pluto, Terry. *Loose Balls: The Short, Wild Life of the American Basketball Association*. New York: Simon and Schuster, 1990.

Reeve, Simon. *One Day in September: The Full Story of the 1972 Munich Olympics Massacre and the Israeli Revenge Operation "Wrath of God."* New York: Arcade Publishing, 2011.

Salzberg, Charles. *From Set Shot to Slam Dunk: The Glory Days of Basketball in the Words of Those Who Played It*. New York: Dell, 1987.

Stern, Steven, dir. *:03 from Gold*. New York: HBO Sports, 2002.

Stradling, Jan. *More Than a Game: When Sport and History Collide*. Millers Point, Australia: Pier 9, 2009.

Ströher, Manfred, and Hans-Dieter Krebs. *Dr. h.c. R. William Jones*. Munich: FIBA, 1998.

Turrini, Joseph M. "'It Was Communism Versus the Free World': The USA-USSR Dual Track Meet Series and the Development of Track and Field in the United States, 1958–1985." *Journal of Sport History* 28 no. 3 (Fall 2001): 427–71.

United States Olympic Committee. *United States Olympic Book, Munich, Sapporo*. New York: USOC, 1972.

Walton, Bill. *Back from the Dead: Searching for the Sound, Shining the Light, and Throwing It Down*. New York: Simon and Schuster, 2016.

Wallechinsky, David, and Jaime Loucky. *The Complete Book of the Olympics 2012 Edition*. London: Arum Press, 2012.

West, Gary P. *Better Than Gold: Olympian Kenny Davis and the Most Controversial Basketball Game in History*. Sikeston MO: Acclaim Press, 2014.

INDEX